Wild Card

Dorothy Hewett was born in Perth, Australia, in 1923, the daughter of a wheat farmer. She was educated by correspondence, at Perth College and at the University of Western Australia. She has worked as a journalist, mill-worker, advertising copywriter and political organizer and for nine years she was a senior tutor at the University of Western Australia.

In 1945 Dorothy Hewett joined the Australian Communist Party, but resigned from it in 1968, after the invasion of Czechoslovakia. In 1949, she left her first husband and travelled to Sydney with her lover, a boilermaker. They lived together for nine years and had three sons. During this period Dorothy Hewett wrote *Bobbin Up* (1959), her only novel, in response to a writing competition. It is based on her own experiences of working in a large Sydney spinning mill, her membership of the Australian Communist Party and life in the working-class suburbs of Sydney. *Bobbin Up* has been translated into Russian, Hungarian, Bulgarian and German, and Dorothy Hewett is currently writing a musical and a film script based on the book.

Dorothy Hewett began writing poetry and short stories as a child. A well-known Australian playwright, she is the author of fifteen plays (including two for children), several of which have been performed at the Sydney Opera House Drama Theatre. In 1974 she received a three-year grant from the Literature Board of the Australia Council and in 1984 was awarded a one-year fellowship by the Literature Board for autobiography. Dorothy Hewett was Writer-In-Residence at Wollongong University during the same period. She is the author of five poetry collections and editor of *Sandgropers* (1973), an anthology of Western Australian writing.

Married to the writer Merv Lilley, she has five children and has lived in the inner suburbs of Sydney since 1974. At present she is working on *The Toucher*, her first novel for thirty-two years; a trilogy of plays, *The Wire Fences of Jarrabin* for the West Australian theatre company; and a new collection of poems, *The Peninsula*.

By the same author

Poetry
What About the People? (with Merv Lilley)
Windmill Country
Rapunzel in Suburbia
Greenhouse
Alice in Wormland
A Tremendous World in Her Head: Selected Poems

Novel
Bobbin Up

Anthology
Sandgropers (ed.)

Plays
This Old Man Comes Rolling Home
Mrs Porter and the Angel
The Chapel Perilous
Bon-Bons and Roses for Dolly
The Tatty Hollow Story
Pandora's Cross
Joan
The Golden Oldies
Susannah's Dreaming
The Man from Mukinupin
Golden Valley
The Fields of Heaven
Zimmer (with Robert Adamson)
The Song of the Seals
The Rising of Pete Marsh

Operetta
Christina's World (with Ross Edwards)

Wild Card

AN AUTOBIOGRAPHY ♥ 1923–1958

D·O·R·O·T·H·Y · H·E·W·E·T·T

VIRAGO

Published by VIRAGO PRESS Limited 1990
20–23 Mandela Street, Camden Town, London NW1 0HQ

A CIP Catalogue record for this book is available from the British Library

Typeset by Bookset
Printed and bound by Australian Print Group

To Hal Porter,
whose idea it was, and
to Merv Lilley,
who helped me carry it out.

ACKNOWLEDGEMENTS

Thanks to the Literature Board of the Australia Council for the grants that made this book possible, to Neilma Sydney for three winters in her 'writers' retreat' on the Victorian Peninsula, to Rollins College, Florida, for the Writer-in-Residency, to Pauline Dugmore and the English Department of the University of Western Australia for assistance with typing, to my son Tom Flood and my sister Dr Lesley Dougan for comment and criticism.

The poems quoted before each Part come from the following publications: 'Testament' and 'Legend of the Green Country', *Windmill Country*, Overland, 1968; 'This Version of Love' and 'In Moncur Street', *Rapunzel in Suburbia*, Prism Poets, 1975.

The photographs between pp 38–39, pp 134–135, pp 182–183 and pp 230–231 are from Dorothy Hewett's private collection. The photographers vary: refer to captions.

The cover photograph was taken by Betty Picken, 1945.

'What does it matter if you do not believe me? The future will surely come. Just a little while and you will see for yourself.'

(Aeschylus, The Orestia)

On winter days on tables and floors she builds endless card houses, propping one card carefully against the other, simple houses with sloping walls and a space left for a door and chimney.

Inside there is always a small clean enclosed space of filtered light.

She plans to swallow a bottle called 'Drink me' and crawl in there, but instead she stays like Gulliver, a giant amongst the Lilliputians. If she got in she could never get out.

She tries to build a second storey, but it holds only for an instant, then topples into ruin. She keeps building them up. They fall into heaps and are lost, and the game has to begin all over again.

PART I

The flat stones on the hill were black
With rain, the she-oaks
Dripped and murmured with an aged
Dim loneliness: we rode our horses,
Hunched in the saddle, through the swollen creeks,
And smelt the steaming wet smell of the earth,
The heavy body of the soil, like a giant bell
Behind the old house creaking in the wind.

'Testament'

THE first house sits in the hollow of the heart, it will never go away. It is the house of childhood become myth, inhabited by characters larger than life whose murmured conversations whisper and tug at the mind. Enchanted birds and animals out of a private ark sail out on tides of sleep, howling, whistling, mewing, neighing, mooing, baaing, barking, to an endless shimmer of wheat and cracked creek beds. Through the iron gate on the edge of Day's paddock we enter the farm, and drive past the giant she-oak split in two by a strike of lightning. The house lies in the bend of two creeks. The sheepdogs are barking from the verandahs. Beyond is the stable yard with the well in the centre where you let down the bucket to bring up fresh clear water. Large animals move there, draught horses big as the Spanish Armada champing forever at mangers full of oats, licking at rock salt, or rolling ridiculously in grey sand, hoofs waving in air. Liquid or wild-eyed, the cows file into the cow bails with curled horns and names like Strawberry, Buttercup and Daisy. The sheep jostle together in the pens, the kelpie running and snapping across their backs. The sun reflects off the corrugated iron of the shearing shed till its tilts and topples, crazy as a glasshouse. In the chaff house it makes eyes that glitter and run like mice across the floor.

The haystacks prickle and gleam behind the 'chunk chunk chunk' of the chaff cutter feeding an endless belt through cogs and wheels. Magpies are sitting carolling on the York gums. At the back of the stable yard is an old, half-rotted horse race where Yarriman, the Aboriginal horse-breaker, drove the wild horses down from the low hills before we were born. To the right of the path through the house paddock where our father staggered with a bloody eye kicked in by Jack, the rogue horse, there is the married couple's flat-fronted, flat-roofed weatherboard humpie, with one door and two eyes for windows like a child's drawing. The red-headed Pommy, Mrs Rogers, is running in and out of the house like a weather woman bringing her underclothes in off the line so that my father won't see them; inside Peggy Rogers is eating her peas off her knife, because 'the fork might prick me tongue'. Outside in the yard their electric-blue Tin Lizzie is parked waiting to carry them away for ever.

Near the high wire stable gate are the murderous gallows, dripping blood and fat; where the sheep hang with their throats cut. On the other side of the gate is the blacksmith's shop with the grinder and the forge and the black anvil shooting sparks, the floor littered with curls of wood shavings. We hang them over our ears like Mary Pickford. On the left is the ant-heap tennis court where I tried to jump the tennis net and broke my arm and had to be driven fourteen miles over bush roads to the local doctor, with a deal splint my father cut from the wood heap bound round my elbow. My mother sits on the sidelines barracking 'good shot' and 'butterfingers'. Past the tennis court is a dry abandoned dam full of rusty tins where Nancy the black-and-white cow fell in and had to be hauled out, mad-eyed and lowing, with ropes and a pulley.

The little gate opens into the garden with the pink Dorothy Perkins rose climbing on the wire fence, the Geraldton wax bush blooming. The house is ringed with almond and fig trees. In spring the almond blossom falls in white bruised drips on the couch-grass lawn. In summer the twenty-eight parrots crack nuts over our heads till our father goes for the shotgun. At Christmas time we sit on the verandah preparing the nuts for the cake with a silver nutcracker. The twenty-eight parrots flash green and black as they fly away, the nutcracker flashes silver in the sun. We carry the almonds into the kitchen, plunge them in boiling water and peel off the skins, till they curl like brown tissue paper and the almonds emerge smooth and creamy white.

The fig leaves are rough like cows' tongues and the fig skins tingle and burn in our mouths. At night time our father carries us shoulder high to the outside dunny singing 'When the moon shines over the cow shed' and 'There's a little black cupid in the moon'.

The house is built with two wings, the old house and the new. The old house has two corrugated-iron rooms. In the ramshackle sleepout, my grandparents live in an old iron bedstead with silver balls for decoration. The shelves are made of butterboxes filled with paperbacks, and copies of *Bleak House* and *Little Dorrit*, with the ominous Phiz drawings. The Swiss Family Robinson build their treehouse, menaced by giant snakes and jungle. My grandmother's tin trunks are crammed with eyelet-embroidered petticoats with yards of handmade lace, pale leather button-up boots, pearl-buttoned kid gloves and VAD nurses' uniforms from the First World War.

Beside the old sleepout is the little back verandah where the quinces and Jonathan apples are stored to ripen on open wooden shelves. I hide there reading *All Quiet on the Western Front*, and a paperback stolen out of the butterboxes with a cover drawing of a droopy, yellow-haired girl playing the piano, mooned over by a handsome Catholic priest.

Go through the French doors, pleated and dark with dusty muslin curtains, into the enchanted centre, the playroom, the children's domain packed with forty-three dolls and a huge box full of *Alice in Wonderland, Tom the Water Baby, Treasure Island, Wind in the Willows, Peter Pan, Emily of New Moon, A Child's Garden of Verses,* Ida Rentoul Outhwaite's *Elves and Fairies,* Andersen's and Grimm's *Fairy Tales, A Child's History of England, What Katy Did* and *What Katy Did at School, Seven Little Australians, Norah of Billabong, Dot and the Kangaroo, Pollyanna, Daddy Long Legs, Anne of Green Gables, The Tales of Pooh, Robin Hood, Robinson Crusoe, Gulliver's Travels, The Arabian Nights, Little Women* and *Good Wives, Coral Island* and *Tom Brown's School Days, Lamb's Tales from Shakespeare* and all my mother's English *Schoolgirl Annuals.*

The dolls are made of rag, celluloid and china. The china dolls' eyes fall in and rattle about in their heads. On the rag dolls' plaster faces the painted eyes run blue when they are left out in the rain. A black mechanical toy car called Leaping Lena bucks across the playroom floor. There is a train set with tangled rails, a double-storeyed, butterbox dolls' house with wicker furniture and a magic lantern, its wavering images clicking on and off across the wall.

Here is the open whitewashed fireplace where our father roasts potatoes in their jackets under the coals in winter, and in summer piles up gum branches to break the fall of Father Christmas as he tumbles down the chimney. We put out a bottle of beer and a piece of Christmas cake, iced and decorated with silver cashews, to reward him for his trouble.

In summer we sleep in the big sleepout completely enclosed in flywire so that at night we feel as if we are floating in air above the garden and the quiet orchard, borne away by the call of the mopokes. In the morning we wake to a wash of light, a magpie perched on the clothes prop, a rooster crowing from the chook yard at the bottom of the garden. In the dim light we watch the cured hams swaying from the iron hooks above our heads.

An old weatherboard verandah runs right through the centre of the house where the sheep carcasses hang in blood-spotted calico. A big water bag with a long spout swings by the tank stand, the rainwater tasting of wet hessian. The bathroom has a claw-footed enamel bath and a chip heater, where our mother develops her sepia photographs in an enamel dish on the marble washstand.

The new wing of weatherboard and fibro was built when I was five. There is a big farm kitchen, a black stove with two huge boiling kettles, a long lino-covered pine table, and a jarrah dresser with a recess underneath where we can crawl and hide. Our father sits in the corner, puts the headphones on, and listens to the test cricket on the crystal set.

In the pantry there are sacks of flour, nuts, sugar and potatoes, rows of home-made preserves and jars of jam. The kettles hiss on the blackened stove, the bread rises in the pans set out on the hob, the wheat is ground into meal for our morning porridge, the sheep's head floats in the white basin, muslined from the flies, the cream is slapped into butter between the wooden pats.

The flypaper hangs from the ceiling and catches in our hair. Blowflies buzz angrily outside the flywire door. Through the kitchen window you can look out on the cannas growing beside the drain, the wattles marking the orchard boundary and the edge of the creek.

In the hall there is an etching of Gladstone, who always chewed every mouthful thirty-six times, and two oil paintings, 'The Stag at Bay' by Great-Aunt Eva and 'The Deer in the Snow' by Great-Aunt Dora, who died of TB in Wooroloo Sanatorium. Eva's stag has a crooked leg.

The hall is the best place to be when the temperature hits 114 in the shade. We lie on our bellies on the jarrah boards listening to *In a Monastery Garden*, *Cavalleria Rusticana*, *Humoresque* and *The Laughing Policeman* on the wind-up His Master's Voice gramophone. Sometimes we play lady wrestlers, or impersonate Two-Ton Tony Galento on the strip of Persian-patterned carpet.

On the other side of the hall is Great-Aunt Eva's bedroom, all polished lino, cheval mirror and oak bedroom suite, reflecting the light. When Aunty Eva comes, once or twice a year, she lies in bed with us reciting *The Schooner Hesperus*, *Hiawatha*, *Horatius at the Bridge* and *Little Jim*, while we pull out her grey hairs one by one.

In the bedroom next door that I share with my mother and sister I have a little single bed where I lie sweating at night, keeping one eye on the griffins on the wardrobe door, which are likely to metamorphose into real monsters, and the other eye on the square of light from the bedroom window, which is likely to let in all things that go bump in the night. The little oil night-light with its round milky glass floats luminous above the dressing-table, where my mother sits singing ... 'There's a long, long trail awinding into the land of my dreams.'

On the right of the hall is the sitting room where we are allowed to go only on special occasions, or when the Salvation Army chaplain calls in overnight. Then my mother plays hymns and makes mistakes on the iron-framed German piano. My grandfather's favourite is

'Rock of Ages', my father's is 'Abide with Me'. There is a leatherette sofa and two armchairs, an oval jarrah table and six high-backed dining chairs. The table is always draped in an orange tasselled cover with a leather centrepiece in a cut-out design of fruit and flowers. On the walls are prints of 'The Watcher on the Hill', a group of wild horses with flying manes and rolling eyes, a herd of Highland cattle fording a stream, some Victorian English girls in frilly muslin pinafores toasting chestnuts in front of a fire grate, a sunflower painted on glass, and Great-Aunt Eva's out-of-perspective painting of a huge Newfoundland, paws outstretched under a half-drowned girl, a ship's funnel smoking in the distance.

The fire grate has fleur-de-lis tiles, and elephants from Bombay on the mantelpiece. The bow windows are hung with pale yellow linen curtains bordered with William Morris fruit. They frame the lightning-struck she-oak and the line of salmon gums, shiny and creaking in the wind, their bark hanging in rags like giant beggar women.

Under a broken-backed wattle in the orchard we have our cubby: an old dunny, cement-floored with a row of tulip tiles behind the seat, and a tent made of sewn wheatbags. By the swing is the wrecked Willy's Knight chassis that once belonged to our grandfather. I play Death and the Maiden laid out on the cracked leather seat, dressed up in my mother's crepe de Chine wedding dress, pleated from neck to hem, with the remnants of a gossamer train.

The orchard is heavy with peach and apricot, nectarine and mandarin, quince and pear. A silver balloon hangs for a moment on the quince tree and floats away. The grapevines are pendulous with pale green ladies' fingers. The orchard is thick with paddy and pig melons. I suck the transparent globule of gum prised off the jam tree. The moon rests on the stable roof like a great ruby bubble. My mountain pony Silver steps out daintily, pulling up clumps of cape-weed, her hoofs curling like Arabian slippers. She has foundered in the wheat.

Every spring the magpies nest in the almond tree, raising naked-necked fledglings, their beaks gaping for worms. The tomtit builds its hanging nest and lays three warm speckled eggs amongst dry grass and feathers. A wagtail balances on the toprail of the wire fence hung with dew drops, chirping 'sweet pretty creature'. The drops hang, glisten and slide. The plover nests in the furrows made by the plough. The quail settles down in the long grass over her eggs. The peewits are crying over the wheat. Rain's coming – the black cockatoos sweep down from the rock hill and collect like black rags on the gums. The racehorse goannas are racing through the orchard, switching their tails. A silver-green tree frog leaps into the pink ivy geranium hanging by the tank stand. I am running to the end of the farm, I am running to the end of the rainbow where there is, apparently, a pot of gold. I am holding the silver balloon on the end of a long string. 'The crow flies home to the rooky wood', and Trix, the sixteen-year-old shearers' tabby, sits patiently in the doll's pram under the almond trees, a frilled baby-doll's bonnet tied under her white whiskers.

My grandfather goes out to feed the poddy calves, the milk bucket clanking at his thigh. In the kitchen garden Mr Wrigglesford leans on his spade on the dry manure heap telling me stories of bardies and earthworms and furry black caterpillars. An old mate of my grandfather's, he goes on monthly benders, and swims, making tracks like a goanna, through the dust to his camp on the other side of the machinery shed. One day he will mysteriously disappear, and we will sit mourning over his tent props and his blackened billy on a cold heap of ashes.

In summer the centre of our house shifts from the kitchen to the verandahs. We sit waiting for the Albany Doctor to blow up, rippling the tops of the wattles along the creek, while the voices murmur on and on telling their endless tales of past and present. The trees lift up their roots and come closer to the house to listen. Then legendary characters stalk the Avon Valley, the ghosts of the gold miners on the road to Kalgoorlie with their wheelbarrows, riding, driving their drays, to camp at Split Rock at the bottom of our orchard; Joe Anchor, who lies buried under Joe Anchor's rock at the edge of the farm, was he seaman or drifter?; the Ridleys and Bells and Hothams who take over the country like crows; the Mundy brothers with their bell-bottom trousers swaggering through the towns; the silvertails playing golf and holding cocktail parties, dancing to their doom, while their farms are taken over by the banks and the rabbits.

We lie in the hammock flying out above stars and wind, listening as worlds coalesce, floating us down the avenues of sleep. The houses of childhood all have this mythical quality lost under the mist of time – the wooden house on the shores of the Swan River and the holiday cottage behind the sand dunes on the beach at King George's Sound.

As long as I can remember we have had these holiday places. Every year in October we go to the Perth Royal Show and stay in my grandfather's jarrah house on the river at Como, where we learn to swim with water wings at the end of a spindly jetty. Globules of jellyfish litter the sand, transparent and quivering. It is the same jetty where my mother went, travelling with her father as a little girl, driving over the causeway in a spanking horse and buggy that left all the other drivers for dead. The air of that house always seems full of the sound of Indian doves cooing. There is a small jarrah forest on the other side of a wooden stile, where we run to catch the tram and ferry to the little city. The rooms are dark and cool, a long living room furnished in oak, a primitive lean-to-kitchen, the bedrooms lined, floor to ceiling, with pale green pressed iron. Our water comes from a stone well with a hand pump and a bucket at the back door. We carry fluted pink and white shaded oil lamps from room to room.

At night strange bleeps and muffled screams come from the back bedroom, where an ancient caretaker, called Lapp, tunes in on his home-built crystal set. We sit with the headphones on for hours trying to decipher something from the rushing airwaves, but we never hear anything that remotely resembles a human voice, or the sound of music. But we are fiercely loyal to the end, and indignant when the grown-ups make fun of Lapp's invention.

There is a copse of wattle between the house and the river. Through the door and across the verandah an old donkey grazes in an empty paddock, like a framed picture. On the other side of the wattle grove lives Mrs Pooley, a tall thin woman with wisps of yellow-white hair, who breeds Pekinese behind a blue convolvulus hedge.

The zamia palms drift their fronded patterns across the white sand.

After the harvest, we travel 250 miles to the South Coast and live for two or three months in a tiny cottage of two rooms and a kitchen beside the sea. The landscape is forbidding and melancholy, with black rocks and low dark scrub lit by the occasional gleam of sunlight on granite or wave or sand dune. The places around us have magical names like Torbay, Nornalup, Nannarup and Two People Bay. Lagoon and ocean, seabird and scrub, lonely and deserted, are surrounded by great karri forests where you can drive a car through a hollow tree. A petrified forest covers the sand dunes. We fish on mirror-smooth rivers. In their green depths white drowned forests drift, quivering. A great kingfish breaks the surface and flashes through sunlight to land jiggling on the end of a line.

At night the lighthouse on Breaksea flicks on and off across the Southern Ocean and steamers with smoking funnels sail by on their way to the ends of the world. The beach on one side is ringed by a scrubby headland like a resting emu, on the other by Bald Head, a sheer crag of black rock. In the distance the tiny island of Dunder Rock glitters in the setting sun. Behind it rises a mountain glimmering like Shangri-la. At Emu Point there is a spring where the Dutch explorers called in to water their ships and Green Island where the colonial ladies fled from a black ambush. The beach is an arc of hard white sand stretching along the bay. Cars drive to the point when the tide is out but often, on their way back, they meet their doom. Bogged or caught in the incoming surf, they wash, bobbing ludicrously out to sea. Pacific gulls fly low over the dunes, pods of whales are sometimes beached, dark-humped and dying in the shallows. We gather white crenellated shells and put them to our ears to hear the sea sighing. At night we lie in bed listening to the surf breaking and lulling against the beach. Sometimes the sound is so loud and the house is so small, we feel as if we are rocking on the surface of the sea, going out with the tide. Next door is a wild tract of reserve covered in eucalyptus and prickly bush twined with purple clematis. We build elaborate cubbies floored with moss and roam with our boy cousins playing wild horses, Robin Hood and Maid Marian and the Merry Men. Behind the house, on the wet bracken hillsides at Miramar, we go blackberrying and run down the slopes to fling ourselves into the surf, the salt smarting the bramble cuts on our legs and arms. At night our father makes big fires of driftwood in the open fireplace and we sit, flushed and stinging with sunburn, in wicker chairs, playing rummy and Rickety Kate on the round oak table.

At the South Coast, where a honeymoon couple once whirled to their death in the blowhole, the sea rushes in under giant granite causeways, sucking and swirling through gaps and holes. If you lean out over hummocks of rough grass on the headland, you can see Jimmy Newell's Harbour where he took shelter, running in under the knoll from a raging storm. King waves sweep over coastal rocks, drowning intrepid fishermen. At Frenchman's Bay there are the stone remnants of jetties and huts left by the French whalers. The wild sea and historic past seem to merge together in one glamorous tale.

At the end of the summer we pack up our shells, call 'Steamer, steamer' for the last time, and go back to put them on the farm mantelpiece, listening to the suck of the surf in our faraway inland country.

My grandfather's house on the Swan River disappeared long ago under high-rise apartment blocks. The wooden house by the sea still stands unchanged, silvered with age, but the beachfront is thickly settled and a caravan park cuts off the house from the dunes and the sea. The farm is long since sold and the farmhouse derelict. The new owners have shifted to a kit home beside Rock Hill, away from the creek and closer to the electric-light poles.

Is it still there on the far side of Day's paddock in the bend of three creeks, unchanged, unclaimed except by the weather and the starry wastes of sky? Do the ghostly draught horses wheel and gallop through the dark? Through the open French doors swinging in the wind is a scratchy 78 still playing the Hallelujah Chorus over and over again . . . Hallelujah, Hallelujah?

CHAPTER

1
♠

A skinny ten-year-old, carrying the billy of tea in one hand and trying to keep her brown lisle stockings up with the other, I am taking the afternoon smoko to 'the man' ploughing the hundred acres across the creek.

I've never worn stockings before and I've forgotten the garters (or perhaps I never had any). They concertina around my knees and fall to my ankles. The billy bumps, scalding, against my thigh.

I am very conscious of the eyes of the handsome Italian farm labourer watching my stump-jump progress, hiding his smile with his hand. He is kind to me, the first of many men who will find my aspirations forgivable, even charming.

But they are neither forgivable nor charming; no interesting hobby, no spare-time dilettante scribbling under her hair after the important business of being a woman is over for the day.

Daughter, sister, lover, wife, mother, grandmother, domestic treasure, I will be suborned into all of these roles (except perhaps domestic treasure . . . there I am always clumsy and half-hearted), but I have my vocation. It is outside sex, and yet my sex is part of it. It is already fixed, brutal, implacable, complete. There is nothing I can do about it, except to get better at it. It shakes me, seductive as love. Words fall out, I am possessed by them.

It is 1933 and I live at the ends of the earth. This is really another country, all the wenches *are* dead, and I am a misfit . . . a little girl who will grow up to be a writer, brought up on a wheat and sheep farm at Malyalling via Wickepin, the Great Southern of Western Australia . . . New Holland, Terra Australis, the Great South Land that the Dutch explorers touched at, blown out of their way to the fabulous spice islands by the Roaring Forties.

As far as the eye can see stretch our three thousand acres. We are amongst the richest farmers in the district. We *know* who we are. At least everybody does except my father, who has been given a share of sandplain across the railway line, plus a grace and favour residence with us all in the old farmhouse.

My father is driving the new Twin City tractor five paddocks away, my mother is ironing the doilies edged with lazy daisies on the kitchen table till the pattern comes through on the hot undersheet, my grandmother is setting the bread dough to rise in front of the black fuel stove, my grandfather is feeding the poddy calves in the stable yard, letting them suck the milk off his fingers, my little sister is doing correspondence lessons at her butterbox desk on the verandah. I carry the billy of tea to the Italian ploughing the one hundred acres.

He came to us from timber-cutting amongst the giant karri forests in the south-west, and sucker-bashing with Ab Walsh and his blue heeler. Ab is a middle-aged bachelor, a prodigious swearer, who pisses (so they say) in the same enamel chamber pot he uses to brew his tea. He has taught the Italian to speak English, so that the first night around the kitchen table he asks my grandmother to, 'Pliss pass the fuckin' butter, Mrs Coade.' I am tremendously impressed by him. A vigneron's son from outside Venice, he has beautiful manners and sings like an angel. One of the romantic young *fascisti* who followed Gabriel d'Annunzio in the attempted recapture of the port of Fiume after the First World War, only to be betrayed by Mussolini, he has been given the choice of firing squad or permanent exile and has chosen Western Australia. Anyway, that's his story. He will work on our farm until he has saved up enough to rent a run-down property from my grandfather. Eventually he will rent our farm, overstock it, make his fortune out of wool during the Second World War, and become the richest farmer in the district, with an Australian wife and two mistresses.

Now he sings Italian opera as he puts out the horse feed. On a ledge in the darkest corner of the stable there is a whole boxful of French letters. The chaff falls from the sack like the sound of a wave. I sit on an upturned wheatbag and suck rock salt; the line of horses' heads, rhythmically chewing, watch me with their liquid eyes. Their tails swing in unison against their warm rumps in the half-darkness.

The district is full of migrant Italians, little fat swarthy southerners who bring their big wives to sit in our kitchen, speechless and eternally smiling, a crescent of sweat under the arms of their black satin dresses. Their earrings flash off the afternoon-tea things. The kitchen range blazes with heat under the giant iron kettles.

There is a Depression. Everybody talks about it. I ask my father what it means, but his explanations don't sound rational. He argues politics with Cecil Elsegood, the Country Party member, outside the Yealering Co-op. I stand and listen. My head reaches up to my father's waistcoat button. My hair twines around it. I can't move. It seems like hours before he notices.

Cecil Elsegood says, 'I'm a politician, Tom. When I move into the sandplain country I'm bright red, in the middle districts I'm palest pink, but when I travel through the rich farms of the Avon Valley I'm white as driven snow.'

He wears a spotted bow tie, and looks seedy. For years he stays in my mind as the image of 'the politician'.

'Sorry, Nip,' says my father, carefully unwinding my hair.

The swaggies are out on the roads, calling into the farms for 'a few stores, Missus'. When she sees them coming across the paddocks my mother rushes us inside, locks the doors in terror, and shouts through the keyhole, 'The men are down in the stable yard.'

The farms on our boundaries have been given over to the rabbits and the banks. The farmhouses fall into ruin, the fences sag; as season follows season, the bush takes over. My father says the bankrupt farmers are 'silvertails' who spent their time going to grog parties, playing golf, buying flash cars, and getting off with each other's wives. They have all been punished, working for wages down in Perth, or even, in a hushed whisper, 'on the dole'.

Some of them hang on grimly because they have nowhere else to go. My father talks about 'those redraggers further out', and years later I discover that many of these poorer farmers, ex-miners from Kalgoorlie who'd taken up this marginal land, fought a fierce struggle with the banks in the 'Hold Your Wheat' campaign, defending the wheat stacks at their local sidings, armed with pitchforks and desperation.

Once a year when we travel to Perth for the Royal Show, the pavement artists line St George's Terrace, their crude chalk drawings of rising suns and sinking moons over black bush washing away in the rain.

'Look, darling, give the poor man a sixpence,' says my mother and I drop it into the Havelock tobacco tin, embarrassed – for him, for ourselves, and for the gulf that divides us. Along the Causeway where the Dutch once dragged their sailing ships over the sand banks, the corrugated-iron humpies and smoky fires of the unemployed cover the swampy little islands in the Swan River.

It is my grandmother's heyday. We have liens on crops and farms. We own a cinema in Perth and grocery shops in little wheatbelt towns like Corrigin, Wickepin and Lake Yealering. We will never go broke. It is our reward for industry, thrift, morality and brains. Years later I travel through these towns reading poetry in Country Women's Association halls for Adult Education. Two old men nod sardonically in the front row. 'You're Ted Coade's granddaughter. He was always ready to lend y' money . . . at ten per cent.'

The breath of their irony reaches out over the years. And I suppose he must share the blame. After all, he was her front man . . .

my grandfather, charming, sociable, affectionate, the ex-alcoholic, drinking lemonade and covering up for my grandmother's devastating tactlessness. They are a formidable combination.

'She's got a brain like a man,' says my father. High praise indeed!

'I don't know why he married me,' she says, her Japanese eyes crackling. 'He had such beautiful girls.'

Years later I find his love letters in her writing box, written in that perfect copperplate that has no character at all. They are full of excuses.

> *Dear Marie,*
> *How can you say I don't love you, when I am always thinking of you. I'm sorry you waited so long under the clock last night, but I will explain when we meet.*

> *Dear Marie,*
> *Please forgive me. I met an old mate from Beechworth last night and he insisted on standing me a dinner. We had a beautiful meal with a glass of port afterwards. I hope you were not too disappointed.*

'Dear Marie' . . . I wonder how she ever got *him* to the altar. My Great-Aunt Daisy hints darkly about it after their deaths. 'Poor Ted, he never stood a chance. Oh! but she was a wicked, scheming woman, your grandmother.'

The stories about her . . . her stepfather forbade her to go to a dance with the butcher's boy, so she tore down the velvet dining-room curtains and, like Scarlett O'Hara, made herself a ball dress and went to the dance anyway.

The family live in genteel poverty in South Melbourne and Mary is 'delicate'. She is anaemic and has to sleep without a pillow but, heartened by the astounding success of the ball dress, she sets herself up in a little room as a professional dressmaker. Eventually she is 'making' for Melbourne's most fashionable clientele. The family are horrified, but nothing can stop her. She has the bit between her teeth. My sister and I reap the benefit of these Melbourne years. In the corrugated-iron sleepout with the swifts scrabbling in the roof, we rifle the contents of her old trunks and bursting suitcases.

I invent implausible tragedies. Playing 'improvised theatre', we parade down the roads under the peeling salmon gums, waving our pearl-buttoned gloves imperiously. The temperature is 112 degrees in the shade. Polly of the Circus, bare-breasted, a pasty of sequins over her crotch, crashes to her doom from the highest York gum. In another year, gawky in my unbecoming wool bathers and rubber bathing cap, I will have real breasts, crossing my hands to hide their swell from the other kids.

The sleepout is our Pandora's box, unleashing our wildest imaginings, the first stir of my sexuality. When my sister, playing some male surrogate, bends me over backwards on the iron double bedstead to murmur extravagant compliments in my ear, the cracks on the corrugated-iron roof wink with a thousand glittering eyes. What does she think about it, this dark plump little girl with the bluebag around her eyes to keep off the blowflies? I take her with me on all our outlandish adventures. She is told what to think, what to say, what to do, who to be, a dozen times a day. I torture her when I don't get my own way, pretend to leave, packing a bogus bag, crying like Tosti, 'goodbye for ever', as I stride off across the paddocks into nowhere. 'Don't go, come back,' she sobs. I wonder when she will be old enough to call my bluff.

But she gets her revenge with the silent treatment, a revenge I will never be able to cope with, so that eventually I am reduced to writing begging notes for forgiveness on all the garden paths.

'Please forgive me. I love you,' I write with a sharpened stick into the dust until, eventually, she relents and speaks again.

When we play Jack Jackson and his wild horses, she is Jack, a sensible, solid sort of chap, and I am all the wild horses, with names like Starlight and Black Beauty, tossing their manes and galloping across the couch-grass lawn.

We have forty-three dolls of all shapes and sizes in the playroom, but we are not very interested in the usual 'baby-doll' games. Our dolls are actors and actresses. Some come from remote foreign lands, brought back to us from 'abroad' by my spinster Great-Aunt Eva, my grandmother's half-sister.

There are a pair of dancing dolls on an elastic string, an Italian doll we call Lucia di Lammermoor and a French china doll in a blue knitted silk dress hung with bells we call Suzette de la Falaise. We bury a wax doll one winter under the almond trees with full funeral honours and when we dig her up in the spring her face has melted. We call her Scarface, and she becomes the heroine of innumerable tragedies.

In the chooks' grave at the bottom of the orchard we construct wobbly crosses over dead pullets, a twenty-eight parrot who bit my finger to the bone, then keeled over and died, and a grey chinchilla rabbit overfed with lucerne.

We invent the None-Go-By Club with its motto – 'Let none go by while this house lives, who need what this house needs to give' – and spend days piling the dead wattle leaves at the bottom of the chook run into crackling heaps preparatory to building the None-Go-By House for the shelter of passing travellers. But the leaves fall down and very few travellers 'come by' in any case . . .

My Great-Aunt Daisy, my grandfather's half-sister, arrives from Perth with her teenage daughter, exhorting her to 'breathe in the good air, Friedelle'. Her son Howard speeds in occasionally on his motorbike, looking a lot like my grandfather, and her eldest daughter, Beau, leaves the handbag counter at the Bon Marché to sit eating chocolates and reading paperback romances on the verandah. A real Hollywood beauty, Beau, with her stilt heels and flyaway satin panels. When she gets bored she makes us up with her astounding array of cosmetics. My mother uses only Pond's cream and almond lotion and 'Naturelle' face powder. Beau, of the many admirers, makes a disastrous marriage and dies of cancer. Howard is killed in the air force in New Guinea.

'My dainty Beau, my poor Howard,' weeps Aunt Daisy, the tears coursing down her powdered cheeks.

My grandfather's nephew, Jack Pemberton, and his best friend, Kev Mardling, arrive from Melbourne to learn about farming. Handsome, laughing Kev Mardling has 'a bad chest' and the dry, clear wheatbelt air is supposed to cure him. Jack Pemberton sits on the verandah at night and tells us the legends of the stars – how the crash of thunder is Thor pushing great boulders around the sky.

But when they shift on to one of my grandfather's run-down farms they spend their time careering wildly into Wickepin to the pub, driving home at dawn, drunk and singing, in a battered old tourer called the Grey Ghost.

When Kev Mardling dies, coughing up blood in the Wickepin Hospital, Jack Pemberton goes back to Melbourne and the Grey Ghost, shat on by the turkeys, lurches into the dry grass in the farmyard, like the ghost of all those golden boys who come to dust.

They are all the visitors who go by, and I can't really imagine any of them living in an igloo of dry wattle leaves at the bottom of the chook yard.

When I begin to read I people the world of the farm with characters from Hans Andersen and Grimm's *Fairy Tales*. They are everywhere in the dim green light of early winter, a peculiar sensation because I both love and fear them. Of course there is always a price to pay in bed after dark with only the night-light between me and Big Klaus and Little Klaus, making shadows; long, thin, squat, obscene. Afterwards, when I see Toulouse-Lautrec's Moulin Rouge posters, I recognize that elongated top-hatted shadow of the dancing man behind La Goulou as the image of my nightmares.

I float down through still green stagnant water with the taste of that curiously childish sin in my mouth. It's like the taste of Henry James's *Turn of the Screw*. They are all sexual stories ... Andersen's ... and he is the evil sophisticated child skipping in the enclosed garden where Kay and Gerda sit with the hearts of roses eaten out by canker; Kay, a little blue-black boy crouched immobile in the centre of the frozen lake, the Snow Queen mesmerizing him with all that white corruption in her face; the sea maid, tongueless, feet spiked through with knives, and her soulless death dissolved in foam, punished like Catherine Earnshaw for a love that annihilates the self.

There is a special smell in the pages of Andersen, the smell of well water and muddy woods. The hobgoblin on the cover caught in the slimy forest is metamorphosed into a white gum as big as a house that can burst its tree fetters and come striding across the paddocks from the line of timber as dusk falls.

I am afraid of the woodheap behind the wash house. When I am gathering wood, and the sky behind the creek is streaked red, I race inside, dropping the chips out of my pinny.

My sister Lesley, who is going to be a doctor, keeps her evil-smelling concoctions in dozens of empty medicine bottles under the tank stand; tea leaves gone sour and green, parsley, mint and piss mixed up together. It's nothing real I'm afraid of, although it is the place where beheaded chooks run in a demented circle with their neck stumps bleeding. There seems to be a presence out there and my heart won't stop thumping until I see the faces bent over the kitchen table in the splashy light from the gas mantles that shrivel up and turn black without a moment's warning. I slip into my place at the table and am ashamed. My fears feel silly now. Later the woodheap will be the place where I masturbate and discover a clitoris. Menstruation will be God's punishment for these forbidden thrills.

My father recites a nursery rhyme:

Who goes round my house by night?
Only poor old Jim ...

I know exactly what old Jim looks like. He is a loony with a hairless head like a dome, who runs in circles round the pigsty baying in the moonlight, a wide vacant grin fixed on his drooling mouth.

The squealing of the pigs at night is the sound of Jim, running round and round. When my father gets rid of the pigs because he hates them, I am relieved. In the daytime I'm not often afraid . . . only of Jack Frost, who lives in the toolbox on the old harvester, and the Haunt of the Owls. But these are rather delicious fears because I have created them myself. Somebody or Some Thing has locked Jack Frost in the toolbox and we never dare go too near in case he jumps out, white, glittery and vengeful.

The Haunt of the Owls is really where the mopokes nest in a section of the creek bed choked with dead branches. The slime on the stagnant pools is oily and rainbow-coloured. Here the mopokes perch, staring down at me with glowing eyes or flapping off into the bush with a curious unearthly sound. There is the Wishing Tree, a little bent-over deathly bush with twigs sweeping the ground. I never climb through the orchard fence into the Haunt until I have danced three times round the Wishing Tree and made a cross of bent twigs to carry with me. The Wishing Tree has fallen on its side in the floods, roots exposed, smothered in some bright-green parasite my father calls knottygobble. Once I try to climb it, but feeling the creeper twining around my arms, legs and hair, I hurry down again before I am changed, like Daphne.

I am halfway there already. Burying my face and my skinny body against the trunks of the trees, I always feel more like a tree than a child.

One summer, deciding to put away childish things, I climb on to the harvester and, eyes tight shut, open the lid of the toolbox. A tiny circle of sunlight comes through a nail hole in the side. There is a cobweb spun across the bottom. I look down at my little sister, waiting, goggle-eyed at my daring.

'There's nothing there,' I say stupidly, and see the faith die out of her eyes. After all, it has been *my* story and now there seems nothing else to do but grow up.

In the summer we sleep in the sleepout in a double bed, the helmeted profile of Apollo-brand corrugated iron repeated endlessly above us. My father wraps himself in his blankets on Gallipoli and fights the Turks all night. He shows us the black dots of shrapnel buried in his forearms.

When I have toothache he packs my hollow tooth with oil of cloves and tells me stories about Dan McGrew, who slept under the lee of a jam tin on Lemnos and put his head in front of a cannon and blew his brains out, or Jeanne, the little French girl whose parents were shot in the moonlight to the strains of *Cavalleria Rusticana* because they were German spies. Sick with nostalgia (maybe), he sings us songs about Bendigo – 'Take me back, back, back to Bendigo' – and talks about green fern, flowing water and luminous girls in big hats on the Yarra, Nellie Stewart, and Melba singing High Mass in

Melbourne. We think he must be mad. What could be lovelier than our great, dry, golden country with the wheat paddocks stretching to the horizon and the little humps of grey-black Aboriginal hills rising out of the landscape like an afterthought?

Sick with a migraine headache, he staggers back from the paddocks, swallows his Aspros and lies in the sleepout with a wet cloth round his head.

The steam trains run through the farm, lighting dangerous fires. My mother remembers when the First World War ended ... the engine driver drove across those flats blowing 'Yankee Doodle Dandy'.

It's four years since the last time I remember being perfectly happy, coming down the verandah singing between the old farmhouse and the new wing. I compose poems in bed and wake my parents in the middle of the night; patiently they write them down, marvelling, no doubt, that they have produced a swan. They buy me Jean Curlewis on the rules of prosody and try to make me scan. 'Tee dum diddle de dum'. How I resent it. I won't listen to the rules or let them transcribe any more. I will learn to read and write, painstakingly transcribing the lines of copperplate into my copybook.

Now I make up my poems to the drone of the separator out in the wash house, mesmerized by the underground rhythm. But sometimes they flash upon me out in the paddocks miles from home, words, images, lines tumbling out in a frenzy so that I have to run back, gasping for pencil and paper. If my sister is with me she has to remember the lines as I say them, over and over, and pity help her if she doesn't.

Who is Jean Curlewis anyway? The daughter of Ethel Turner, who wrote *Seven Little Australians* and made me cry over the death of Judy and long for a brother like Pip. Later I read Jean Curlewis's *Beach Beyond* and spend years looking for a boy who'll walk with me into the sea. But they're all afraid.

> I walked home with a gold dark boy
> And never a word he'd say,
> Chimborazo Cotopaxi
> Had stolen his soul away.

I think of my first memory. I am standing up in the back of a car, almost too small to see over the front seat. My father is driving through a huge storm. The rain pours down the windscreen. Blurry shapes of storm-driven trees whirl past. He is driving carefully and my mother is afraid. It's his first car and he's only had two driving lessons. My grandparents sit on either side of me in the back seat. I can feel their warm knees pressing against my sides. There is no sister. She isn't born yet and I am safe amongst all these large people who love me and my father who is so cleverly driving on and on into the night where nothing can happen to us because he knows everything. I am probably two years old.

Another thunderstorm. My mother is hanging out the washing on the verandah. I run and hide my face in her green cotton dress. She often wears green. For years it becomes the colour I hate most because I associate it with her. But now she looks down smiling as a clap of thunder shakes the farmhouse. She takes me by the hand and we go into the bedroom. My baby sister is sleeping in her wooden cot, her short black curls fall against her chubby face. She has long, sooty black eyelashes like a sleeping doll.

'Ssh!' says my mother. 'Isn't she beautiful? Don't wake her. *She's* not afraid.'

I pretend to agree but she seems alien to me with my yellow hair and thin body, and I am surprised by jealousy.

The new farmhouse is being built. The old one stays where it is, corrugated iron and a weathered, grey jarrah verandah. The new house beside it smells of sawn timber and asbestos walls. I take my crayons and draw all over the lovely whiteness. How thrilling it is.

My father takes my hand and speaks to me seriously. 'Look what you've done, Nip,' he says. 'You've spoilt the beautiful wall.'

I shake my head. I want to cry. Can't he see that I only wanted to make it even more beautiful?

'I want you to promise me you'll never do such a thing again.'

Molly, too light for a plough horse, has a new foal. I go with my father, tiptoeing through the early-morning frost. 'Be very quiet. Don't frighten her,' he says. I hold my breath. They are standing in the clearing. The foal is perfect, a white star on her forehead, her forelegs trembling. Everything is bright green. The sunlight, slanting through the clearing, outlines the foal's coat with silver. The scene holds, trembles, reflected in the glass of the morning.

'Can I have her?' I whisper. 'Can she be my horse when she grows up? Can I ride her?'

'We'll see.'

I will call her Star. But he is only being diplomatic, because, later he sells them both to the Dutchman on the neighbouring farm.

Another memory. I am walking at dusk to the stables with my pet joey hopping through the dust beside me. I am just like Dot and the kangaroo. The joey has a leather collar around its neck and it follows me everywhere, but the dogs pull it down and kill it. Nobody tells me where it has gone, but I know.

An old woman in a large black silk dress and a white lace cap sits under a walnut tree in a Beechworth garden. Her face, when she turns, is fragile as paper. 'This is Great-Aunt Kate,' they say, pushing me forward, and she takes my head in her hands and speaks in a strange lilting voice; the voice of my grandfather when he speaks the Cornish of his forebears. 'Where's goin' thee? Goin' tay matin'. Hear chillun singin' luvely.'

I am five years old and we have gone on our trip to the eastern states to visit my father's relative at Korong Vale and the last of the Coades in Beechworth.

Beechworth ... the magic town where my grandfather lived when he was a boy. His mother kept the pub and it still stands, The Star Hotel, a youth hostel now, where once the drinkers gathered round the bar and cheered the actors in the playhouse at the back.

Blanche Coade was a Cornish servant who married a miner old enough to be her father. He died when my grandfather was only two, so she married again and had several more children. When her second husband died she was in her fifties but she married my grandfather's best friend, who was only in his twenties, and my grandfather cried for a week. I stare at her photograph: a stout, unbelievably ugly woman with a big coarse face and a knob of hair. Why did he marry her? Was it the pub, or did she have unknown female charms that just don't show? Afterwards my mother says darkly, looking at me, 'It must be in the blood.'

She drank and died of asthma and her young husband outlived her but she must have made the most of it while she could, my ugly Cornish great-grandmother. A pewter beer mug blessed, they said, with the lips of Ned Kelly, still stands on the shelf in my study, all I have inherited from her except that suspect blood.

The evening is full of bats flitting like tiny, eerie birds through the air. The poddy calves frisk in the home paddock, lifting their tails; amongst them is Blucher, the son of Amen. Amen is the crooked cow with the hollow back, so named by my father because she looks like 'the last word'.

My grandfather starts up his new Willy's Knight and drives it like a stump-jump plough straight at the wooden gates that lead on to Yealering road. My father runs to open them but he drives straight through, one gate hanging lopsided over the radiator. He doesn't stop but grins out of the driver's window. 'Don't worry about opening the gate, Tom,' he yells and waves and is gone in a spurt of dust, driving with one hand into the distance, his nicotine-stained moustache-ends streaming in the wind.

Dew falls in the garden, swimming with the scent of sweet peas, stocks, carnations and love-in-a-mist. The dusty asparagus fern shakes by the tank stand.

2

◆

IN 1912 my grandfather rode out the fourteen miles from Wickepin with his two brothers-in-law, and took up three thousand acres of virgin land. They called it Lambton Downs. The rather pretentious name was significant. These first-generation Australians always referred to England as 'home', and the Lambton came from my grandmother's background. Her stepfather was once owner of a plaster works at Lambton in County Durham.

He migrated to New Zealand, where my grandmother was born, and then to Victoria, where the new plaster works in Melbourne apparently went close to bankruptcy. His portrait in the family photograph album shows a white-bearded patriarch with gold watch and chain looped across his waistcoat, his arm clasping a round-faced, doll-like child – my mother.

It's interesting, and I suppose understandable, that my grandmother, that purveyor of dark family secrets in her corrugated-iron sleepout, should have kept the secret of her own birth inviolable. She was the illegitimate daughter of Margaret Thompson, a Methodist Irishwoman from Belturbot in County Cavan.

Margaret Thompson, known as 'the Bolter', ran away with an Irish sailor and her name was for ever expunged from the family Bible. She became housekeeper to Robert Tindale at Lambton, and when he emigrated to New Zealand she and her lover went with him. Two daughters, Elizabeth and Mary, were born in the new country. The sailor deserted her and she married Robert Tindale. They sailed for Victoria, where she had five more children and died of cancer in South Melbourne. My grandmother nursed her and, in response to her pleas for a merciful release, administered the overdose of morphine that killed her. The death certificate was signed, without question, by a sympathetic doctor.

The version my mother told me had a significant twist. In her story, Bess and Mary were the legitimate offspring and the five children of Robert Tindale and Margaret Thompson were the bastards, which would have made the second marriage, if it occurred, bigamous. But according to the Irish connection, my mother's story was fictitious. My sailor great-grandfather disappeared into history and I don't even know his name.

I only saw Bess once, in Melbourne: an ugly, great bully of a woman lying in an airless, darkened bedroom. A professional invalid who hadn't got up for years, lording it over an unfortunate daughter and son-in-law, she took to her bed – the last refuge of the strong-minded woman.

Apparently neither Bess nor Mary got on with the rest of the Tindale family, particularly their half-brothers. They were considered difficult, headstrong and unwomanly.

Mary solved her problem by marrying Edward James Elgin Coade, a charming weakling, and becoming shadow minister of the family fortunes. When they met he was a counter-jumper in a Melbourne draper's. She came in on her birthday to buy a length of dress material and discovered it was his birthday too, although he was a year younger (a secret she kept hidden all her life).

He was a bit of a dandy. Her half-brothers called him Mary's ten-bob-a-week toff. He used to swagger down Swanston Street on a Saturday afternoon in a silk bell-topper, twirling a walking stick. That top hat lay on top of the wardrobe for years, battered but still debonair, until my youngest son wore it to a fancy dress party, and our dog Alf ate it.

There was a general strike and a bank failure in the East, but an El Dorado had opened up in the West. Ted and Mary set sail for Fremantle with their baby daughter. He had been offered 'a billet' as a window-dresser in the Perth branch of Bon Marché. Still Mary wasn't satisfied. 'You'll never better yourself while you're working for wages.' So Ted went partners in a tiny general store across the railway line, and sussed out the goldfields in the nineties rush, not for the chimera of gold, but for the lower-middle-class realities of 'trade'. His reminiscences were laced with wild stories of Paddy Hannan lighting his pipe in the bar with fivers and carriage horses, shod with gold, flashing through the streets of Kalgoorlie.

When the line went through, they followed it one hundred and fifty miles to Wickepin, and set up their own general store. Ted used to go out in his horse and dray selling stores at one hundred per cent profit to the navvies along the line.

Whisky was the problem. It had always been the problem. My mother had a lifelong horror of 'strong drink'. 'I'm a wowser, and proud of it,' she'd say, with her irritating self-righteousness. She was an only child and every afternoon she came home from school to an empty house to get the tea and then it was off to the pub to stand outside in her frilly white pinafore and button-up boots, plaintively asking for 'Farvie'. Her mother sent her because of the moral persuasion, and maybe because of her own unshakeable pride. Besides, René was his darling, his 'pet', the apple of his eye. They went everywhere together, spanking over the Causeway Bridge with Dolly, the ambler. Racing the other turnouts, they arrived triumphant at Como to go crabbing off the end of the jetty.

When they shifted to Wickepin she was sixteen years old. He'd come back from his travels up the line, roaring drunk. He was quite good at hiding it, and Mary was never perceptive, but René always knew. Ginger, his big, rawboned chestnut, brought him home but the next day the retribution . . . Farvie vomiting, with a sore head and the terrible remorse.

The whisky made him belligerent, so there were black eyes in the pub and blood to cope with as well. His last and most famous exploit was the ride he took for a bet into the bar of the Wickepin pub. Ginger reared and shat on the turkey-red carpet, sending the bottles and glasses flying.

He won the bet but then came the morning after . . . the item in the local paper, the publican's bill for the carpet and sundry breakages. It was too much. Mary and René packed up and left to catch the train. Tearful, he found them at the station. They drove a hard bargain. Not another drop as long as he lived . . . and he kept his word. For the rest of his life Ted drank only lemonade.

His daughter's reaction was strange. For the rest of *her* life she told the story to anyone who would listen. When she buttonholed perfect strangers in Boan's Department Store and retold the tale of her father's wild ride, her eyes would glow with excitement. This was her dream father, a kind of 'man from Snowy River', thundering up the turkey-red carpet, throwing his hat in the ring, the red horse rearing, glamourized and frozen for ever in that one magnificent gesture.

He was the surrogate lover she longed for – not Percy Blake, the Manchester goods traveller, who kept dusty acid drops in his pocket and loved her romantically . . . not even my father, the Black Prince, riding through Corrigin on his black stallion, the war hero with his DCM and his Croix de Guerre, playing his mournful cornet in his single, rented room over the main street.

Which was, I suppose, why she fell in love with a charming young drunkard who came to keep the books in the Wickepin store. He wanted to marry her, but the other side of her – that streak of natural caution – dictated the answer. They said goodbye on the beach at Cottesloe, and when she'd gone he waited till the tide came in and obliterated the last trace of her footprints.

Years later, she was vindicated. She saw him driving a rubbish cart along St George's Terrace, hunched over, in a shabby overcoat in the rain. It was a cautionary Dickensian tale.

I am programmed to play that role in her life, to inherit the romantic non-cautionary side of her, to live out that part of her personality and to be both loved and hated for it. But there is a streak of caution in me, if only she'd known it, that will guarantee my survival. The struggle to come to terms with my mother dominated most of my life. Her switches of mood from protective love to destructive hatred bewilder me. I learnt never to trust in her benevolence because it was sure to be followed by persecution.

Often it seems to me I have two mothers. There is the mother who lights the little night-light sweetly singing 'There's a long, long trail awinding into the land of my dreams', and wakes us in the mornings, pulling back the bedroom curtains, with:

Good morning merry sunshine
What made you wake so soon?
As yet the early rising sun
Has not attained his noon

and the mother who calls me 'a great gawk' and, frothing at the mouth, her face red and swollen, beats me with an iron-edged ruler, then clasps me to her sobbing, crying that she is 'a wicked mother to treat her little girl like this'.

These strong, dominating (even domineering) women are perpetually fuming with an excess of energy and nothing satisfactory to use it on. My mother continually admonishes us 'not to get married and have a family if you want to get on'. My grandmother is a shrewd, calculating businesswoman and without her there would have been no family fortune. But in all the years of partnership, her name never appears on the shop awning or the business letters. She is truly, although nobody believes it, 'the silent partner'.

Still she has *Science and Health, with Key to the Scriptures*, and the *Christan Science Monitor* sent from America and Saint Mary Baker Eddy, the crazy epileptic – 'God is love' and 'There is no sensation in matter' – to transfigure her worldly empire.

Yet in comparison to most other women of their class and time they are emancipated, unusually powerful because they are financially independent. My grandmother virtually runs the family business. 'If you want to get an answer, go to Mrs Coade. She's the real boss.' So much so that years later the image of her, senile, bewildered, resentful, sitting at the dining-room table with my mother literally guiding her hand while she signed over power of attorney, was never to leave me. Or do I imagine it? Was my grandmother really incapable by then of understanding what was happening to her? And yet I do remember it clearly, my mother's implacable face ... and some primitive atavistic part of my grandmother that understood only too well that abdication of power.

As the child of wealthy parents, my mother always had her own money ... a separate bank account, property and shares. For years my father regularly placed the same pitiful amount of housekeeping money on the table. He had no idea of the real cost of living and she kept it hidden from him, augmenting the weekly sum from her own purse so that he, who had started with a debt of one hundred pounds to my grandfather, went on quietly amassing a considerable fortune of his own.

I take down the photograph of my mother in her wedding gown standing alone. My father always hated having his picture taken and refused to stand beside her for the traditional wedding portrait.

She poses there, uncertain: the round, sweet, vulnerable face, the large hazel eyes, the long Irish upper lip, the dark curling hair. 'Men shot themselves in the scrub on her wedding day,' says my grandmother, with dramatic overstatement. In another faded sepia print, dressed in riding breeches, khaki shirt and wide-brimmed felt hat, she's pretending to swagger, smoking a pipe. There is a fox terrier at her knee. She loved dogs and there was always a Nip or a Rex in her life. She was a good swimmer and a good rider, refusing to ride sidesaddle or wear the prescribed divided skirt.

What have these images to do with the angry overweight woman who loved cream sponges and ham sandwiches and fought a neurotic battle against fat all her life? But then I never knew my mother in those earlier days. Perhaps I don't really know her now.

Marriage destroys her. She has no talent for it, and she married the wrong man anyway. She loves company and talk and outings and travel. She is outgoing and affectionate, while he is almost a recluse, introverted and moody, a bookworm who finds it hard to show his real feelings and can never understand what she finds to do all day 'in town' – mostly window-shopping. Was he always like that or was there another man I glimpsed once at the Bowling Club in the bar, telling stories and jokes, the life of the party? He loves to argue, changing his political opinions like a weathercock according to his opponent, and when visitors come (the ones he approves of) he is often transfigured. But at home he grows more and more silent.

My mother has always wanted to be an interior decorator, and she has a real talent for it ... furnishings, colour schemes, china. I cruelly mock her taste in paintings – 'Bluebell Wood' and 'Autumn Fires'. How pitifully proud she is when she exchanges them for Van Gogh's 'Sunflowers', how she waits for my approval – and gets it, grudgingly. She often goes to art exhibitions, and buys me a Namatjira 'Ghost Gum' and an Elizabeth Durack oil of a young Aboriginal girl sitting naked on a rock. 'Girls can do anything better than boys,' she tells us firmly, but we want to be boys. Was that why she took us to the Boys' Department at Boan's Department Store and bought us khaki shirts and serge trousers with braces? The male shop assistant was scandalized as we triumphantly tried them on in the changing rooms. 'They're more sensible,' she told him. 'We're from the bush and they're always climbing trees.'

And yet she was the victim of her upbringing. Years later, when my father was dead, she told me plaintively, 'If only I had a son to advise me.' I raged at her: 'You've got two daughters, one's a doctor, one teaches at a university. Most people consider us quite bright, you know. How dare you insult us by saying you need a son!'

There were great advantages in living in a close-knit three-generation family who were all obsessive oral storytellers, but it also meant that we lived at the centre of inherited traumas. The relationships were all on the maternal side. My father's family were the outsiders. On summer nights we lay in the hammock on the verandah listening to the murmur of adult voices endlessly recounting the web of stories that crisscrossed the generations.

My father resented my grandfather, and who could blame him? It must have been galling. Every time he didn't accede to her wishes, . or dilly-dallied in the carrying out of some task, my mother circumvented him with 'I'll ask Father'. It was Father who was always roped in to pack the car when she went on holidays because he was 'such a marvellous packer'. It was Father who was always asked for advice.

As for the running war between my mother and my grandmother, it had a hundred malicious variations, in which I was often the pawn.

In the butterbox bookcase in my grandmother's sleepout I found an old sepia photograph of my father's family – eight brothers and three sisters.

'Who's that?' I said.

'That's your Uncle Harry. He went mad and had to be locked up in the asylum. He had sunstroke.'

My father had never mentioned Harry. Long afterwards, when I asked my mother about him, she told me that when my father first drove her out to visit his parents, there was a barred room in the house and Harry emerged only once to sit at the tea table with downcast eyes, saying nothing. She was never introduced. 'Who's that?' she asked, driving home again. 'Oh! Just one of the boys,' my father said, his face darkening.

It was obviously a sore point, but there was a streak of instability in the Hewett boys. Frank, the eldest, locked his wife and daughter up and pushed food under the door to them for weeks at a time because he believed they were having sexual relations with his sons. When we visited Uncle Frank (which was seldom) there was a weird atmosphere in the place. He sat at the head of the table, dark, round faced, overweight, with a peculiar, sly smile that made me feel uneasy. His four sons hardly spoke and his tall, skinny daughter was silent. Under Aunt Lizzie's oil paintings of white horses with rolling eyes, her own eyes rolled hysterically.

In 1954, sitting in front of the fire in the study of my parents' big house in Heidelberg, where I had fled from my own disastrous nine-year liaison with a paranoid schizophrenic, my father talked to me once about his eldest brother.

He was living and working in Melbourne when he got the letter from his father saying that Frank was ill and was coming to Melbourne for a rest and a holiday. Would Tom look after him and see that he saw a doctor? He went down to the docks, but there was no Frank. That night a note was pushed surreptitiously under the door. Frank couldn't contact him yet. He was on the run from Lizzie. She'd followed him from Western Australia and was trying to poison him.

Late one night he turned up, mad as a hatter. Under some pretext my father got him to a doctor.

'Your brother is suffering from a paralysis of the insane,' the doctor told him. 'It's caused by untreated VD but it's been left too late and there's nothing I can do.'

'How could that be true?' My father stared into the fire. 'There were no women living out there in the bush. Until he married Lizzie he'd never even have seen one.'

'What do you think caused the madness then?'

'Sunstroke,' he said. 'And that was what did it for my brother Harry.' It was one of the few times in our lives when we talked intimately together.

My paternal grandparents had immigrated to Western Australia after the First World War, following their two eldest sons to Kunjin, a wheat and sheep district in the Great Southern. Land was cheap and the dairy farm in Korong Vale outside Bendigo could hardly support so many sons. They called their new farm 'The Vale'.

I always felt that my father was ashamed and uneasy with his family. He had never got on with his mother and left home at fifteen to be appreciated as a carriage builder in the Newport Railway Workshops in Melbourne. The Hewetts didn't speak properly, said 'was' instead of 'were' and besides, they were dreamy Esaus and he had crossed over and given his allegiance to the Jacobs . . . the money-makers and the landowners who lived not by the morality of the true dissenters but by the Protestant ethic of 'getting on'. He was the bright one, who had educated himself at night school at the Working Men's College in Melbourne, and married into money.

There is a streak of religious mania in the Hewetts – fanatical Protestant dissenters who, in the next generation, would become Exclusive Brethren. Seventh-Day Adventists and Jehovah's Witnesses, they built ugly makeshift jarrah churches and drove their children to the services three times a day on Sundays. No wonder my father says, 'In religious matters we can be left to make up our own minds.'

His father was the son of a Methodist minister from Norfolk, but his mother was the centre of this religious fanaticism. It was a cheerless religion, with no cards, no drink, no movies, no theatre, no dancing and a lot of sin and fire and brimstone. Vengeful lay preachers, Methodist and Baptist, grew up like mushrooms in Kunjin, the Baptists dipping their sheet-wrapped congregation in the muddy waters of the local creeks.

Vale Farm has cool cement verandahs and pepper trees scattering their red seeds at the gate. My grandmother comes out, a tiny dumpy woman in a dusty black dress, bent double with rheumatism, snow-white hair pulled back in a bun, dark-skinned nose like a hawk, velvet deep-set eyes. I never liked her. Once she holds me between her strong knees and forces castor oil (the supposed cure for all childish ailments) down my throat. I vomit it up all over her.

But my grandfather, Ephraim Hewett, is a delightful, whimsical man, small and wiry, with a high soprano voice and a shock of grey-black curls. He can toss pancakes over his shoulder to land in the pan and, even at the age of seventy, can take a running jump at a horse and land squarely on its back. At night he piles huge mallee roots in the fireplace that is as tall as a man, till the sparks fly up and the little parlour, crammed with furniture and china knickknacks, grows hotter and hotter. There are hideous coloured photographs of all 'the boys' (except my father and Uncle Harry) glaring from the corrugated-iron walls in oval frames lined with velvet. I can hardly keep my own eyes open as the eyes of 'the boys' goggle and swim like genies in the firelight.

My grandparents live with their two youngest sons and an

unmarried daughter. Aunt Alice has never married because she is bald and wears a white cotton cap on her head. When she was a girl she had radiation treatment for eczema of the scalp. The radiation burnt her scalp so badly that she lost all her hair and eventually died in agony in the Corrigin Hospital. A sweet-natured woman with a handsome face like my father, she had one middle-aged boyfriend, but my grandmother put a stop to that. She is needed on the farm. She takes us to feed the pigs at dusk, her white cap bobbing above her thin, black-clad frame.

One winter's night we stay so late at 'The Vale' that we have to sleep over – my mother, my sister and I – three to a bed on a sagging double mattress. The room is stuffy, the tiny window is jammed shut and my mother and sister keep rolling me out of bed as they turn. There is a peculiar acrid smell in the room and my mother says the sheets are damp, but what else can you expect. Next morning when she finds the chamber pot under the bed, brimful of ancient yellow liquid, she swears we'll never stay overnight again – and we never do.

My father always left Vale Farm in a rage because he usually discovered my grandfather up on the twenty-foot tank stand fixing the windmill.

'Why don't you let the boys do that, Dad?'

'Oh, they reckon they get dizzy.'

'The boys' were Uncle Roy, who had a hump on his back from a TB infection as a child and died young, and Uncle Don, who died at forty of poliomyelitis in an iron lung in Royal Perth Hospital.

It was at 'The Vale' that I discovered Alfred Noyes's ballad of 'The Highwayman' in an old annual that must have once belonged to 'the boys'. It tingled my spine for years afterwards. Whenever I thought of the highwayman lying dead on his blood in the highway with a bunch of lace at his throat and Bess, the landlord's daughter, plaiting a dark red loveknot into her long black hair, or Tim the ostler with hair like mouldy hay, I'd be back again in the weird, green half-light of evening, with the pigs squealing from the yard, 'the boys'' eyes watching me from the walls of the blazing hot parlour and their treasure trove of dusty annuals waiting to be devoured.

They were all olive-skinned and black-haired, the Hewetts, and there were dark hints of 'black blood', 'a touch of the tarbrush' that was supposed to come from my grandmother ... wild stories of Aborigine blood or Maori or even a tall tale that we were the descendants of Hiawatha. A more plausible explanation is that Alice Hughes, my paternal grandmother, was the daughter of a Scotsman and a German Jewess who migrated to Bendigo in the Gold Rush.

At Lambton Downs I read the Billabong books and wish I had

two brothers like Norah of Billabong. My father gets books sent from
Perth and reads *The Seven Pillars of Wisdom*. A rogue horse called Jack
almost kicks out his eye. He tells us how to walk long distances,
stepping out heel to toe, but our mother says it's unladylike and you
should point your toe first. She seems to be getting madder. She beats
me often now, her face flushed red, her eyes crazy. She is menopausal
at only thirty-five, but I don't understand why she hates me. My
grandmother beckons me into the sleepout and I try not to go. She
has betrayed me too many times already but it is so seductive, the
sympathy, the bogus understanding. I know I am being used as a
weapon in some deadly struggle, but I seem powerless to control it.
Why do I go into the warm double bed smelling of old people? Why
do I weep and show her the ruler marks on my arms and legs?

'You great lout!' screams my mother, and I lie in bed at night
feeling clumsy and unloveable, pulling my legs up, trying to will them
to stop growing in case I turn out to be like Uncle Frank's daughter,
my six-foot cousin Vera. 'She'll be as tall as Vera,' they say, but they
are quite wrong and I needn't have bothered. It is disastrous for a girl
to be six foot. It narrows the choice of males and means you are
unfeminine and can never wear high heels. I have decided I don't
want to be unfeminine. I want to be a kind of superfemale, but still
small, desirable and tender.

Tea at night, and the men are in from the paddocks. I hear my
grandmother's silky voice across the kitchen table: 'You should see
what your wife has been doing to your poor little daughter today,
Tom. The weals on her legs are terrible.'

I dare not raise my eyes from the mashed potatoes I hate. They
stick in my throat.

'What have you been doing?' my father says.

'Nothing.'

I swallow the potato in a burning lump. My mother's terrible eyes
are staring at me.

'She's a disobedient girl,' she says.

'She doesn't mean to be, do you, pet?' My grandfather is my
friend and ally, the only other blond in the room. Dark, dark, dark,
they all sit, relentlessly masticating their food. I try to slip away.

'I'll see you in the bedroom,' hisses my mother. She goes ahead of
me, carrying the night-light. She is standing by the dressing-table, her
shadow huge on the white walls. The carved heads of the griffins are
grinning at me from the doors. The wind blows the curtains in and
out, out and in. She is holding a tiny bottle in her hand, full of some
brownish liquid. I think of *Alice In Wonderland* and the white rabbit.
Her eyes blaze.

'This is poison,' she hisses. 'Tell me what you told Nana or I'll take it now.'

I lunge at her, trying to reach up and snatch it away. She holds it higher and tilts the bottle. Her eyes are watching me.

'And you'll always know you killed your mother,' she whispers.

'No, no!' I scream.

She clamps her broad hand over my mouth. I am struggling in her grasp. 'What did you say?'

I can't speak. I am choking. Why doesn't somebody come?

She takes her hand away. 'Tell me.'

I will tell her anything at all, as long as I don't have to carry this burden of guilt past her grave, because I *am* guilty. I hate my mother. I have sometimes wished she was dead.

'I told her I wished you would die,' I say, and I'm glad to say it, even though it is a lie, because her face is so shocked. She drops me. She stares. I have got through to her at last. 'Get into bed,' she says, through her teeth. I put on my flannel pyjamas. She stands watching like Judgement Day. I hide in the little bed against the wall I sleep in. My sister shares the double bed with my mother under the window. She is angry with me because I've refused to share it too. I can't breathe with big bodies beside me. I must sleep alone. It's my only independence. I wonder if my father feels the same out in his single bed in the sleepout.

They have never slept together in all the time I can remember, and they never will. She is writing something by the night-light on the dressing-table. I lie absolutely still. Perhaps if I don't move she might go away. But no, she is pinning the paper to the bedhead. I don't move a muscle. 'Read it,' she says, holding the night-light high above her head. I twist round. The words are printed . . . big, jagged, black: I MUST NOT TELL LIES AGAINST MY MOTHER. I sob. This is the worst of all. I must sleep under this all night, maybe for ever, like a brand on my forehead. 'If you pull it down I'll beat you till you're black and blue' – and she goes out of the room.

The farm is the centre of our existence, our Garden of Eden, but I always know that under the bridal creeper and the ivy geraniums, the black snakes wait and slide.

CHAPTER

3
♣

EVERY year, after the shearing is over in October, we leave for the Royal Show, staying in the old Como house with Lapp and his crystal set.

Lapp is an eccentric, our friend and ally, a failure in the great game of life. Absent-mindedly he fries up his spectacles with his breakfast egg and bacon, reads our poems and stories, and writes us enthusiastic letters, illustrated with his own cartoons. An ex-journalist whose fiancée faded away in a TB sanatorium, to us he is a deeply romantic figure. Standing in the dim kitchen with his high domed forehead and flyaway hair, telling his endless stories, he is my first critic and my first fan.

In the city I am a divided being with a terrible contempt for 'the townies'. Yet I have intuited that there is something different about us. Are we awkward 'bushies', country yokels? Is there something wrong with our clothes? I roll my long white socks around my ankles to be a 'bobbysoxer' like the other girls, but my mother asks me what I have done with my garters.

I stare solemnly in the shop windows trying to decide what is wrong with us. When the shop assistants say, 'what a lovely day', and my mother answers, 'no good for the crops', I wince with embarrassment.

I am looking for heroes and heroines and one evening, full of doves' cries, I go hand in hand with my father through the stile and the jarrah grove to find them.

My little sister screams as I disappear in my tiers of pale-blue muslin dotted with tiny, darker-blue roses. The night is full of glamour. I am going out alone with my father to see *The Desert Song* at the Capitol Theatre. I have toothache but I'm not going to let on in case I have to stay home. It's almost as if I know that a signpost is about to appear in my life pointing towards a most peculiar destiny for a little bush girl living thousands of miles from the rest of the world.

I sit transfixed as the curtain rises and the Red Shadow, on the Capitol stage, rides out in his crimson cloak, mounted on a real snow-white horse. This, then, is where it has all been leading: the make-up games (as we call them), the dress parades under the salmon gums, Suzette de la Falaise, and Lucia di Lammermoor, the wax doll with her face melting under the almond trees. I have found my destiny.

When J. C. Williamson's play *The White Horse Inn* has a season at His Majesty's I am there in the audience, heart in my mouth, transmogrified into those illuminated beings up there on the stage; the tiny blonde doll-like actress playing the lead dances and sings like an angel with her tiny blond leading man.

When the curtain falls and we go out into the streets, it seems to me that we have left the real world behind us, that this world everybody else considers 'real' is only a world of phantoms.

On our train trip to the eastern states on the Trans-Continental a miracle occurs: the whole cast of *The White Horse Inn* is on board, rolling across the desert to Melbourne. I bask in their golden presence, sitting on the glamorous laps of 'the girl' and 'the boy' (as I call them) eating chocolates with soft centres in silver wrappers, treated like a princess. 'The girl' has a blonde, bobbed cap of hair and wears very short skirts so that you can see her jazz garters. 'The boy', in silver-grey flannel bags and a white silk shirt, looks just like Scott Fitzgerald (only I don't know it yet).

For a few brief illuminated days I share the life of these magic beings 'on tour' and then they disappear into the darkness at Adelaide, never knowing the permanent dream they have created in the breast of one five-year-old girl.

Perth, for me, is a mecca of new experiences, and the centre of it is 'West's', my grandfather's cinema and open-air picture garden in the working-class suburb of Subiaco. Here I am transported into another legendary world . . . the silver screen. I become a dedicated and knowledgeable film fan: my dream heroine is Greta Garbo. I consume everything about her – Greta Gustafson, the gawky milliner who, living on a lake called Stillfarden, is discovered by Maurice Stiller, the famous Swedish director, and taken to Hollywood.

I go home to the farm and write a musical, *Lynette the Gypsy Dancer*. On my birthday the kids come from the neighbouring farms and are dragooned into playing in it – with only one afternoon's rehearsal – before an audience of our parents. My sister and I play the leads, of course. She is Lynette and I am Tam, the Gypsy Prince.

Every year on my birthday I am given another Film Annual. My father calls them 'Dorothy's Bible'.

And now my inventions in the sleepout become even more outrageous . . . divorced couples, extramarital affairs, blazing love stories proliferate under the corrugated-iron ceiling until Marjory Day from the next farm is not allowed to play with us any more because we are 'too sophisticated'. But this is not a great tragedy. She doesn't seem to get the hang of it anyway, can't remember her lines and is a hopeless actress. Besides, ever since I hit her over the head with a claw hammer when we were playing 'doctors', she doesn't really trust me – and who can blame her?

My dreams have an architectural construct now. When I grow up I will be a famous writer *and* a famous actress and live in a mansion called Fairhaven on the banks of Lake Stillfarden. I will never marry but I will have many lovers and many children and many servants to do the hated housework. In the evenings I will lounge on a crimson velvet divan in the Red Resting Room receiving my lovers and the other celebrities in a cloud of incense under the wavering light of the candelabra.

Fairhaven has a distinct resemblance to the picture palaces built in the thirties to feed the Depression dreams of the disaffected masses. My grandfather's cinema is restrained Art Nouveau with artificial garlands of pink roses and classical statues from Tindale's plaster works, miraculously born again in Perth under the ownership of my great uncle, Robert Tindale. He is also responsible for the design of the Ambassador's, a blue-ceilinged fabulous rococo with artificial clouds and false stars that really twinkle. Draped terracotta Grecian ladies gaze down from carved alcoves, and a stuffed macaw swings on a bamboo perch in the upstairs lounge.

The Tindales are really rich. They go on yearly sea trips to Europe and their wide verandahed house in Mount Lawley is crammed with bronze statues, naked except for a fig-leaf, standing with dim, pointed lights like ice-cream cones in their hands. When we go to visit we are taken into a sitting room full of overstuffed furniture and have to sit on leather pouffes from Aden and yell, terrified, into Great-Aunt Edie's ear trumpet. She is almost stone deaf.

My father always refuses to go with us. When my mother was married from this house, Great-Aunt Edie followed him down the hall, sweeping up the mud from his boots with a brush and pan. Insulted, he never went back again.

We share our father's contempt for their snobbery and there is something a bit creepy about Uncle Bob, sitting at the head of the table, cracking jokes under the bronze bust of 'The Frowning Boy', something not really benevolent about his portly frame. For Uncle Bob is a tyrant and a bully. He has stopped Great-Aunt Eva marrying her boyfriend because he is 'common', and promised her 'a home for life' if she gives him up. Uncle Bob's acne-scarred daughter Marjie, with her affected Perth College drawl, doesn't marry until he is dead and buried. I wonder if Aunty Eva in her mauve bedroom, treated like a kind of superior servant, thinks she has made a good bargain.

Sometimes we are taken to be 'baby-sat' at the home of Great-Aunt Mabel, with her shingled hair and her magnificent bust, in black silk decorated with a strand of pearls. She lives in Como with our Great-Uncle Ned, an abrupt, dark-browed, silent man in glasses, the only one of my grandmother's family to go to university. They all went without to get Ned through his degree and he has repaid them by becoming chief engineer of the Public Works Department, designing the Fremantle Bridge and the Canning Dam. But these visits end suddenly when Aunt Mabel divorces him and everybody remembers that she was a barmaid in Kalgoorlie and her name is not spoken again. Ned lives alone in a melancholy house with jarrah floors, shaded by pines, and even my mother, who was once his favourite, is afraid to visit him now.

During the year of the Great Fire my father has rheumatics so badly he has to hobble on broomstick crutches. We live for months at Como while he takes the mineral-water cure at the baths. When nothing seems to work and the doctor tells him he'll have to have all his teeth out, he comes back from the dentist with a false set and we sit and weep because he can't be our father. His face is so changed. Now he can't play Schubert's 'Serenade' on the cornet in the sleepout any more. His false teeth slip on the mouthpiece. But his rheumatism gets better and bothers him only when the weather changes.

On sweltering summer nights we sit in the farm kitchen waiting for the line of trees to stir along the banks of the creek. We are waiting for the Albany Doctor to roar up 250 miles across forest and scrub and sandplain from the Indian ocean.

After the harvest we leave for Albany to live hugger mugger in the tiny cottage facing the sea behind the line of sandhills. Albany is full of wheatbelt farmers. Our cousins are there from Kunjin, and the Dougans, the Irish connection from Corrigin, have their beach house next to ours – the last two houses set apart on the beachfront next to the Katanning Reserve.

We build cubby houses of moss and creeper and vines and play Daddy Potstick and cricket and rummy and Rickety Kate and Strip Jack Naked, when it rains.

The dunny is up the back on a low hill and our Irish cousins pull up the wooden flap behind the pan to see our bottoms. They flick up our skirts and try to see the colour of our pants, yelling 'Poppy Show', till I get tired of it and dance on the wooden table used for cleaning the fish, holding my dress up high and screaming 'have a good look!' till they are abashed and slink away.

They are not really Irish and they are our cousins fourth removed, the sons of Jimmy Dougan, my grandmother's first cousin from Armagh, nephew of the famous 'Bolter'. He is something of a 'stage Irishman' with a heavy brogue who runs Mackay's Farm Machinery Agency in Corrigin and married the local schoolteacher.

The interior life of the farm disappears altogether. Albany is all action, winning races and sand-castle competitions and signing the pledge at the Temperance Union Picnic. Our father goes fishing at Emu Point and turns green when he sees the fishing boats bobbing in the channel.

Along the roads in Denmark the Pommy migrants drive their spring carts and the Pommy kids in their hessian rags stare at us as we pass. They have been given a block each in the karri forest, with a cow and an axe, by Premier Jimmy (Moocow) Mitchell in his disastrous land settlement scheme, and now they stand there, dressed in sugar bags, with the sun slanting between the aisles of the karri trees, their faces pinched in the rainy light.

Once a week I go to learn drawing from Miss Brenda Holland in the house with the ruby-red pane of glass in the door, on the hill overlooking the town and the Princess Royal Harbour. She is a kind, vague spinster with a red mottled face under a hand-woven reed hat. She sets up the still life of fruit with a jug and bowl, a cup and saucer, and tries to teach me perspective and shading, but it all goes wrong. On the walls are her oil paintings of the last of the King George's Sound Aborigines and sepia etchings by Van Raalte of eerie white-limbed karri forests.

After a storm the beach is littered with shells and at night we lie in bed listening to the surf. Once a pod of whales are driven up mysteriously on to the sand and lie there, dark, mournful monsters, dying.

Then it's time to lock the house and leave the bay with its ring of dark mountains. Two People Bay, where one day ornithologists will find the Noisy Scrub Bird, and the mountain I call Shangri-la luminous in the far distance.

We are going home for another year, driving up the road past the old she-oak, hearing the sheepdogs barking with excitement. The farm wraps itself round us once more. My father reads the rain gauge under the almond trees and taps the tanks to find the water level. The old patterns of dream and reality reassert themselves.

Once a week we go into Yealering for our stores – one street with the pub, the Co-op, the saddler's, the blacksmith's shop, the store rented by the Irishmen, Kingston & Salter's that belongs to my grandfather. Paul Kingston, with his wisps of pale hair and his long, high-coloured Irish face, runs the café at the end of town where my father buys us our favourite acid drops and his favourite 'spiders' . . . lemonade laced with ice cream.

This is the dark side of the town where the Aborigines and poor whites gather. I stand watching from the road, fascinated by the lint-haired, half-Aboriginal children with their dark, flat-nosed faces. Their black mother in a man's felt overcoat and old felt hat sits in a sulky, waiting, outside the pub. On my way home we pass Jack Baxter's weatherboard house with the stable leaning sideways and take bets on when it will all fall down. We might pass Miss Burrows, her face weathered by the sun, reined in on a big roan horse, or follow the crooked track of Jack Swannell's dray cart, with its wobbly wheel, Jack Swannell sitting up front, an albino in black glasses, staring over his draught horse's rump.

Dolly the ambler is dead and buried at the foot of the orchard. Ginger has rheumatics and my grandfather goes out in the frost each morning and props him up in the paddock.

There are moments like Wordsworth's 'spots of time' that emerge from the flux of the seasons. We are standing in front of a colonial two-storeyed house in a bright green home paddock. Our father is buying us two mountain ponies, one grey, one pale chestnut, from the Guildford landowner Walter Padbury. The ponies have been broken in by Hugo Throssell, the VC winner and husband of a writer called Katharine Prichard who lives in the house he built for her on the Old York Road. Katharine Prichard is a Communist and they call her 'the Red Witch of Greenmount'.

We take the ponies home but Goldie is a vicious little creature so we sell her to the butcher's boy. Silver is my pony, a delicate stepping grey. My father buys my sister Lesley a Shetland called Jimmy who puts his ears back and gallops like the wind. We call my sister the Prince of Wales because she is always falling off her pony.

I am driving down Hay Street with my father in 1933. There are canvas signs strung across the road that read SECESSION and 'Westralia for the Westralians'. My family are all eastern staters who have been transformed into patriotic West Australians. They are secessionists who believe that all the farmers' troubles can be traced back to Canberra. There is a referendum to separate West Australia off from the rest of Australia. The secessionists win and petition the Crown for separation, but the Crown rules that it is unconstitutional, and the secessionists lose.

My grandfather puts a carnation in his buttonhole and wears his best suit with the gold watch and chain. He belongs to the Freemasons. He is going to his Lodge meeting in Wickepin to 'ride the

My paternal grandparents: Ephraim Hewett, son of a Methodist minister from Suffolk, and Alice Hewett (née Hughes), his 'little Jewess'.

'These first generation Australians always referred to England as "home".' Mary, René and Ted Coade on their trip 'home' to London in 1911.

My father, Tom Hewett, the 'Black Prince', during the First World War.

'My mother was a dark round girl in a country town', (from 'Legend of the Green Country'). René Coade, aged twenty-four, in 1920.

My mother said that just before the photographer clicked his camera I deliberately tousled my hair. Myself, aged two.

'The air of that house always seems full of the sound of Indian doves cooing.' Myself and my sister Lesley on the verandah of my grandparent's house by the Swan River at Como, Perth 1927.

'The first house sits in the hollow of the heart.' Lambton Downs in the 1930s. Photo: René Hewett

Doing correspondence lessons at my butter-box school desk on the verandah at Lambton Downs. Myself, aged seven. Photo: René Hewett

Hiawatha and Lynette the Gypsy dancer in full regalia for the Yealering RSL fancy dress Ball. Myself and my sister Lesley in the farm orchard with Gwenny Hobson, the 'married couple's' baby, in the doll's pram, 1930. Photo: René Hewett

goat'. He looks magnificent. I have an image of him careering round a room full of beery, red-faced men, keeping his seat on a great, white, bucking billygoat with fearsome horns, his coat tails flying as he rides.

I can't add up or subtract. It's all a mystery to me but every year I win second prize for illustrated stories and poetry at the Royal Show. Only Alice Bland always beats me. We both have our poems published in a Correspondence School publication called *Brave Young Singers*. I despise Alice Bland's poetry. It's all about helping her mother and being a domestic treasure. At the Royal Show I am introduced to her in the Agricultural Pavilion. She is a wholesome-looking brunette with short bobbed hair, several years older and taller than I am. Impossible, though, to see her as a rival. It doesn't make sense.

My father is clever at arithmetic. At Korong Vale school, when they couldn't teach him any more, he became a pupil teacher at thirteen. He tries to explain it all to me but his methods are extraordinary; masses of little black figures march mysteriously up and down the page. My mind goes blank.

'Add it up,' he yells. 'Tell me the answer. Any baby could do it.' His dark face thrusts itself into mine, swollen with rage. 'I'll make you answer.'

He throws me over his knee and starts beating me hard with the flat of his hand. I am outraged. Although it hurts I can't even cry.

My grandfather bursts into the kitchen. 'Stop bullying that child.'

'She's my child and I'll do what I like with her.'

I feel like an object. My grandfather wrenches me off my father's knee. 'Don't interfere,' my father says. 'I'm warning you.'

'Get out of the way, Pet,' my grandfather says gently.

I love him more than anyone else. We look alike. We are the only blonds in the whole family for generations back. We have the same thick, curly golden hair, the same blue eyes, the same natural joyousness (when I can forget the black blood of the Hewett clan). I love to look in his photo album: all those faded sepia crowds of young men in boaters and striped blazers drunk on Sydney Harbour on holiday, their arms round wasp-waisted girls. I can always pick him out. He's the happiest and the drunkest of them all.

But now his eyes blaze. He and my father are facing each other in the middle of the kitchen floor, exchanging punches. My mother screams. 'Tom ... don't touch him ... Father!' My grandmother moans. The two men glare at each other like wild animals. Then my grandfather turns on his heel and walks out of the kitchen. There is a white line round my father's dark mouth. His eyes are crazy.

I lie in the sleepout, sobbing. Outside, through the flywire, I can hear my grandfather pacing up and down in the moonlight. I can smell the smoke from his cigarette mixed with the scent of dewy stocks and carnations.

My mother comes out into the garden. I strain my ears but I can hear only bits of the conversation.

'We'll pack up and leave tomorrow,' he tells her.

She is crying. She doesn't want him to go. 'Oh, Father!' she sobs.

Then I hear footsteps beside the bed. 'You wicked girl, you're not asleep,' she hisses. 'Do you know what you've done? You've driven your grandparents out of their home, and it's all your fault. Remember that.'

I lie in the darkness. Nothing will ever be any good again.

It's lonely after they've gone. Except for the sound of the swifts on the roof, the sleepout is empty. I hide on the back verandah amongst the stored apples reading my father's copy of Remarque's *All Quiet on the Western Front*. I'm horrified but I can't stop reading. So this is what war is all about . . . not my father's funny stories about Bracegirdle, the conceited Pommy Major who kept his own chooks in a private pen on Lemnos, not the Scotties playing the bagpipes in a skirl of sound as my father marches on Anzac Day with his medals gleaming, not the picture of the American doughboy in Arthur Mee's Encyclopaedia with the caption 'The man who won the war' that makes my father smile sourly, but a filthy mass murder with wounded men screaming on the barbed wire in no-man's-land. I decide to be a pacifist.

Life goes on. My father takes out the poison cart to poison the rabbits. Sometimes we help him pull up stinkwort, pile up the mallee roots in heaps in the paddocks, or ride out to bring in the sheep with the new lambs draped over our saddle bows. Once my father brings home the last of the sandalwood left by the sandalwood cutters and we sit by the fire in the playroom with the strange blue-green flames leaping and dying and the exotic scent of the sandalwood filling the shadows.

He teaches us the names of the trees . . . salmon gum, York gum, white gum, wandoo, marri, she-oak, jarrah, jam. In September my mother goes with us to pick wildflowers in the bush . . . spider orchids, donkey orchids, clumps of pale blue leschenaultia, eggs and bacon, smoke bush and golden morrison. We fill the house with the scent of the delicate bush flowers that come up from the scrubby earth like miracles in the spring.

We climb up to look inside the bowl-shaped magpie nest at the ugly featherless babies, but when we take the baby tomtit out of its hanging nest and hold it in the palm of our hand, feeling the beating of its heart, the tomtits never come back to the almond tree again.

Sometimes I long to be by myself. I hide in the dunny and read the comic strip about the Phantom and his black panther, Fang, and Jim and Buck and the Ivory Patrol, or run across the orchard and climb through the sagging netting to the Haunt of the Owls. I sit there in the silence – listening. I can hear my sister calling and I feel mean, but I hug my aloneness and pretend I can't hear her. I run further away to Windy Ridge and stand under the salmon gums, staring up through their sparse high branches, watching the crows cawing and rocking in the wind.

We have named every inch of the creek ... Brownie Wood, Buccaneers' Island, the Magic Mirror, the Dell of Memories.

My father is worried about the salt rising and the erosion cutting into the paddocks. He has a plan for reafforestation. Let the Agricultural Department provide the native trees and each farmer be responsible for looking after them, but the Agricultural Department laugh at him. They think he is a dreamer. 'In fifty years,' he says, 'the Great Southern'll be a desert,' but they don't care. In fifty years they won't be there.

My mother has so much more to do now that my grandmother has gone. My grandmother did all the cooking and made and mended our clothes. It's true that there's nobody to boss my mother around and tell her to 'get on with her work' when visitors come, but she still rages at me until she falls on the floor in a kind of fit, screaming and drumming her heels and frothing at the mouth. She does it only when nobody else is around.

Sometimes she lies, white as a sheet, with her eyes closed, on the sofa in the sitting room, and sends me to bring her clean towels from the linen press. Soon they are soaked and stiff with blood and I have to run for more. I am terrified, but there's nobody else to do it. My sister is too young and my father is working out in the paddock.

One day I am lying on the warm verandah, smelling the wood-bugs, with my face buried in the weatherboards. A hornet is buzzing backwards and forwards, building her clay house above my head. I look down and see a trickle of blood. I freeze ... Is this God punishing me at last? Am I going to die, and if so will it be soon? There is a dark stain spreading on the crotch of my pants. It feels sticky and uncomfortable. There is a dull ache in my stomach and groin. I wait all afternoon, afraid to tell my mother about it. Is this something else wicked and terrible that I have done? When I have to go in to her at last, she looks sorry for me and gives me a quick hug, but she seems embarrassed. 'You're a woman now,' she says. 'It's terrible, but it happens to all of us and it always makes me feel better when I think the Queen has to put up with it too . . . don't tell your little sister'.

I am eleven and a half years old. It is the beginning of the violent period pain which would plague my life for the next ten years. Once a month I'd have to get half-drunk on gin and lie writhing in bed with a hot-water bottle clasped to my stomach.

Charlie Fuller comes to work on the farm. He is a Pommy with a gammy leg who teaches me how to play table tennis. Sometimes he brings his son Lou to stay with him – a big twelve-year-old with a pleasant open face. When we go to town for my father's Returned Services League meeting Lou takes me into his back yard under the wattle tree and twists my arm and gives me a Chinese burn. I realize it is some strange love ritual, and refuse to cry. He doesn't know what to do. He leads me into his bedroom and we wrestle together by the bed. The navy-blue holland blinds are pulled down against the heat. He presses himself against me and I feel the excitement as his hands move all over me. Then his mother calls us for afternoon tea and we sit with flushed faces at the kitchen table, staring at the oilcloth, eyes averted, eating the hot scones and pretending nothing has happened.

At night we stay at the Kellys' and play 'make-up' games with our friend, Rae, who is almost as good at it as we are. Arthur Kelly is the Co-op manager, an ugly charming man like a bullfrog with a reputation as a ladykiller. I put on Mrs Kelly's dress and her high-heeled shoes, make up my face with powder and rouge and lipstick and put up my hair in a golden bun.

Mrs Kelly laughs and brings me into the sitting room. 'Look at this, Kel,' she says, twirling me round.

Arthur Kelly stares at me like a connoisseur. He has never looked at me like that before. 'Why, she's going to be a real beauty, Tom,' he says.

My father looks embarrassed and uneasy. My mother isn't a bit pleased. 'You'd better go and take it all off,' she says curtly.

I stare at myself in the dressing-table mirror. Is it true? For the first time in my life I feel powerful, triumphant. I remember the look in Arthur Kelly's eyes. I have a weapon to use. I smile. Yes, it *is* true, and suddenly I feel frightened.

CHAPTER

4

WHEN my mother announces nervously: 'Mother and Father will be coming back next month,' my father's face grows close and dark again. 'Then we'd better get packed up and leave,' he says, and goes off down the paddock. But before the month is out we are living behind the family store in Corrigin and I am suffering my first traumatic experience of primary school.

It's a family crisis. George White, the lessee of my grandfather's shop in Corrigin, has changed sides, gone across to manage the dreaded Co-op, and is trying to take the newspaper franchise with him. It's all high drama. Our grandparents arrive at the farm to look after us while our parents leave for Perth and Corrigin to save the family fortunes. There is nothing like a financial crisis to force the middle-class family to bury their differences and close ranks.

As for us, we have a wonderful reunion, sitting up late in front of the kitchen fire, sliding over the lino on skis made of kindling tied on with binder twine. 'While the cat's away the mice do play,' crows my grandmother, her little eyes snapping. We ride out to shift the sheep, my grandfather dressed up in his riding trousers and leggings, sawing at Ginger's hard mouth and bawling contradictory orders to the dogs. But there is something sad about it. Change is in the air. The world outside is starting to close in and open up in a kind of pincer movement that leaves me alternating between dizzy excitement and bleak terror. I have been aware for a long time that it's hardly possible for me to be the writer and actress of my dreams and live isolated for the rest of my life on Lambton Downs, but it's always been something that could be faced up to in some far-distant future. Now the future is becoming the present at an alarming rate and I'm not ready for it.

The only way to save the newspaper franchise is to shift to Corrigin and run the store ourselves. Soon I find myself sitting amongst rows of country children droning out spelling and tables, already (the shame of it) put down a class because I can't do the arithmetic. For every spelling or arithmetic mistake the teacher, a bad-tempered martinet with a head like Beethoven, lines us up on the school verandah and canes us unmercifully across the palms and the bare legs as we file past. Ironically, when my mother hears about this she visits the school and demands that the caning stop. So now I am an Ishmael. I line up with the other kids and pass unscathed, longing for the sting of 'the cuts', conscious of the scorn and hostility for the privileged and protected.

Everything seems to mark me off as different. When we play games out in the playground I don't know the rules; I am invariably running the wrong way, passing the ball to the wrong side or sending it soaring into the wrong goal post. We walk to school with Edna and Irene McLimmens, whose father is a part-Aboriginal truck driver for the Shell Oil Company. Irene puts apples inside the front of her dress. 'Look!' she giggles, strutting along beside us. I am scandalized, but secretly wish I had the courage to do the same. When the McLimmens take us home to the humpy they live in across the railway tracks, I see, for the first time, a woman unashamedly suckling a baby. The McLimmens' mother has a foxy pointed face under a cloud of bright red hair. Her pendulous, milk-white breasts, blue-veined and freckled, hang out of the front of her dress like pears.

My mother is horrified when she hears the story and refuses to let us visit again. I think I should have had the sense to shut up about it. She wants us to be friends with the bank manager's and the garage proprietor's daughters, but on Saturday nights, when the farmers all come into town and the pubs are wickedly full, the cars parked bumper to bumper in the main street, we are out over the rooftops with Edna and Irene. 'You've got blood on your pants,' says Edna. 'You better tell your mum.' It's my second period. Until now it has never occurred to me that this will go on month after month. I thought it was only a one-off affair or, at worst, an occasional female curse to be borne.

When Edna is caught secreting a worthless, almost empty scent bottle belonging to my mother, and lies about it, the McLimmens are banned from the shop and banned from our lives for ever. How we miss them, our first school friends. The dim cave of the store and the wide streets of Corrigin, built under a hump of granite rock, throng with the legendary stories that have spun the web of our childhood.

This is the town full of drunks and remittance men who could read Latin and Greek, where all the eligible men were in love with my mother, where old Tom Allen, a hanger-on of my grandfather's, was found blind drunk, playing 'My Gracious Redeemer' on the piano in the sitting room with his boots off, 'to save the carpet'.

Down in the creek bed a harmless madman has camped, trying to solve the secret of perpetual motion, tuning in to Marconi on a matchbox. One night, screaming 'Marconi, Marconi, must I kill?' he leaps over the town picket fences in his white nightshirt and tries to break into my mother's bedroom. She hangs on to the doorknob with all her strength till the danger is averted. 'Marconi says I must not frighten the ladies,' the madman whispers, and – overcome by a town posse – is taken off to the lockup.

This is the main street where my father rode, the Black Prince on his black horse, home from the war, and saw my mother in a rage kicking a flaming primus stove across the road. She was the local postmistress and the primus stove, used for heating the sealing wax for the post bags, kept exploding and was almost useless.

This is the shop where he called for her on their first date; the black horse prancing and flighty in the shafts of the sulky, they drove hell for leather out to Kunjin and Vale Farm, where she had to endure a family prayer meeting.

This is where he came to borrow one hundred pounds from my grandfather when he went broke in the building business and his partner drank all the profits. He came into my grandfather's office with odd socks on, and my grandmother passed judgement: 'There's a handsome feller.' My mother took her father aside. 'Lend it to him, father,' she whispered. 'He seems a decent sort of chap.'

Here is the shop where, at two years old, I carried out armfuls of shoe boxes into the street and gave the boots and shoes away to the passers-by – a story told long afterwards to prove my infant socialist leanings. Here is the closed door between the shop and the living quarters, where I pounded with my fists, screaming 'Mummy, Mummy,' till she couldn't stand it any longer and they left the shop, which my father hated anyway, and moved to Lambton Downs.

Sometimes we are allowed to serve the town children with lollies and comics. I sit behind the counter reading. The stories terrify me – 'Vull the Invisible' and 'Spider Web', a hairless creature, like a human spider who hangs in the centre of a giant cobweb, luring his victims to their doom.

Our next-door neighbours are the Greeks who run the café. They cut pictures of Princess Marina of Greece marrying the Duke of Kent out of the papers and paste them up on the pressed iron walls.

We dance the lancers in the Town Hall, an edifice of pale pink stone, and one never-to-be-forgotten night Max Montesole and his wife come to town and play 'Excerpts from Shakespeare . . . The Strangling of Desdemona'.

At school somebody passes me a brief love note down the rows of desks. It's from a boy with pale red hair called Duncan Waldon. 'Will you be my girl?' he writes. I crumple it up scornfully, but I am secretly thrilled and flattered. I watch Duncan Waldon out of the corner of my eye and when he leaves school and goes to work at the Co-op, I hang around in the dusk with the midges biting my bare legs, hoping for a glimpse of him in his white apron, shaking a broom at the Co-op door. But it's too late. I've missed my chance and he has put away childish things. Only George White, the Co-op manager now, stands there in the doorway, his flaming red crest of hair on end, looking quite benign and not at all like the Judas he has been branded by my family.

In three months it's all over. We have sold the shop and gone back to the farm, but the web is broken. My mother stands staring out of the kitchen window at the cannas blowing in the sludge of the open drain and the sombre line of bush marking the creek bed. A fox's sharp thin bark or a dingo's howl trembles from the low hills. A curlew wails in the night so that my father takes his shotgun and runs down the creek, thinking it's a woman screaming.

My mother hates it all and wants to shift to Perth. The excuse she uses is that she can't teach me correspondence lessons any more because I've got 'past her'. She left school herself when she was just fourteen.

I want to go as a boarder to a girls' school and live an adventurous life like Katy in *What Katy Did at School*, but my mother won't even discuss it. This is her last chance of escape, and she means to take it.

I sit out in my grandparents' sleepout, empty now except for the books still piled up in the butterbox bookcases, and read my grandfather's leather-bound copies of Dickens . . . *Little Dorrit, Great Expectations, Nicholas Nickleby, David Copperfield, The Old Curiosity Shop, Oliver Twist* . . . all those lost tormented children in a world of manic adults. I understand it very well. My father gives me a copy of Adam Lindsay Gordon's *Collected Poems* for my twelfth birthday – 'For the Glory of God and of Gwendoline' and 'Brown Britomarte lay dead in her straw, next morning they buried her, brave old girl' – but my favourite poet is Alfred Lord Tennyson, bound in morocco with gilt-edged pages and a brown silk bookmark. I learn big slabs of *Maud*, all of *The Lady of Shalott* and 'You must wake and call me early, call me early, mother dear . . . For I'm to be Queen o' the May', and weep for the death of the young and innocent.

I discover L. M. Montgomery's *Emily of New Moon* and identify with Emily, a girl living in an isolated place (Prince Edward Island in Canada) who dreams of becoming a writer. My favourite book is *The Dream Girl's Garden*. It has a story about a fairyboy called Nim who has a wicked heart but a beautiful face and body. Gradually, like Dorian Gray, his face distorts and his body twists grotesquely to match his cruel deeds. Only when he begins rescuing beetles, ladybirds and dragonflies from pools of water does the tide turn. He recovers his great beauty and becomes a boring Goody Two-Shoes. The morality tale is completely lost on me. I love the wicked Nim . . . the brilliant face with the beautiful, lying eyes.

But the days are numbered. We can feel them passing, and everything we do seems to be haunted by . . . 'for the last time'.

I ride out on Silver and come home at dusk when that weird primitive fear of the Aboriginality of the Australian bush shuts me out and sends me riding fast into the lighted circle of the farmhouse, that little stockade of European civilization.

We read about the Spartan children who took wolf cubs to bed to bite at their hearts all night in order to make them able to endure pain. We devise our own system of torture: a plank over the bullants' nest, where we have to lie still as statues while the bullants crawl all over us. I'm often ashamed because my little sister is so much braver physically than I am. While I shut my eyes and grit my teeth and die a thousand deaths, she lies down quite calmly amongst the swarming ants or jumps off the edge of the silo, hanging on to a rope, without turning a hair. While I hesitate and hide my eyes, trembling, when our Pekinese pup runs bouncing and barking, tail in a ridiculous plume, amongst the bolting draught horses in the paddock, she runs straight in and rescues him, the hoofs missing her head by inches. She doesn't seem to be afraid of the dark or have to hide under the bedclothes, sweating, with her eyes darting from window to door, waiting for something to come in out of the night.

That summer in Albany I am told that if I go swimming with my 'pain', as my mother calls it, 'the blood will run up to my head and I'll go mad'. I run away and hide amongst the sandhills and peppermint bushes on the Katanning Reserve. I feel unclean.

My father finds me there, tear-stained and tragic. He says nothing about it, but walks beside me identifying the different trees and plants. I am wildly grateful to him, this dark silent man whose sensitivity and fierce pride match my own.

We go to Yealering for the last time. Jack Baxter's stable is still standing upright. I stare out over the salt lake with the dead trees half drowned in the middle. Next summer on Boxing Day, Kingston & Salter's will take out their toy launch for cruises on the lake, there will be egg-and-spoon and sack races, the swings will creak on the reserve, other children will swim and scream and pull off the leeches, our cousins will come from Kunjin and Corrigin, clinging like turkey chicks to the tray of their old Ford truck, but we won't be there.

At the Fullers' house we say goodbye. Lou has been sent away to work on his uncle's farm in the south-west. His felt hat with the holes in it is hanging on a peg on the back of the kitchen door. I wish he was there to give me a Chinese burn. I stare at his hat with a lump in my throat. Time seems to be accelerating, hurrying us at the speed of light into another world.

The farm has been leased to Tony Sartori, but before we leave there is the auction sale to be endured – all these strangers fingering the bargains, bidding away our lives, violating the house and the stable yard. The giant black kettles are boiling up oceans of water for the afternoon teas. Our kelpie, Scamp, who has been belted, pinched, bullied and petted by us until my father says he's no good for anything except killing chooks, bites a little girl savagely on the leg – and I'm glad.

I sit up in the broken-backed wattle, and survey the familiar world of the farm. The wind tears through my hair. I run down the creek to make a last wish at the Wishing Tree. The mopokes are watching with their burning eyes from the dead branches. A plover gives a piercing cry from the fallow, a kingfisher flashes. It's autumn.

We pack up our books and the best of our dolls, give away our bikes, our doll's pram and our treadle car to the Sartori kids. I take the first chapters of the new novel I'm writing, called 'Wheat', and the Old Gold Chocolate box with the picture of a jewel box with ropes of pearls spilling out of it where I keep the drafts of my poems. We say goodbye to the dogs and the ponies. The team has been sold already, replaced by two new tractors. I have made a pact with my father that when I grow up we'll come back, and start a horse stud on the three thousand acres, but of course we never will.

I have given my heart once and for all and I know I will never have another real home in the world again. I am grief-stricken but incredibly light, like a snail who has lost her shell. I float out into the world, lost and unencumbered, and write a bad poem in my poetry exercise book:

> I left you in the sunshine
> And the soft sweet breeze
> With the purple shadows lolling
> Beneath the cool green trees.

I know there's something wrong with it. It is like a bad copy of all the poems I've ever read and besides, it sounds too much like England. But one day I'll do better. I'll make legends out of this place . . . the Golden Valley of my childhood with Nim, the boy with the owl on his shoulder and the falcon on his wrist, buried at the foot of the orchard beside the chinchilla rabbit, the white pullet and the twenty-eight parrot who took fits.

I'll write poems and plays and stories full of ghosts. The Munday brothers will swagger down the one main street of Yealering, Duncan Waldon will stand for ever in the doorway of the Co-op in his white apron, Great-Aunt Eva will recite 'It was the schooner *Hesperus*', the Wirth girls will hang twirling by their teeth from the Big Top (just as they do every two years when Wirth's Circus comes on tour), Desdemona will be strangled in the Corrigin Town Hall, those tiny gilded figures, 'the boy' and 'the girl', will shimmer behind the footlights at the Maj, the madman will murmur 'Marconi, must I kill?', and at the dark end of town, the Aborigines will gather outside Paul Salter's cool drink shop.

Under the smug, snub-nosed gables, through the picture windows, past the circular rose bed in the middle of the front lawn, the river runs silkily in summer or leaden in winter. Squalls blow up and it boils with mud. 'There's the Great Southern,' my father says, 'running into the Swan.'

Twice a week my sister has piano lessons from Mr McDonald, a small dark man with a big frowning head. I stand by the German piano with the unlit gilt sconces, singing 'Danny Boy', Tosti's 'Goodbye', 'The Little Silver Ring' and 'Pale Hands I Loved Beside the Shalimar'. 'Goodbye for ever, goodbye for ever, goodbye, goodbye, goodbye,' I cry out wildly through the autumn tonings. I am a contralto with no middle range at all. Mr Concannon, my singing teacher, is trying to turn me into a mezzo-soprano. For him I sing 'Who Is Sylvia?', 'Ave Maria' and 'The Walnut Tree' in a high, thin choirboy's soprano. 'When she is forty,' he says, 'her voice will mature very nicely.' But forty seems like the end of the world. I give up singing lessons and concentrate on 'Night and Day', 'Chloe' and 'That Old Black Magic's Got Me In Its Spell'.

I've never had a room of my own and long to have one. Yet it never occurs to me as strange that I share the sleepout with my father and sister, three single beds under the canvas blind bumping in the wind off the river. He dresses in the dark master bedroom. When we burst in on him inadvertently, he modestly turns his white bum, hastily pulling up his trousers. Our mother sleeps in the single bedroom looking out over the back garden, where the big jacaranda carpets the buffalo grass with fallen blossoms. At the end of the garden, past the passionfruit vine and the Queen Anne's lace, is the underground air-raid shelter, smelling of wet earth, with its shelves of tinned food that will never be used. We sit there imagining what it must be like to live in London, where the bombs are falling.

On weekends we play tennis rather badly on the gravel tennis court. We wish we had long legs like the French mannequins we have seen sliding up and down like panthers on the catwalk in the Bon Marché. We try out Elizabeth Arden's cake make-up and stare at our faces for hours, squeezing blackheads, in the bathroom mirror. The bathroom is a shrine in the centre of the house, ultra-modern in green and fawn mottled tiles, a terrazzo floor, a green bath and an etched glass door on the shower recess. I lie luxuriating in the hot water until my mother bursts screaming through the door, accusing me of trying to procure an abortion. Her face swells, flushed with rage. She looms over me, beating at my bare shoulders with a wire hairbrush. She truly believes I am the Whore of Babylon. As she lies raging in the bedroom that should be ours, I throw a shoe at her head. She ducks. It misses. Her pink rubber corsets with the pinpoint breathing holes lie on the back of the bedroom chair, her dark serge dresses with the dress-preservers sewn under the armholes hang in the polished wardrobe. On her dressing-table are the first plastics, her imitation ivory hairbrush, comb and powder box, a round silver hand mirror embossed with winged cherubs and a bottle of witch hazel. She will die in that bed like her mother before her, while I sit watching. 'You know I've always loved you, don't you?' she whispers.

'No, I don't.'

The house throbs like a bruise, like a boil swollen to bursting point with our hatred. My father escapes first to golf and then to bowls, with his own generation of old soldiers who fought on the Somme and at Gallipoli. There he argues politics, tells endless stories and even shouts a couple of beers in the bar. He gets tinea in the golf club showers and sits on the back lawn, the jacaranda patterning his still handsome face, his long white feet with the bunions floating in a basin of phenol, his disinfected socks and old-fashioned black lace-up boots placed neatly beside him.

The Liberal Party politician next door lends him his Hansards, but he throws them into the rubbish bin and still votes Independent.

I escape from that hated house, where it is impossible to have any secrets, to 'Cathay', my grandparents' house across the road; three-quarters of an acre with an apricot, a fig and a mulberry tree. A retired civil servant from the East India Company built it for his bride in the shape of their honeymoon ship, the *Cathay*, which brought them from Bombay to Fremantle. She died of TB on the journey and so he lived on there, an aging alcoholic with the bossy nurse he eventually married. There is a little wicket gate at the bottom of the garden where he used to sneak out for a drink.

The house is set deep in a hollow with a crooked path edged with yellow daisies. A sandstone wall covered with a mauve creeper drops down into the shadowy kitchen, the windowsills lined with pots of 'cuttings' from my grandmother's 'green fingers'. She is a tiny, squat, thickened woman with Chinese eyes like an idol, who always carries a roll of banknotes hidden in the top of her stocking, because 'the banks failed in the nineties'. My grandfather comes out from under the house in the grey flannels he wears summer and winter. 'Give sixpence to the nice gardener,' says the woman passing with her little daughter, and he takes it, grinning. He has thick, curling silver hair, and a shapely white leg disfigured with an ulcer.

No one will ever be able to take it away from me. I'll hear again my father's dreams and nightmares of trees and salt, remember the weatherbeaten Miss Burrows, the only woman farmer in the district, reputed to be mingy with her farm labourers. Did I really see her once, sheltering on horseback under a she-oak with the rain dripping off the leaves on to her felt hat, darkening her sour mouth?

I open the iron gate for the last time. Through my tears, the farmhouse blurs in a hollow of sunlight, the iron roofs glinting. In these last months I've been so sad, my father has taken to calling me 'Mona' and 'Dorothy Draggletail'. I hate those names. I wish I had been christened Hermione or Deirdre of the Sorrows.

I close the gate. When the azure blue summer bird migrates back to the dry creek bed, I won't be here. We drive away through Day's paddock into the future.

PART II

I have seen her, wonderful!
A waterfall of hair, body like glass,
Wading through the goldfish pools in winter,
Her white sharkskin dress dark wet above her thighs,
The very shape and effigy of love:
Or turbaned, earringed, lying on the lawn
Among the clover burrs, her bangles clacking,
reading Ern Malley.

'This Version of Love'

THIS is the house of my adolescence, tantrums and tears – House and Garden, 1935 – a monument to the thirties, an Art Deco museum in the dress circle facing the Swan River. 'Autumn tonings', my mother says, and autumn tonings it is.

Textured walls, tapestried fireplaces, folding leadlight doors, an orange and brown geometric pattern carpeting the sitting room. The picture rail is hung with 'Autumn Fires' and 'Bluebell Wood'. The light fittings look like upturned orange soup plates or yellow iceblocks. In the sitting room, dancing to 'Sympathy', I experience my first kiss. On the back verandah one summer night, sitting out on the top step in the moonlight in my white sharkskin tennis dress, I fall in love.

My father reads the newspaper in the breakfast nook, rolling cigarettes on his rolling machine. They droop off his bottom lip as the ash falls, burning charred round holes in his shirt. In the evenings he reads Sir Philip Gibbs and Edgar Wallace by the gas fire under a standard lamp bent like a yellow tulip over his chrome smoker's stand.

We dream of flinging open the double doors, rolling back the carpets and hostessing wonderful dances on the polished jarrah floors, piling up six records on the console radio/gramophone. We will sweep into the modern waltz and the foxtrot in low-cut taffeta and voile with lamé insets made by our grandmother. We stand patiently for hours while she fits and fiddles, her mouth full of pins. But our father wins the State Lottery and buys a billiard table, smack in the middle of the dining room like a household god. Night after night he and my grandfather circle the green baize, my grandfather cheating surreptitiously to get an extra thrill out of it.

The house is cool and dim with a bed of blue hydrangeas under the dining-room window. On the walls are black-and-white photographs of the Swan River settlement. The sitting room is long and blue-coloured with polished jarrah floors, dark-blue Indian rugs and a carved teak fireguard with an elephant's head as the centrepiece. Is it these or the ceiling fans in all the rooms that give it that vague colonial atmosphere? On the wide jarrah verandah, high-set over the river, my grandparents sit out on summer nights and count the cars passing along the Riverside Drive. It is as if they are wonderingly counting the years of their lives, from the horse and buggy to this mechanized age of planes and fast cars they can hardly comprehend.

In winter my grandmother heats bricks covered in flannel in the gas oven and puts them to warm the iron-framed beds in the sleepout. I push down to the bottom of the bed through the crackling cold of the linen sheets and feel the brick hard against my toes. The sleepout is musty with a sweet old people's smell.

'Goodnight, pet,' they call from their shadowy double bed at the other end of the room. The wind whines and creaks in the ropes of the canvas blinds, the stars are ice-cold and blazing through the cracks. Raindrops spatter against the flywire. The camphor laurels rush through the night. The house is like a ship at sea with the wind in the rigging.

This is my 'safe' house. Here I am the beloved. I can do no wrong. I always call in on my way home from school to sit reading under the apricot tree or pedalling on the player piano, singing 'Overhead the stars are gleaming, bright as blossoms in the tree' or 'Tea for two and two for tea, just me for you and you for me', while my grandmother fixes my new dress on the headless dress dummy. There is a silver wattle by the limestone wall, a sapling that grows as I grow. I press myself against its thin trunk, staring up at the evening sky, a crescent moon caught between the branches. What magic waits for me? The excitement of it takes my breath away.

Across the road on the other side of the street lives the millionaire racehorse owner with his fat, fluffy wife. Every morning a taxi arrives from the Esplanade Hotel with a covered silver tray delivering her breakfast. She eats it in a pink negligee on the front porch, the taxi waiting by the kerb.

'The world is so full of a number of things, I'm sure we should all be as happy as kings,' I chant, going home reluctantly through the yellow daisies.

The house in the hills outside the city is the first house I will ever own. We see it advertised in the *West Australian* and my father drives us out through the shimmering summer. We dip down into the valley and see it, an acre and a half surrounded by a random rubble wall, stones all shapes and sizes toppling crazily at its foot. 'Something there is that doesn't love a wall, that sends the frozen groundswell under it,' I recite, running up the slope, over the tiny creek with the rickety wooden bridge, and into the dwarf's house, gnome's house, troll's house, smothered in pink dog roses. It is a ridiculous house, a crazy house – two rooms with a tiny cement front porch, built of grey weatherboard and golden Darlington stone. My father smiles tolerantly but understands my excitement. He, too, is taken up with the enchantment of the tiny house.

For a while we go up only on weekends, sleeping in the single iron bedstead on the front porch.

In early summer I pick the pale pink dog roses and fill vases and bowls with them but they don't last long, the petals whiten and fall on tables and floors. We are like the dog roses – four seasons in the enchanted house and we have parted. Leaving it all behind us, we go our separate ways, and I cannot bear to look back.

On my fiftieth birthday I burn candles and hold a wake in my mother's house, scattering memorabilia on the windowsills – John Buchan, Sir Philip Gibbs, Peter B. Kyne, Lloyd C. Douglas, Edgar Wallace and Ethel M. Dell. The guests are asked to come in mourning. To bury it all I have to make a black joke out of it. But still the ghosts walk, so we sell it. It is still standing on the brow of the hill, built to last. The jacaranda they planted still blooms each spring in the back garden. Are the new owners ever troubled by ghosts? Do doors slam and shoes thud against walls, are voices raised in fury, does an ambulance pull up in the driveway on dark nights and carry away an attempted suicide, does a girl rock in misery by the gas fire and an old woman dying in the second-best bedroom still murmur, 'I haven't gone yet?'

My sister and her husband lived at 'Cathay' for years but the rates escalated, so they sold it to a developer, who crammed its three-quarters of an acre with ugly two-storey town houses.

On a drive through the hills, I stop by the stone wall and look up at the magic cottage. It looks like a real house now, a pergola out front, embowered in the full-grown trees and shrubs we once planted long ago.

So we pick up the cards and build again, but the clear outlines have vanished. The houses seem to be so crowded now – full of images, noises, footsteps and change. I can hardly separate one year from the next, scarcely decipher what happened when. As it gets closer, everything moves further away. It is a mystery – this remembering. It plays weird tricks with perspective.

If I struggle hard enough, I can bring back an image suddenly spotlit. There is a big, white, dead cat swarming with maggots at the side of a house with a false attic in a street in Melbourne.

If I listen hard enough I can hear a dog bark hoarsely and the little steam train whistle as it leaves the station. The creek, swollen with water from the hills, gurgles under the wooden bridge in Darlington.

There is the sound of boots going away down an endless, dark, frosty street. There is a baby lying asleep in his pram with pollen dropping on his cheeks. There is . . . what? – I don't remember.

5
♠

Perth in 1936 is an innocent little city, not much bigger than a large country town, lost in time and distance, floating like a mirage on the banks of the Swan River. We live in a middle-class suburban street south of the river, lined with lopped-off plane trees, in a hideous, dark, liver brick bungalow I immediately christen 'The Castle of Despair'. I have never known such misery. School is a nightmare. I stand in the girls' playground, under the pines, watching the other kids play . . . French and English, fly, knucklebones, marbles, skipping games, passball . . . I don't know any of them and am too shy and awkward to join in. Many years later I will go back and see my eldest son, a wan, lost little figure, standing under those same pines in the boys' playground, hiding behind the trunks just as I did, suffering the identical horrors of the different child who doesn't fit in. I will long to be transformed by that little bottle labelled 'Drink me' into a twelve-year-old again, so that we can share our terror and our loneliness. But instead I turn and go home, knowing there is nothing I can do to help him. At least he never has to suffer the ignominy of being taken out of the 'scholarship class' and put in with the 'dummies', because he can't do arithmetic. He becomes a Doctor of Pure Mathematics. I get two out of twenty for mental arithmetic, even in the dummies' class.

Every morning my hair is pulled and twisted into two curls with tight rubber bands and I suck the ends obsessively. My mother tells a story of a girl who sucked her hair and had to be operated on and a huge hairball removed from her stomach, so I suck my handkerchiefs into holes instead.

I have to wear long, black, narrow college shoes that pinch my feet unbearably. I have gone barefoot all my life, but the feet that were horny and tough, that could walk over rocks and stubble and hot sand, are now as soft as any 'townie's'. My legs ache with what the grown-ups call 'growing pains' and when I stick my burning college shoes out into the school aisle, the teacher trips over them and I get into trouble. There is a girl who pinches and sticks pen nibs into me, and another who has 'things' in her hair that crawl out and across her forehead before my fascinated stare. When it's composition or spelling or dictation, I move up to the top of the class; when it's anything to do with the hated sums, I plummet to the bottom, which means

I always end up somewhere in the middle, just over the border from the real dumdums or those who refuse, out of some wild principle of revolt and despair, to learn anything at all. But Mr Lewis, the miniature teacher with the bright red face and sandy hair, likes me, so I am nicknamed 'teacher's pet'.

There is a vicious fight in the school playground between two girls. One of them is the bad girl of the class, with narrow eyes and twisted mouth. I'm horrified and without thinking I run between them, my face white and my eyes blazing. They are rolling over and over on the gravel, biting, kicking, screaming, pulling out each other's hair. I wrench them apart.

'Stop it, stop it. You should be ashamed,' and, miraculously, they stop. The bad girl is amazed. She grins crookedly. 'What's up with you?' she says, and after that, if there is ever any trouble, she always defends me.

Malcolm McAuley, tall and handsome, with a larrikin's lopsided grin, smiles at me. When I come to school one morning there are signs written in chalk all over the girls' shed . . . MM LOVES DH. I try to rub the chalk off the weatherboard walls and pretend to despise him, but I watch him with a secret glow and suffer when he gets the cane.

My mother takes us to dancing lessons with Miss Frizell in the local hall. She is a stringy bottle blonde with knobby knees in her forties, who dances 'The Dying Swan' with her boyfriend, Maurice. He is a tough in a black beret who pretends to be French. In bobby socks and frilly dresses, we do Shirley Temple tap numbers and sing 'On the Good Ship Lollipop'. My father is ashamed of us and, dimly, I realize why.

I catch everything – measles, whooping cough, pleurisy and, almost, pneumonia. I get paler and skinnier day by day. My mother worries that I am anaemic.

When my grandparents buy a dim, cool house in the dress circle above the golf links and the river, we shift out of 'The Castle of Despair' and life starts to improve.

I love 'Cathay', but my father is building another house for us on the block opposite. When my sister and I see the size of the land, we sit on the low scrub and cry. Exiled from three thousand acres, we think it is like a prison. But the house goes up, with its snub-nosed gables and its plate-glass picture windows.

Our old friend and mentor, Lapp, drops dead in the Como kitchen, and the house is rented out to strangers. We never even have a chance to say goodbye.

My grandparents shift into 'Cathay', and I lie in bed at night in the new house and cry for the farm. I feel as if I have been turned out of Paradise into the dark world beneath. I wish I could be like Hans Andersen's mermaid, become foam on the flood water of the Swan River and flow back, dissolving, lost in the creeks of my own country. I wonder if my father is as homesick for the bush as I am. He never says so but seems to have settled for a book and a chair, or a game of golf at the Royal Perth Golflinks.

As my mother passes his bed, he grabs at her arm. 'Nothing's been any good since we stopped sleeping together.'

She pulls away. Her face flushes red. 'Don't be silly, Tom.'

My grandmother says, 'Men are funny. Always wanting to put you on their knee and kiss you,' or 'Your grandfather's never touched me since your mother was born. He knew another one would kill me.'

Pamphlets on sex instruction for adolescent girls are sent through the post. My mother tries to give them to me but I run away, and won't read them. I feel as if some secret part of me is being violated. She presents me with *The Way of the Eagle* by Ethel M. Dell as some kind of substitute, and I do read the palpitating, hothouse nonsense she calls a love story. I sense some unpleasant prurience in both the sex manuals and Ethel M. Dell. There is some nasty secret here, like the time my mother slapped my face for discovering her douche bag in an old tin trunk.

At High School I'm not much happier. I can't do French or Algebra or Geometry. I have to sit in the classroom for a whole week with a sign round my neck because I can't remember the French verbs.

Miss Bonus – blonde bun, horn-rimmed glasses, pale, hand-knitted suits – says: 'Stand up, Dorothy Hewett. Are you a moron when it comes to Maths?' I bite my lips, struggling against tears, but they drip down my face and she looks ashamed.

I love the English lessons. When we do *The Merchant of Venice* I play Shylock, creeping crookbacked between the desks, hissing: 'Signor Antonio, many a time and oft/On the Rialto you have rated me . . .'

I borrow Miss Bonus's bathers to play the Amazonian female lead in the school play. The other teachers seem astounded at the transformation. I hear them discussing me as I dress for the opening night: 'What a lovely little figure she's got, and so mature for a thirteen-year-old.' I am filling out. I have breasts, a small neat waist and swelling hips. I take off all my clothes and stare at myself in the cheval mirror. There is a soft fuzz growing between my legs and I don't like the look of it. My grandmother, dressmaking, with her mouth full of pins, says: 'She's got a sway back. She needs a little pad in her lower spine.'

I've learnt to play French and English, and fly and knucklebones, but at lunch time I often sneak away to the old graveyard behind the school and sit amongst the gravestones writing poetry in my English exercise book. At school assembly we sing 'God of our fathers, known of old,/Lord of our far-flung battle line,/Beneath whose awful hand we hold,/Dominion over palm and pine', or 'Bring me by bow of burning gold'. I look up at the names of famous women engraved in gold letters around the Assembly Hall . . . Boadicea, Florence Nightingale, Madame Curie, Queen Elizabeth, Elizabeth Barrett Browning . . . and my voice soars out under the stained-glass windows. Some day, I think, with absolute certainty, my name will be up there.

I have vague friends, but I'm not really close to anyone. There is one girl I admire – slender, dark, alive, laughing. She's won an Eisteddfod Speech Medal. I wish I could really get to know her. She's always playing jokes on the form mistress and getting into trouble and there does seem to be some unspoken underground allegiance between us. Maybe it's because we both love acting and Shakespeare. In my second year at university, when I'm enrolled in Abnormal Psychology, I see her again at Claremont Hospital for the Insane. She sits in front of the students . . . heavy-bodied, dough-faced, speechless, with her stockings drooping over her institution shoes . . . paraded before us as an example of incurable schizophrenia. She haunts me for a long time after that.

My parents visit the school, worried about my tears in bed at night. 'She's not suited to a state school,' says Miss Bonus, a snob at heart. 'Send her to college, where she'll fit in. She's so sensitive.' So I am enrolled in the Business Course at Perth College in a white middy blouse, a gored navy-blue skirt, a panama hat and the black stockings of my dreams, to learn typing, shorthand and book-keeping.

Perth College is a double-storeyed red-brick building with an ivy-covered chapel, a swimming pool and an avenue of pines where the Church of England sisters pace, black habits in winter, grey in summer.

I have a kind of friend called Edith Budge, a poor minister's daughter, who doesn't fit in either, but for different reasons. Typing, shorthand and book-keeping remain a complete mystery to me, so I am moved into the 'professional' class. The teacher reads my essay on Titania and Oberon aloud. The classroom rocks with laughter. The following week I write an essay on 'The Most Unforgettable Character I've Ever Met' (a theme borrowed from the *Reader's Digest*). I write about Ann Craig, a tall, leggy, brusque girl from one of the 'old families', who is destined to be School Captain. I have a secret crush on her but now it is secret no longer. The class titter and look sideways, but they are beginning to be afraid.

I have a poem published in the school magazine: 'A little thorn needle, a little grass thread, for the Queen of the Fairies will Oberon wed.' In the school playground I sit alone, reading a book of poetry, pretending to ignore them all. Edith Budge has been left behind in the Business Course, a cut below these girls who will go on to the Leaving and perhaps even university.

I have a nickname, 'Hermit Hewett', but they know nothing about my secret life – reading Mazo de la Roche's *Jalna* series under the apricot tree at 'Cathay', drowning myself in that dark world of Gothic romance, dressing up and parading in a white spotted tulle evening dress, skin tight to the knees with a fishtail flounce, handed on from my second cousin, Marjorie Tindale, copied from Joan Crawford in *Susan Lennox – Her Rise and Fall*.

I twirl in the folding, mirrored doors of my grandmother's wardrobe, seeing myself reflected, image after image, like shots in a movie – twirling tulle, bare arms, gold coiled hair. When my mother is pleased with me, she calls me Honeytop. I lie in bed, curled up in the sleepout with the striped canvas blind bumping in the wind, and make up fabulous stories about my life as a great writer and a famous actress in the capitals of the world.

I write *Han the Chinese Fisherman* and play the female lead in a matinée in the school hall. My father takes me to a meeting of The Fellowship of Australian Writers. We sit in a basement café with a mural of ballet dancers painted on the walls as I listen, breathless with excitement, to these heroes of Australian literature reading their works: a big, dark, handsome man from Kalgoorlie called Gavin Casey, who has won the Bulletin Short Story Competition; tall, cool, aristocratic-looking Henrietta Drake-Brockman, who has written a novel about the first settlers called *Younger Sons*; an old woman called Mollie Skinner, who looks like a boobook owl and has actually written a book, with D. H. Lawrence, called *The Boy In The Bush*.

My father sits uneasily, silent, proud and still handsome amongst these gifted paragons. Dimly I realize what a strain it is for him. He knows nobody. He doesn't fit in, but he is putting himself through all this because perhaps, in some strange way, he does believe in me, although he never says a word about it. Then we have to turn our backs while a sad, saggy-looking man in bifocals reads his radio play.

After it's all over, he approaches us as we stand awkwardly on the edge of the meeting. 'My daughter wants to be a writer,' says my father, in explanation. The saggy man looks at us sadly. 'Don't ever let her be a writer,' he says. 'Nothing in it.'

I go out into the night air, flushed with indignation. He has spoilt

my wonderful evening. I fume all the way across the Causeway.
'Anyway,' I say. 'I didn't think much of his radio play.'

My father grins.

'And I *am* going to be a writer.'

'Okay, Nip,' he says.

A distant cousin invites me to the annual Hale School Ball, but he
is embarrassed by my stumbling, my dress and my hairstyle. My
grandmother has made me an orange, puffed-sleeved, innocent
crepe de Chine. My mother has wound my hair in coils over my ears.
They are called 'telephones'. I look like an awkward spinster and I'm
only fifteen. I spend most of the night dodging being a wallflower,
sitting on the toilet fighting tears or powdering my nose obsessively
over and over in the powder room. But I'm watching and learning.
Next year I'll be the belle of the ball in the same 'apricot' crepe de
Chine, remodelled with silver lamé shoulder straps, a silver corselet
cinching my waist. Two golden braids will hiss on my bare shoulders
as I dance the cross chassis and lock, learnt at the Wesley College
dancing classes.

My family have built the Regal Theatre, an Art Deco picture
'palace' with a crying room for mothers and babies, double plush seats
with no arm between for lovers, a sweeping staircase from foyer to
lounge with a huge gilt-edged mirror at the top. The manager, Mr
Appleby, in his grey suit, is bowing in the foyer. Mrs Appleby is
eternally smiling in the ticket box, the fireman stands guard at the
bottom of the stairs, the identical twin usherettes tear the admission
tickets in half, and up in the bio-box the operator and his assistant
have one eye on the film and one on the blonde woman with the big
tits across the street, undressing without pulling down the blind.

On silver sandals with baby Louis heels I float down the stairs in
my pale-green, ballerina-length crepe de Chine to see Fred Astaire
and Ginger Rogers in *The Gay Divorcee*:

> Bon-bons and roses for Dolly – she floats down the stairs like a
>   dream,
> The people all rise and as I close my eyes she's there in her green
>   crepe de Chine.
> Her pageboy bob is on her shoulders, she's there making eyes at the
>   men,
> Silvery sequins, a-glitter, circle the swish of her hem.

The King of England has abdicated to 'marry the woman I love'
and become the Duke of Windsor. I thrill to their love story and hate

old Stanley Baldwin. There is something called the Spanish War but I don't know much about it. Hitler and Mussolini are giving Fascist salutes and bombastic speeches on the Fox Movietone News, but it's obvious that they are just buffoons and nothing much to worry about.

My greatest worry is the Junior Exam. Algebra and Geometry are a torment. I can't remember the theorems, let alone understand them. My French grammar is non-existent and my accent appalling. I'm always late for school, dawdling to the tram stop, waving back to the tree on the corner . . . 'Goodbye old tree, goodbye,' missing the early ferry, panting through the school gates with my pyjama top still on under my school blouse, missing Chapel, and sneaking into the back of the classroom.

My only real happiness is when I call in at 'Cathay' on my way home, pushing open the little green iron gate in the picket fence to find my grandmother planting out her 'slips' on the kitchen window-sill or my grandfather pottering underneath the house in his baggy pants and flannel shirt, the shield slipping on his ulcerated leg.

I sit at the player piano and sing 'Hustling Hinkler, up in the sky', 'That Certain Party', and 'Velia, oh! Velia, the witch of the wood/ Would I not die for you dear if I could'. The piano rolls are turning and turning as I pedal for dear life in the blue sitting room.

Sometimes my grandmother, with her famous tactlessness, puts her foot in it. We are sitting out on the slope of the lawn gazing down at the river. 'And Lesley will get her scholarship,' she purrs, 'and you'll *pass* your Junior.'

I go home in tears, and of course, that is exactly what happens. Lesley becomes a scholarship girl enrolled at Modern School, the High School for 'brains', while I just scrape through the Junior with the minimum five subjects (failing Maths and French). Why can't I be clever at everything like my sister, instead of this weird freak who shines only at English Literature?

With the Junior looming, my grandmother suggests I am taken to see a Christian Science practitioner who will have 'the right thought' and be paid to pray for me. I am shocked at this revelation. Is nothing sacred? Can everything be bought and sold in the market-place, even the goodwill of God?

Except for the obligatory grace and prayers before bed when we were little, religion has never played much of a part in our lives. We used to recite 'Thank you for the world so sweet', and bless all our relatives every night. It took a long time because there were so many of them and you couldn't leave any of them out in case you hurt their feelings.

Gentle Jesus, meek and mild
Look upon a little child
Pity mice and 'Licity

I was quite prepared to pity the mice, but who was 'Licity?

Of course my grandmother was always going on about 'error' and 'science', and now here is Mrs Love, sitting behind her desk, rolling in fat, with sleepy heavy-lidded eyes like a female Buddha. I gather my courage and my indignation together and start asking questions: 'Why does she think she has the right ear of God? Why is she paid to pray? Why can't I pray for myself?' Generations of Protestant dissenters stand at my back. My intellect soars and demolishes her. She is terribly glad to see the back of *me*. My mother looks shocked and slightly amused. I have a feeling she is rather in awe of my cleverness. My father laughs and Christian Science goes out of the window.

In the September holidays we go home to the farm, crawling across the wheatbelt in a shabby country train, through paddocks green with the spring rain, arriving at Malyalling siding, sleepy in the dawn, to be met by Tony Sartori.

His wife Hilda and his sister-in-law Pommy, huge women out of a Drysdale painting, cook boiled meat in the farm kitchen, wash up eternally, and swing the teapot in rhythmic circles round and round above their heads to make it brew . . . 'When was that . . . that was five years ago on a Fridee in May or was it Saturdee over home at six o'clock . . . and poor old Mum said . . .'

We still have most of our old furniture stored in the sitting room. We sleep there under 'The Stag at Bay' and 'The Watcher on the Hill'. The sitting room, that sacred place where we were allowed to sit only on special days, has become a lumber room. It seems like a kind of sacrilege. My mother decides to try again with my sex education. Maybe it's the insistent bawling of the bull in the back paddock that turns her mind to it.

'You might as well know what terrible things can happen,' she says. 'There was a man and a woman stuck together like dogs on the Esplanade and when they found them in the morning, her insides had come down and trapped him. They had to cut *it* off.'

The orchard well and the well in the stable yard have both gone salt. The orchard, the garden and most of the trees along the creek bed are already dead. It has all happened just as my father predicted.

Peter, our clever sheepdog, has been poisoned with a bait left out for the foxes. Strawberry's horn is growing back into her head. A kelpie pup is strangled by accident, dangling from a rope at the back of the truck. Hordes of rabbits leap in front of the headlights, squashing and bumping under the tyres.

But when we ride out to help bring in the sheep, our ponies flatten the pink and white paper everlastings under their hoofs, quail and plover rise up in front of us, the new wheat quivers like a green sea whispering to the foot of the rock hill and we are back in our own country.

Except that it isn't really our country any more. Everything has changed and even though Tony Sartori brings out the bottle of Chianti after tea and pours me my first glass of wine (while my mother frowns), I don't really belong. It's not my farm.

In Albany, at the end of that year, I imagine I have some kind of transcendental experience. I am walking along the beach alone in the evening, the sand glistening as the tide recedes, when I hear a voice that comes from the sky. I write a poem on the wet sand, given to me like automatic writing, but the surf washes it away and by the time I get back to the beach house I've forgotten it. Sitting on the end of the jetty staring at the dark water while my father fishes, I feel I am experiencing the mystery of the universe, but after that, until I fall briefly in love with a Catholic who plays 'Souvenirs' on his violin, I set my face against all organized religion.

I want to leave school. My mother takes this seriously and has a long private interview with a prospective tutor behind closed doors. The young woman, who needs the money desperately, wisely advises her that it would be better for me to learn to mix with my peers.

But it is my father who really talks me out of it . . . my father, who has a great respect for education, who went to the Working Men's College at night and wanted to be a doctor, only there was never any money, and then the war broke out, and nobody had ever heard of a doctor who came off a little dairy farm in Korong Vale anyway. 'Try it for another year,' he says, 'and see how you go,' which is just as well, for before another year is out I am the resident eccentric genius of 5B and have fallen in love with Lilla Harper and Ken Tregonning.

CHAPTER

6
◆

GRADUALLY the school takes shape around me. Miss Sainsbury and Miss Porteus are smoking their secret cigarettes in the shrubbery on the way to the swimming pool, Sister Rosalie stands at the foot of the altar, bending her hooded eyes on the crocodile of girls as they file up the aisle of the school chapel. We are supposed to bow to the name of Jesus and curtsy before the altar. The Anglican hymns soar up to the chapel roof. The bowing and curtsying blows like a Pentecostal wind through the line of girls, our eyes lock. Sister Rosalie is daring me to remain upright. She stares me down and I shiver, but I stand my ground. I will not bow before the altar, I will not curtsy to the name of Jesus.

In 5B we have special privileges. We are allowed to sit by the swimming pool at lunch time and in our free periods, and this is where I gather my audience around me to read the latest chapter in my endless serials. The wind blows the pages out of my hand. They scatter across the lawn. The girls run to catch them and bring them back. 'What's next?' they cry, as I search desperately for my lost pages.

There is something called 'school spirit' which I scorn. After school, in the cloakroom that smells of sweaty sandshoes and menstruation, the head of the school house to which I am assigned corners me. She is a hairy girl who looks as if sprigs grow out of the soles of her feet. 'Where is your school spirit?' she cries. And I smile with that superior, infuriating little smile I am learning to adopt with such success.

In winter we buy buns at the corner tuck shop and toast them over a mingy fire in the classroom. In summer we sit endlessly by the swimming pool drowned in a blinding light that leaves nothing untouched and has no shadows. It dances across the chlorinated water and on to the green lawns. The Sisters pace up and down, moving like owls along the avenues of pines, their hands clasped passively together.

Mrs Russell-Smith is an MA from Oxford. She teaches us English, History and Geology. Sitting up in front of the classroom with her little fat legs dangling and her shrewd face enclosed in layers of plumpness, she tells us about Eliot and Yeats, Wordsworth, Keats and

◆

Coleridge. She teaches us Shakespeare. She tries to give us some idea
of a world that exists outside our closeted classroom and our closeted
lives on the banks of the Swan River. She is, in a way, our only link
with culture.

Sometimes we are invited to visit her house at Guildford, on the
outskirts of the city, and there we have 'afternoons', where her
bloatfaced son plays the piano or Stephanie James, our resident
musical genius, cracks her knuckles and plays themes for each one of
us. For one there is 'The Girl with the Flaxen Hair', for another there
is Rimsky-Korsakov or Chopin or Tchaikovsky or Beethoven. The
evening comes down and we drink coffee and tea, and was it cakes or
scones we had on those long-ago weekend afternoons? We leave and
wade across acres of green Guildford grass to the train and go back to
our suburban homes feeling that we have been privileged to touch the
edge of some kind of larger life which in our own houses seldom, if
ever, reaches us.

Her wry, deflating comments on my school essays keep me in
line: 'Beware of rhetoric! You seem to be in some danger of regarding
literature as a drug addict regards his drug – a perpetual stimulus to
unreality.'

Only once do I triumph. The essay topic is: 'What will you be
doing in ten years' time?' 'Last Christmas,' I write,

> I saw myself lying dead in a flat above Piccadilly Square. The
> Christmas before that I saw my name in sky signs on Broadway.
>
> Now I am dead I have time to do all those things I never had
> time for when I was living. I think how strange it is that I wondered
> about dying and whether there was anything after it. How stupid I
> was ever to be afraid of death. After all, this is all it amounts to, one
> feels a little disembodied, perhaps, a little lost and naked, running
> about without any covering. There is no one else to see except the
> other spirits and they don't bother me much. They say I cannot
> become born again until my name dies out of electric lights and I am
> forgotten. They say it would be too much of a handicap for a new
> spirit carrying all that around inside her.

At the end of this opus, Mrs Russell-Smith has only one line to add: 'I
am incapable of evaluating this.' Ah! triumph. Ah! secret, sly delight.
I have silenced her at last. But little by little, so that I am hardly aware
of it, she is shaping my style, she is influencing my ideas. She is
cleansing me of hyperbole and rhetoric. She sits up there watching us
through her half-closed eyes, the folds of her fat wrapped around her
and misses nothing. She is a great cat ready to pounce. Only once in
those two years did I ever see her shaken. She cried on the day France
fell.

My two best friends are Mary Vetter and Betty Picken. Mary is a dark dove of a girl who wears expensive black silk stockings and has a deformed hip and an exaggerated limp from childhood osteomyelitis. She lives in a grandish house on the south side of the river with manicured lawns swooping down towards the water's edge and cool, embracing verandahs. Her father is Otto Vetter, an eccentric *bon vivant* of German extraction who sits smoking cigars in his library (they actually have a library!). He wears a velvet smoking jacket with a green velvet cap, and a gilt tassel bobbing on his crown – the epitome of eccentricity and exotic good taste.

Betty Picken, on the other hand, is the daughter of a bank manager. A thin, fair, nervous girl with high cheekbones, she dreams of being a famous woman photographer. At the back of the classroom sits Lilla Harper, descendant of the first families, the First Fleeters who brought their pianos, portraits and antique furniture to rot on the blistering sands of Garden Island. Her grandfather built Woodbridge, a mansion on the banks of the Guildford River – now a prep school for Guildford Grammar, the most aristocratic boys' school in the whole of Western Australia. The Harpers live in a sprawling bungalow with polished jarrah floors and a rose garden where Mrs Harper walks in her green divided skirt, snipping off the dead roses with her secateurs. It is she who gives me a copy of Elizabeth Barrett Browning's *Sonnets from the Portuguese*, taken on her honeymoon to read to the enigmatic Walter Harper who, apparently, never listened. It is a beautiful edition with gold-rimmed leaves and a deep-red morocco cover. In it she writes, 'Those whom the gods love die young. As you seem to be in some danger I am presenting this to you now.'

I am entranced by the Harpers, by their moodiness and mystery. As they move around their dim verandahed rooms, their thin faces with the twisted mouths, pop eyes and pale skin reflect like shadows the faces of their ancestors, hanging in framed oval miniatures on the walls. They are like the characters in Mazo de la Roche's *Jalna* series.

They have a servant, a resident servant! They use finger bowls with a floating magnolia after meals. They have a chaise longue upholstered in pink velvet on which I lie, trailing one arm listlessly in the summer heat. My friendship with Lilla is always secret, never open. Unlike my friendship with Mary Vetter and Betty Picken, it has overtones of smouldering passion. Lilla sits in the back of the classroom, watching me with her twisted smile, her sardonic eyes encouraging me to even more ridiculous flights of verbal fancy. I can see her now: walking along the pine avenue, away from the swimming pool, with her strange sloping walk and upright carriage, or forever regarding me from the back row of 5B, a dust mote floating across her face.

I write endless poems to her, and have long intense telephone conversations lasting late into the night:

> Sitting here in the darkness,
> a recruiting speech on the wireless,
> and behind it a background of music.
> My sister playing dimly
> so that it is sad, some deep thing,
> sitting here in the darkness
> waiting for the telephone to ring,
> breaking this like a sudden shrill hurt,
> then our voices will meet over wires,
> emotional, throbbing, emotionless, empty and full,
> aching and curiously flippant.
> We shall speak as we never do in reality,
> it is like a dream life lived over a telephone, touching
> ourselves like small,
> half heard ghost voices,
> tomorrow we will be strangers hurting again.

'Come to dinner!' yells my father. 'Even geniuses have to eat.'

The war has begun. We have passed through the period of appeasement and Mrs Russell-Smith has been scathing about 'that foolish man with the umbrella who has betrayed us all'. Munich has failed but to us, living so far from the world, it will be a long time before we are conscious of what war is and how it will change our lives. Young men we know will be killed or wounded, disappearing for years or for ever. There will be rumours of Jap invasions, and the Brisbane line. At the university we will crouch in trenches while the Catalinas swarm over our heads from the Yank flying boat base on the Swan River. We expect bombs to fall but they never do. The American invasion will hit Perth. The Children's Court will be full of under-age girls with VD and rabbit-skin coats, whose American boyfriends have shot through never to be seen again.

Until this time the clock has always stood for us at half-past three and there has always been honey for tea. But on the night Chamberlain declares war on the BBC, crackling from London, with Big Ben booming behind him, all that is changed irrevocably. I sit on the floor, reading, deliberately blotting out his English vowels, wrapped in my concept of myself as an unrepentant pacifist.

'Listen,' says my father, 'war is being declared.'

But I refuse to listen. My grey-blue eyes lock with his navy-blue ones. He is furious with me, his face is white with rage. 'I don't want to listen,' I say.

'You will listen! I'll make you listen!' he yells, but I get up and throw the book into the corner and stride out of the room.

He had fought what he thought was 'the war to end war', had been a war hero, endured it all – the trenches in France, the landings in Gallipoli, the lice, the misery, the mud, the barbed wire, the gas and the death, and here was his eldest daughter making a mockery of the main event that had fashioned his life. My father never really recovered from the war. He didn't tell endless drunken stories at RSL reunions, he never spoke about the actual experiences which had given him his medals, but it had obviously altered him for all time. From that moment began the long war of disagreement between my father and myself. Up to then I had regarded him as the keeper of all knowledge, but now my own ideas of the world were beginning to form in my own head, and they would be so radically different from his that gradually we would live together as silent, intolerant strangers, the romantic image of the dark man dissolved under the pitiless eyes of adolescence. My father is manager of the family Regal Theatre. He had dreamt of being a doctor or a forestry expert, but now he sits, night after night, monitoring the sound on the balcony, watching those endless Hollywood movies which fill him with despair and boredom, driving home late at night in a car with a gas distributor on the back or catching the last ferry, in his leather overcoat.

When I bring my girlfriends home, he embarrasses me by his heavy, flirtatious jokes about their boyfriends. I wish he would stop making such a middle-aged fool of himself. He finds it impossible to handle my sexuality. Every lover, every possible husband I bring home, is subjected to his pitiless scrutiny. All are found hopelessly wanting. 'There was only one beauty in our family,' he once told my mother, 'and that was her downfall.'

On May the first, 1939 I fall in love at one of those romantic dances orchestrated on Mary Vetter's wide verandahs with the coloured fairy lights swinging over our heads. 'It was a queer night with rain and the river very dark,' I write in my diary.

There were little cut-up lights all over the roof. I wore a flame-coloured dress and looked the best I ever had. I also wore a cross. I am not a Catholic but I could be. The Merry Widow waltz – a whirling ecstasy of motion. We hardly spoke. Yet it is strange. In the beginning I knew his name but I had never seen him before. I *knew* him. We never spoke except once when I laughed like Garbo, who is my heroine. The last I saw of him he was standing against a pillar, with his head thrown back like a young, brown, Greek god, with the others humped in dark shadows at his feet, and his hair blown into a blond crest. He was supreme.

In my poetry notebook I write:

Oh golden boy walking out of the rain
with the wind in your hair
and the blue-black night in your eyes!

His name is Ken Tregonning, and he is one of the smart young set, the 'Peppermint Grove Push', who live in the wealthiest section of Perth's stratified suburbia. The 'Peppermint Grove Push' are richer and more sophisticated than the rest of us. When they arrive at school dances they tend to stick together, making 'in' jokes we are hard put to understand. They are spoilt and privileged and good-looking and rich, whereas my background is the hard-working, lower middle class who have pulled themselves up by their bootstraps: Methodist preachers, Cornish miners, Cornish serving girls, Irish smallholders, narrow-minded Methodist dairy farmers. No wonder Lilla Harper and Ken Tregonning seem to me to be impossibly glamorous creatures, the dark side and the light side of a social world which I will never be privileged enough to enter and pretend to despise.

I have an everyday boyfriend called Neil Jones, a diminutive, clever boy, son of the ex-schoolmaster at Yealering. We take long weekend walks by the river. We have intellectual discussions about life and religion and whether there is such a thing as reincarnation, a belief which I have adopted as a substitute for heaven. But compared to Ken Tregonning, Neil Jones seems impossibly plebeian and ordinary. How can he compete, even as dux of Hale School, with this sporting hero who is also intelligent and handsome and owns a little yacht, a Sharpie called 'The Cheerio'. He sails out from the exclusive Freshwater Bay Yacht Club on weekends and I dream of going with him but never make it. He does ask me to a Yacht Club dance, which is the social event of the season for the 'Peppermint Grove Push' and those who aspire to enter their charmed circle. We stand on the point, looking out over the water, with the lights dangling twice over in the black surface. A huge red moon rises over the river. It's summer and I wear a red skirt and an embroidered peasant blouse brought back by my Great-Aunt Eva from one of her trips to Czechoslovakia or Hungary, or one of those exotic countries that I dream of visiting one day. Ken Tregonning writes me the occasional postcard in which he calls me 'the gypsy girl' or 'the career girl', but in the end it doesn't come to anything, not even a kiss good night.

For years I kept one of those postcards he sent me, with the painting of a sailing ship on the front of it. 'We must not be ships that pass in the night,' he wrote. However badly he was expressing himself, it was sincere. But he had danced with me when we first met principally because I was pretty and he always danced with the prettiest girl in the room. Now he had found out what 'a corker nature I had'. If only he had really known!

By July 1940, Neil Jones has introduced me to the joys and torments of foreplay without consummation. We wander away in the weekends to the pine plantation, where I lie on the pine needles with the sunlight slanting through the long aisles of trees while he systematically explores my body. On a holiday in Albany he masturbates me under a blanket on the back seat of the car. We drive on and on over sandy beach tracks between the low scrub or along the golden gravel, with the trunks of giant Karri trees sliding past along the road to Denmark, my parents sitting in the front, sublimely unknowing.

Sexuality has taken the place of intellect. I resent his power over me but can't keep away from those probing fingers. While I share his obsession, these experiences hardly rate a mention in my diary. It is still full of my impossible, unconsummated romance with the figure of the glamorous, unattainable Ken Tregonning.

Rottnest is an island eight miles off the coast of Fremantle, a magical place in the youthful memories of West Australians. First discovered by the Dutch explorers, it has a dark history as a penal settlement for Aborigines, exiled from their own country and left to die of pneumonia in the cold winds sweeping across the Indian Ocean. Laced with lakes so salty it is impossible for anything to sink in them, and lonely bone-white beaches with high-stepping water birds that migrate from as far away as China, it had then a feeling of such unspoilt timelessness that it was like living in a dream country on the edge of the world.

> I went to Rottnest, and now I love it, as if it is deep in my heart. The gravestones and the little snails hanging on the salt grass, the green shallow seas, the line of the reefs, the strange grassy uplands, the lighthouse with its fingers at the heart of the whole island, the lakes – blue or Stillfarden-grey.

I jitterbug so madly in my red circular skirt and scarlet blouse, sliding between the legs and whirling over the head of a young man called Dicky Dimmitt, that I am called 'the Red Terror of Rottnest'.

But when he takes me away to a lonely beach and tries to kiss me, I repel him with such fierce virginity that he is astonished.

'I thought that's what girls came to Rottnest for,' he says, and all the way along the sandy beach track he punishes me by walking ahead and letting the peppermint bushes lash my face.

My sister and I decide to have a dance at 'Cathay', hanging the blue room with paper lanterns. The candles burning inside them catch on fire as we dance. I wear an aquamarine dress the colour of the shallow seas over the reefs at Rottnest:

> . . . all night long Ken never came near me, and I went through the agony with my mouth hard, jitterbugging, seeing his face always through the window, staring, always staring. I went and sat on the window seat with Betty Picken. She said afterwards she had never seen anyone sound so hysterical or look so terrible.
>
> And when we walked back to the house, I talked quickly all the time and I can remember the damp stillness of the garden, all around us, and his puzzled farawayness, like a child. And when he said goodbye, he said goodbye as if he really meant it, and I saw him go, never looking back, except once, and we looked at one another and that was the last. And Lilla sat under a red lantern in a green patterned dress.

But there are other things in my life besides Ken Tregonning. I have always acted in the school plays: as Belinda in a hammock surrounded by moonstruck lovers (schoolgirls in drag) and as a thinly disguised lesbian in a play about shop girls called '9 till 5' which fascinates me because I have already begun to ask myself questions about my relationship with Lilla. Am I really a lesbian? Is this one of those forbidden Sapphic affairs I have dimly heard about? And if so, how then am I also in love with Ken Tregonning and unable to keep away from Neil Jones? I try to persuade the school to do a play called *Children in Uniform*, but it is far too sophisticated for Perth College. I try to start a school magazine to replace the boring ineptitudes of the one that already exists, but this is forbidden. Everything is forbidden.

When the Perth Repertory Club decide to put on Irwin Shaw's *Bury the Dead*, the war breaks out and the season is immediately cancelled. How I scorn their cowardice. But I join the Repertory Club, playing a succession of dreamy ingénues and Marigold in *Wind in the Willows*, in a blue silk dress with short socks and a big blue bow in my long hair.

I experiment with one of the fashionable hairstyles. 'We will now cut for zee pageboy bob,' cries the Swiss hairdresser, his scissors hissing over my coils of hair. But finally I decide that all this fashion is boring and predictable and opt for a short haircut, like a boy's,

wearing grey trousers, a boy's grey school shirt and a sports coat to go
with it. I like to think I look like the famous aviatrix Amelia Earhart.

Another spot in time: a school geology excursion with Mrs
Russell-Smith to the Gingin Hills, bare grassy uplands, scattered
outcrops. We move from rock to rock, tapping away with our little
hammers, pretending to be geologists. It's a very ancient landscape,
with a sparse wild beauty of its own. I sit on One Tree Hill amongst
the blond grass with the wind blowing my jagged bronze-wing haircut, while Betty Picken takes my photograph with a box Brownie and
Lilla Harper watches it all sardonically.

> Oh! small dark head against the sky
> And your throat with the blue shirt and the boy's body,
> Petrovicat, why were you a woman? I love you so,
> Blue shirt, long body in the grass. Petrovicat,
> > My soul is sick
> > Don't think of that.

When I go for weekends to the Harpers' house, Lilla and I swim
in the tea-coloured river, choked and tangled with saplings and the
roots of drowned trees. We come back through the paddocks, passing
Woodbridge – fallen into disrepair, turned into an Old Women's
Home, all the old ladies evacuated for the duration of the war; mad
old girls, who buttonhole Walter Harper in his garden and unravel
their fading wits and memories like the rubbish crammed into their
shabby handbags. At night I lie in the sleepout, burning for Lilla's
bed, but we never touch each other. The train whistle blows at
Guildford station and I hear the sound of the frogs and the crickets in
the dark-green grass by the river.

Mrs Harper, *née* Drummond, that fascinating birdlike woman,
tells us scandalous stories about the West Australian First Families,
and I plead with her to write them down. She laughs at me and says
she would never be able to live in Western Australia again. Maybe she
is telling me all this in the hope that one day I will write them for her.
They are astonishing stories, about the Vasse River near Busselton on
the South Coast of Western Australia, a place sacred to the memory of
the pioneering Bussells. On one side of the Vasse lived an ancestor of
the Drummonds; on the other side a Mrs Bussell with her full-grown,
idiot son. They used to take a little boat and row across the river and
have ladylike cups of tea with each other. On this particular day Mrs
Bussell arrived, looking much as usual, and sat in the drawing room.
'Could I have a cup of tea, Mrs Drummond?' she said. 'I just bashed

my son's head in with an axe, and he is lying dead on the opposite side of the river.'

Sometimes the stories are sinister, sometimes hysterically funny. I sit listening in the dim Harper sitting room with the pink chaise longue, the ancestors' miniatures staring from the wall, the green flats outside the window stretching away to the river, and Mrs Harper's bright, birdlike voice unwinding the secrets of the past to my enchanted ears.

Once a month I stagger home from school with violent period pains, to be dosed with gin until my head reels. I have rebelled against the bucket of bloodstained rags soaking in the wash house and emancipated myself with Modess like the other girls. 'Red sails in the sunset,' they giggle together.

Discovering Meds, I decide to risk the 'blood will run up to your brain and you will go mad' theory, and don't go mad at all, only end forever the dreary embarrassment of sitting fully clothed on the beach while everyone else goes in swimming.

Out in the sleepout, drunk on pain and gin, I write:

Pain, the hibiscus bud dies,
And it lies in my hand
Quite dead, a red kiss,
And I thought I never knew
That pain was red before this.

There are amber eyes in the room
Strange amber eyes like the eyes
of a bronze bird,
And a heartfull hibiscus bloom,
And strange white stone of music that
I heard . . .

A sheaf of my new poems clutched in my hand, I am taken by my father to see my first live writer . . . Keith Ewers, the West Australian novelist. We sit in his dim little study and he tells me my poems are 'quite extraordinary for a sixteen-year-old', but to, 'forget about being a writer. There's nothing in it, except heartbreak . . . I've had to work as a schoolteacher all my life'.

I leave, dancing on air, because this bespectacled thirty-year-old with the long, kind face has praised my work. We stand awkwardly on the porch.

'Do you still want to be a writer?'

'Yes.'

He grins wryly. 'Then I suppose you will be.'

If I can't make a living as a writer, perhaps I can be a journalist on the side. My father takes me to see Malcolm Uren, editor of the *Western Mail*. 'It's no job for a woman', he says. 'It hardens them. It's too rough a life. I wouldn't let a girl of mine do it.'

I stare at him, large, dark, expansive, behind his littered editor's desk, and burn with female fury. What right have these pontificating males to condescend to *me*? What right have they to decide my future? I *will* be a writer, no matter what they say, or how many warnings they give me.

I sit on the prow of the ferry experiencing, across the glassy water, the shape and colour of the first small skyscraper against the Perth skyline. This is modernity and I struggle to write it into my poetry – the blocks of pale stone thrusting into the sky, the curve of river and city. There is a language here which *must* be radically different and in a poem called 'The Crane', by John Redwood Anderson, I think I have discovered it:

> It stuns
> The rapt attention, and it lifts
> More than its load of many tons:
> More than the turbine swung on high
> So easily,
> A toy
> In its great grasp of steel.

At the end of 5B I win the English prize . . . a copy of *The Oxford Book of Modern Verse*. It changes my life: Yeats, Eliot, Edith Sitwell, Ezra Pound, the Irish poets.

When Mrs Russell-Smith warns Lilla against me because 'there is something unwholesome' about me, and 'I am not a friend' for normal people, I get my revenge by muttering:

> Oh! fat white woman whom nobody loves
> Why do you walk through the field in gloves
> Missing so much and so much . . .

'Dorothy is a rebel in word and deed. The latter usually tones with time,' she writes on my end-of-year report. My mother is horrified and goes up to the school for an interview. She comes back looking bemused. 'All she seems to have done,' she tells my father, 'is go to the tuck shop during school hours and take off her panama hat on the ferry.'

'I will live in Ringsend with a red-headed whore,' I whisper savagely.

I sit in the dentist's chair, three storeys up, waiting for the injection to work. My teeth are crumbling inside from lack of calcium. Through the window, the gilded weathercock on the spire of the Methodist church is whirling faster and faster, spinning against the clouds. When I come down in the lift my face is numb, but I am walking on air through the glowing streets. It's like coming out of the darkened movie theatre, where I can be anybody I want for a little while – Garbo or Dietrich in a black beret, Joan Crawford with padded shoulders, tragic-eyed Bette Davis, husky-voiced Margaret Sullivan or Katharine Hepburn, tossing her hair and striding off down Hay Street in wide-legged trousers.

I come home with my brain teeming with stories about a lint-haired girl with high cheekbones I've seen drinking coffee in London Court. I call her Sasha, and try to write about her: 'As idle as a painted ship upon a painted ocean,' the ferry bears me home across the river, the city towers reflected in the water like dazzling spires. But afterwards there is always the letdown, when the bright images fade and the world turns flat and monochrome.

Next time I sit in the dentist's chair nothing happens and I feel cheated. The use of drugs for painkilling purposes has been tightened up. Goodbye whizzing weathercock, goodbye cocaine.

It is my last year at school. Anne Gregory, the flamboyant daughter of Captain Gregory, who is immortalized as the romantic sea-captain in Katharine Prichard's *Intimate Strangers*, is no longer head girl, but she has left behind a wealth of legend. The boarders tell how she knotted sheets together and climbed out of the window to go rampaging through the town with her handsome father. He is not allowed past the 29th Parallel, so the gossips say, because he is suspected of being too friendly with the Japanese pearl divers who worked his pearling luggers in Broome before the war. Now Dorothy Patterson is our head girl. The large, serene, clever daughter of a big pastoralist family, she sits at the back of the classroom with her friend Constance Spurway, a theatrical scholarship girl with a mop of auburn curls, who comes from a poor family and is always slightly out of step with these rich descendants of the early pioneers. When Spurway buys a new dress, we all have to troop up to her room and see it, spread out on the bed, a bright-green organdie, transforming her boarder's cubicle. These two are the leaders in the baiting of poor

Miss Hamilton, 'Hammie', the French mistress. But we are all culpable. We all join in, so that she constantly flees the classroom in floods of tears and afterwards I am ashamed, but dare not admit it.

Shirley Forrest is a descendant of Lord Forrest, 'Jarrah Jack' from Bunbury, whose bronze statue dominates the city, gazing out from Kings Park over the Swan. The Forrests are regarded by the Harpers as jumped-up parvenus. Shirley is a vague, pretty, wide-hipped girl with an imagination. In the Divinity class she stands up and challenges the High Church Sister who has just arrived from England.

'Sister,' she says, 'Dorothy Hewett has never been baptized. Will she go straight to hell?'

'Very probably,' says the Sister, who the week before confiscated my Divinity notebook and dropped it, with fastidious fingers, into the waste-paper basket. It was filled with drawings of scantily clad women, their anatomical details plainly visible through the sweeping muslin of their dresses.

We have a new Art mistress, a tall, russet-headed girl in a real artist's smock who tells us fabulous stories about Sydney and her fellow students at East Sydney Tech. Her heroine is Tiger, a rebel with flaming red hair, hooped earrings and mascaraed eyes, who paints like an angel. Our teacher predicts that she will become one of the great new avant-garde women painters of Australia. I can hardly wait for the next instalment. It's like a fascinating serial. Painting my clumsy, abstract designs of white masks, red hibiscus and black panthers, I suddenly see them for what they are ... schoolgirl fumblings! I am disgusted with myself. I will leave this narrow provincial little town, go to Sydney, and sit in coffee shops late at night arguing the meaning of Art and Life with real artists like Tiger.

In September we go for a holiday to a guest house in the hills and I meet Ralph Lang, a twenty-two-year-old Catholic bank clerk who plays 'Souvenirs' on the violin and actually owns a sports car. When we go back to Perth, he invites me to a dance to meet his large Catholic family. Things are getting serious. I walk home from the ferry at night with Father McMahon, the Catholic priest, an Irishman with the squashed nose of a pugilist who plays golf with my father. He talks to me about Irish mythology, fairies and poetry, and I think about maybe marrying Ralph and committing that cardinal sin for all Protestant families, called 'turning'.

After school I tear off my school blouse and my black stockings, buy a sixpenny lipstick from the corner chemist that cakes like dried blood on my mouth, and race through the little gate on the other side of the swimming pool to meet Ralph Lang in his sports car. We whirl away for delirious hours of kissing and murmured promises. 'I may take your chastity,' he whispers, 'but I will never take your virginity.' I only wish he would.

My parents are horror-stricken. They fear the worst, particularly my mother, who has found the fragment of a poem I wrote to Neil Jones after those guilty afternoons in the pine plantation: 'He laughed and pulled my skirt above my hips/and drank again from my soft yielding lips.' She is sure that I am on the way not only to sexual perdition but to religious perdition as well, which seems strange considering that few of my family have gone near a church for years.

A letter comes from the Children's Court. I am charged with 'being an uncontrollable child', Ralph with 'contributing to the delinquency of a minor'. My parents have reported us, have transformed our romantic idyll into a dirty little sexual crime. He is bewildered, hurt, horrified – poor Ralph and his charming, respectable Catholic family! For some perverse reason of my own, I demand to speak to his father on the phone and, weeping, apologize for all the trouble I have caused. I lie in bed in the sleepout, sodden with tears, howling as much for the end of my Catholic idyll as for the cowardice of Ralph Lang, who has promised never to see me again in return for getting off the moral hook.

Slender and tall, with his long, sensitive, wind-chapped face and his passion for music, he has betrayed me and I will never forgive him. We say goodbye at a last secret meeting in his sports car on the Perth side of the ferry. Red poppies are blooming in a garden bed near the ticket office as he tells me he will never stop loving me.

Five years later, selling the Communist newspaper the *Workers' Star* from door to door, I knock at the door of a dingy-looking flat. I can hear children crying, and a harassed woman with a baby on her hip, her fair hair coming undone, answers my knock. 'You'll have to ask my husband,' she says. I go out into the back yard. There is a pair of long legs sticking out from underneath a sports car. The face emerges. My God! It's Ralph Lang! We stare at each other. He is a good Catholic but he buys the *Workers' Star*, looking sad, and flustered and harassed and slightly embarrassed at this ghost of a seventeen-year-old schoolgirl who almost got him into trouble with the Children's Court.

At the time it was all hushed up. Neither of us ever appeared before the Court. In fact my family were as horrified as his at the prospect of all that unpleasant publicity.

My father takes me in his arms. 'It's not fair,' he says. 'You're too little to cope with all this trouble,' but as I weep I despise him and myself for our hypocrisy.

I visit Neil Jones for the last time in the little fibro and weather-board 'Teachers' House' with the lino-covered floors. Sitting nervously on the edge of his bed in the sleepout, I tell him all about Ralph Lang and my broken heart. He tries to kiss me and undo my blouse. He doesn't seem to realize that his power is over. Embarrassed, I pretend that his mother is coming and escape into the kitchen.

She puts me in the master bedroom in a double bed with icy sheets, and a white china basin and ewer on a marble-topped wash stand. I lie there for a long time, staring into the dark until I fall asleep.

When I wake in the middle of the night, my bladder is bursting. To go to the toilet I will have to pass through the sleepout by Neil's bed. He'll make a grab at me again. I lie there in excruciating agony. It seems like hours. When I can't stand it any longer, I get up and piss in the ewer. It's like sacrilege – tinkle tinkle tinkle, it goes on for ever. It will wake up the whole house and now I dare not go to sleep again. What if his mother comes in the morning and finds her sacred ewer brimming with piss? When dawn breaks I creep into the hall, ease open the front door, and carry the guilty ewer across the wet lawn, pouring out the contents and rinsing it under the garden tap. Shivering, stupefied with tiredness, I crawl back under the white bedspread. I leave as soon as I can after a painful breakfast, his brown eyes accusing me all the way to the bus stop. As the bus pulls out I wave, knowing I'll never really see him again, but all I feel is guilt, relief and a curious lightness.

It's time to plan for the future. If I want to be a great actress I had better do something concrete about it. Through an old army mate, my father arranges an audition for me at the ABC. My audition pieces are certainly audacious for a seventeen-year-old – for tragedy, Gemma Jones in *Escape Me Never* (I've seen Elisabeth Bergner play that role in the movie); for comedy, Amanda in Coward's *Private Lives*.

The report comes back: I have talent but my voice needs more training. Again my poor father – pushed, I suspect, by my mother into those entrepreneurial roles for which he is so ill-suited – withdraws thankfully back into his shell.

I talk my parents into allowing me to go on a camp concert tour with the Repertory Club. Driving back to Perth in the hired bus after midnight, I am sitting in the back seat next to a middle-aged actor I admire, a leading light on the theatre committee, when he starts to grope me. I am astonished. I sit rigid with embarrassment and outrage, particularly when I realize he's doing exactly the same with his other hand to the young actress in her twenties on the other side

of him. 'Would you like to come and sit next to me, dear?' calls a
motherly, middle-aged woman across the aisle. Thankfully, I grab at
the excuse.

In line for the juvenile lead in Thornton Wilder's *Our Town*, I am
inexplicably dropped from the cast list and never offered a part in a
Repertory Club production again.

At the end of the year I play the Virgin Mary in the school
pageant, but I never join the Old Girls and never go back to Perth
College.

In those last weeks at school Lilla tells me she has never really
cared for me. Confused and distraught, I climb up the stairs to the
cloisters and stare down into the cement quad, willing myself to jump.
Predictably associated with the pain of lost love, it's my first flirtation
with the idea of suicide. But climbing down again I write my most
accomplished poem to date, which does much to assuage my mortal
anguish:

> The dark fires shall burn in many rooms,
> will they sometimes miss me with my tangled hair,
> still girls in dark uniforms
> crouching in winter with their cold hands trembling,
> still voices echoing as our voices echoed
> and the faded frumped-up form
> of a mistress teaching French.
> Does she remember us or do we pass
> only like dreams of dark figures,
> some with different hair or deep voices,
> or merely countless hats hanging on pegs,
> countless columns of moving massed black legs?
> Our minds are sprawled on unforbidden lawns,
> our voices lie like queer leaves in the clipped grass,
> as we believe so we shall pass.

7
♣

'SEEK WISDOM' says the inscription on the bust of Socrates in the university quad. 'Verily it is by beauty that we come to wisdom' is chiselled into the back of the stone seat by the pool. Wisdom is all around us. Surely some of it might rub off on me. I am entranced by the university – the Spanish mission buildings in pale sandstone, the tall clock tower, the Christmas trees, orange tails blazing against green lawns, the wooden stile that leads on to the football oval with its grazing sheep from the Faculty of Agriculture – all this circled by the calm reflecting waters of the river.

I am enrolled in first-year Arts, an English Honours major, in Australia's only free university. Maybe I will become one of the privileged intellectuals. In a photograph taken at the inauguration ceremony there we are, standing in the front row, Mary Vetter and I, wreathed in smiles, beside tall, demure Julia Drake-Brockman. 'When in silks my Julia goes', we recite to her.

In the back row is Ron Strahan, who will ask me to marry him and then change his mind; Danny Dunn, future Registrar of Murdoch University, who once suggested we might run away together; huge, shambling Mick Wright, who will write romantic poems to me. Here in the centre row is my fourth cousin Noel Dougan, from the Irish connection, who will marry my sister Lesley; next to him is his friend, Bob Blanckensee, who will become senior partner in his father's law firm. He has an adolescent crush on me. On the other side is Klaus Blaumann, who will take me to visit at his mother's studio. Elise Blaumann, a refugee from Hitler's Germany, is an Impressionist painter who will startle Western Australia into Modernism. I stand in her studio entranced by the glowing canvases.

What are we like, my generation of 1941? – romantic, idealistic, fiercely partisan about politics and equality of the sexes, determined to change our world, we are very conscious of being a radical, intellectual minority in a little Australian backwater. If our boyfriends are unlikely to survive the holocaust, then it is up to us to enjoy our youth while we have it. 'Live wildly today, forget tomorrow,' I write. We are existentialists without knowing it.

I scorn the Yanks, pasty-faced boys who seem to think that an orchid or a box of chocolates can buy them anything. I am fiercely independent. Nobody can buy me and I always insist on paying my own way.

I go out a few times with the Americans: once on a blind date to the Independence Day dinner, with glamorous Gabrielle Cunningham, who is half-French and wears black lace bras under her see-through blouses (my partner is a Catalina pilot named Tex, who calls me Dotty and bores me to tears); once to the American Independence Day ball, with Bob Holmquist, a little New England submarine rating, who insists on giving me his class pin, which I don't want. As we are frisked at the entrance to the Embassy Ballroom by two hulking Yank MPs, a woman in front of me drops two whisky bottles out of her fur coat to smash on the marble stairs. Inside, they are pulling up Coke bottles filled with whisky on ropes through the ballroom windows. As the evening wears on, drunken young women, their breasts falling out of the front of their evening gowns, dance with bald-headed generals old enough to be their fathers. I am disgusted. In my own way I am a moralist too.

There are scandalous stories about naked girls, dosed up on Spanish fly, found raped in the bottom of air-raid trenches and wild parties in Mount Street flats, with a champagne fountain where the girls dip their breasts and the Yanks suck off the champagne. The scandal breaks when one well-known society girl sues a passionate Yank who gets carried away and bites off her nipple.

Later, when I am assigned to the Children's Court as a part-time reporter for the *Daily News*, I see the seamier side of the Yank invasion – dozens of teenagers, some as young as twelve, standing in the dock pregnant, charged with being 'uncontrollable children'.

The vice squad roam the parks and river foreshores and enterprising little boys steal discarded panties and shoes off engrossed couples on the Esplanade, for fun or even blackmail. I sit in the Women's Common Room, listening pityingly to the girls with their autographed photographs of handsome American airmen, their tall stories of married lovers who will divorce their American wives and send for them 'back in the States' when the war is over. I prefer Australians, who give neither orchids nor chocolates, who are inarticulate but seem to promise love and even silent understanding.

I am still a passionate pacifist, contemptuous of recruiting posters, canteens and War Loan Rallies, particularly since I've seen Lew Ayres in *All Quiet on the Western Front*, stretching his dying hand over the sandbags for the white butterfly escaping into no-man's-land.

I am terrified I might be 'manpowered' and sent into a jam or munitions factory.

We are mostly the children of privilege, with well-off, middle-class parents who can afford to keep us at school and send us to university. Yet we despise them for their old-fashioned, narrow Victorian standards, their ignorance, their right-wing politics, their pathetic patriotism, their racist, male-dominated society. Between them and us, educated on Freud, Adler and Jung, there is an impassable gulf that can never be bridged again.

I have only just managed to get into university by the skin of my teeth, taking a special French translation test to qualify, but I am here, surrounded by books and paintings; prints of Michelangelo's 'Adam' in the Administration building, Diego Rivera's Mexicans in the Refectory, Gauguin's Tahitians, Van Gogh's 'Bridge at Arles' and Franz Marc's 'Red Horses' in the lecture rooms.

My confidence is shattered in the first weeks. We are all given an intelligence test by the Psychology Department. When I am called in for my interview in the tower with hairy, charismatic Dr McIlwaine, I am told that I shouldn't really be at university at all, I'm not intelligent enough, not anywhere near the top brains in the state. Ashamed and demoralized, I stumble out into the sunlight to sit by the pool, feeling like an outcast amongst all these golden, brilliant creatures. It is as if I have been branded FAILURE before I've even started. I have been brought up to believe that I can do anything. What has gone wrong?

Miserably, I climb the stairs to the library and sit there amongst my beloved books in the English Literature section. Before the year is out, I will have systematically read through the shelves, discovering *Wuthering Heights*, Dylan Thomas, Lawrence's poems, the plays of Eugene O'Neill, Maxwell Anderson, Lillian Hellman, Elmer Rice, Kaufman and Hart and Clifford Odets.

Christina Stead's *Seven Poor Men of Sydney*, Kenneth 'Seaforth' Mackenzie's *The Young Desire It*, and Eleanor Dark's *Prelude to Christopher* will have proved to me that it is possible to write poetic novels about Australia.

Stealing a youthful drawing of him out of his *Collected Poems*, I decide that I am the reincarnation of Dante Gabriel Rossetti. With his long wavy hair and dreamy-lidded eyes (before he grew gross and bald), there is a rather odd resemblance. Lizzie Siddalas 'Beata Beatrix' becomes one of my favourite paintings. Sitting hour after hour cross-legged on the floor by the stacks in a shaft of sunlight, I will devour this enchanted kingdom. Even if I haven't got any brains, I can still read.

I get my revenge in the Psychology Department's Rorschach test.

Dr Kaula, the little German psychologist and a Jewish refugee, calls
me into his study. He finds my interpretation of the ink blots disturbing. Stepping outside the role of lecturer, he wants to psychoanalyse
me. I am flattered. If I can't be intelligent, I can be mad and gifted.
Everybody knows the gifted are crazy.

Every week I climb the stairs to his tower room until one day he
asks me, 'What is your ambition?'

'To be a greater actress than Sarah Bernhardt and a greater
writer than Edith Sitwell.'

In a rage, he dismisses me. He is disgusted. He thinks I am
putting on an act. Maybe there is a certain amount of bravado in my
claims, but in reality I am deadly serious.

However, he does give me one precious gift to offset the damage
of the intelligence test. 'Take no notice,' he scoffs. 'It is a test of
mathematical ability, that is all. Your ability is in language.' Well,
that's fine, I can cope with that. I've been coping with it all my life.
('Dorothy Hewett, are you a moron when it comes to Maths?')

I try and repay the gift. When the jingoistic, anti-Semitic head of
the Psychology Department dismisses Dr Kaula for incompetence, he
appeals to the students for support. 'I am an academic. What else shall
I do? Where can I go? I have a wife and child.'

We take up a petition for him – not that it does any good. Tiny,
sad, bespectacled, with his heavy German accent, he takes my hand.
'We must say goodbye,' he says, 'but perhaps you will remember our
little talks, perhaps they did some good for you.' I can't bear it.
I escape from the tower and stumble down the stairs, feeling vaguely
guilty.

We have a new professor of English who will revolutionize the
Department. Alan Edwards, a scholarship boy from Lancashire and a
Cambridge don in his early thirties, who rides a girl's bike to the
university, is a disciple of Freud and Leavis. Calling my bluff, he lends
me the banned Yellowbook editions of *Tropic of Cancer* and *Tropic of
Capricorn*. I am secretly shocked, but wild horses wouldn't drag it out
of me.

'Well, what did you think?' he asks, with his deceptively benign
smile.

'Oh! I got a bit bored with it all,' I say loftily. 'It was a bit too much
of the same old thing.'

His eyes snap behind his glasses. He considers me an arrogant
little bitch.

Alec King is a lecturer in English. His speciality is Wordsworth.
At his first lecture he tells us that if we want to understand Wordsworth's relationship to nature, we should go out of the lecture theatre,
take off our shoes, and feel the grass springing under the soles of our

bare feet. I am the only student who takes him at his word, striding out across the green lawns, shoes in hand, rejoicing at Wordsworth between my toes.

I have been taken up by the second-year university bohemians – Gregor McLeod, Lloyd Davies and Mary Bell. Gregor is a Communist with a red, squashed, humorous face crowned with auburn curls. His Great-Aunt, Sheila, is famous for having ridden a white horse up the marble steps of the Palace Hotel, naked except for a cloud of long red hair. Lloyd is a law student, short, myopic and witty. He is Gregor's best friend, and Mary, sardonic deflater of all our pretensions, is their constant companion.

I hide my black slack suit and my black velvet beret in my locker, change into them in the Women's Common Room, and sally forth, playing my version of the emancipated woman artist. I long to have a proper dress allowance so that I can choose my own clothes, but our mother always takes us shopping, charging everything to her account. She is usually absurdly generous and we come home parading in our slack suits and beaded dresses, our stovepipe hats and slingback cork-soled shoes, before the bemused gaze of our father.

'How do we look?' we cry, hungry for masculine confirmation.

'You'd look good in a chaff bag at your age,' he says.

When Gregor McLeod lends me Zola's *Nana* and Ron Strahan lends me a sex manual with all the different sexual positions under-lined in red ink, my father rebels with Methodist distaste and fury. He calls Ron up for an interview. 'Do you think this is the right kind of book to lend a young lady?'

'Yes,' says Ron, with commendable courage. 'I think sex is a necessary part of any young woman's education.'

My father is nonplussed. He had wanted 'educated daughters' and now, like the serpent's tooth, I have turned against him.

The Jewish refugees are arriving in Western Australia. 'Hitler had the right idea about those Jews,' he says, folding the *West Australian* newspaper. 'They're coming in here with their fur coats and their diamond rings and taking over the country.'

His anti-Semitism disgusts me. I flare up. 'You look like a Jew yourself.'

He laughs. 'Maybe you're right. My father used to call my mother his little Jewess.'

My parents always refer to Aborigines as 'niggers'. When I protest, they jeer at me. 'What would you call them?'

'Coloured people!' My own racial attitudes are still fairly rocky.

We live in a seemingly gentle, unpolluted, isolated world of space, white beaches and long golden summers, but scratch the thin skin off the top of this utopia and you find corruption at the heart. If you are born black or poor or a woman, it is an impossible world to live in; if you are gifted, if you have a passionate, questioning intellect, it is a vicious world that blocks every avenue.

But there are advantages in belonging to a small provincial university. Our surroundings are calm and pastoral – no brutal architecture, no concrete, force-fed learning factory. Even as first-years, we know all our lecturers. We are invited to the Vice-Chancellor's house for afternoon tea and every month the Professor of English holds play readings for us in his own home. What a glorious world it is after all. Ric Throssell, the handsome son of Katharine Prichard, sits by the pool in the quad holding court with his retinue of Teachers Training College students. We all know about Ric Throssell. They say he is an atheist who refused to be sworn in on the Bible as head boy of Wesley College.

At the end of the year, in the Commonwealth Literary Fund lectures, we listen to Henrietta Drake-Brockman, Mary Durack and John K. Ewers. Gavin Casey arrives, drunk, uproarious and irreverent, and is an instant hit with all the students. The novelist Vance Palmer turns up in Alan Edwards's tutorial. Sitting there in his spotted bow tie, he talks to us in a low-key kind of way about Australian literature, about which we know nothing at all.

I meet Mary Durack, the novelist, the first writer who doesn't tell me to forget all about it. Her sister Elizabeth, the painter, invites me to her studio at the Art Gallery, and I sit there amazed at myself talking about Art and Life with tall, blonde, paint-smeared, elegant Elizabeth.

Gabrielle Cunningham is thrown out of the French tutorial for wearing slacks. In the cause of academic freedom for women, I make a bet with Gregor McLeod and swagger into Alec King's tutorial in my grey mélange trousers, puffing at an ostentatious Camel. He doesn't even notice.

Lloyd Davies presents me with a bunch of dandelions because I am the only woman in the university who will appreciate it. Mick Wright blunders drunk into the Women's Common Room, frightens a young woman out of her wits by professing undying love, and is threatened with expulsion.

I spend more and more time in my favourite place, the little sitting room off the Women's Common Room. Drowned in yellow light, with the Virginia creeper tapping against the diamond-paned windows, I sit there composing my endless poems, my hair in a long

Veronica Lake bob. 'Put a clip in it,' my mother says tartly. 'You'll get a squint if you're not careful.'

I write a play called 'Time Flits Away Lady' (title courtesy the *Oxford Book of Modern Verse*). It is an experimental melodrama that plays ducks and drakes with time and wins first prize in a University One-Act Play Competition. We set up a trestle stage in the refectory and Lloyd, Connie Spurway and myself all play leading roles. Mrs Russell-Smith comes to the first night. 'You were an impossible child to teach,' she tells me. 'It was so difficult to get your attention.'

I hear her opinion of my play on the grapevine: 'It was melodramatic and overwritten, but there was a kind of power about it. You could sense the talent.'

I fall off the trestle stage and sprain my ankle but, hooked by the glamour of it all, write a one-act murder mystery called 'Sarah', a two-act lesbian love tragedy in blank verse called 'Ah Judas!', and a full-length melodrama about a celebrated actress who dies young of TB (shades of Garbo in *Camille*). The play is set in Switzerland, London and Paris, where I have never been. It never occurs to me to set any of these plays in a recognizable Australia, but I have written an experimental novel called 'Daylight' where all the action takes place in Perth and all my contemporaries, thinly disguised, appear in it. There are quotes from Dylan Thomas introducing each chapter. To my astonishment, when I show it around, some of my friends are less than flattered. Even the rambunctious Gregor McLeod is deeply hurt. Mary Bell is furious. She writes me a bitingly sarcastic letter accusing me of egotism and cruelty. 'You are a monster, Dotty,' she tells me.

I can't remember the exact moment when I became conscious of the divided self. There is the girl who moves and talks and rages and loves and there is the writer who watches and writes it down, who even in her most passionate moments is saying, 'Remember this'.

This cold, detached consciousness that always writes it down afterwards without fear or favour, who is she? Does this mean that I will never be able to experience anything fully with sincerity and passion? Whoever she is, she has come to live with me for the rest of my life – analysing, taking account of, describing everything . . . a monster? Perhaps Mary Bell is right.

My first real success comes when I win the *Meanjin* Poetry Prize. I have seen the little magazine, with its row of Aboriginal footprints, in the university library and sent a batch of poems under the ridiculous pseudonym of Jael Paris. 'Dream of Old Love' is a Gothic lyric probably influenced by Edith Sitwell and the Chinese 'translations' of Ezra Pound:

The sunlight hurts me like a diseased hand,
I am the evil Chinese princess
And you the diseased prince,
Richocheting in our turret of courtesans.

The discovery that Jael Paris is an eighteen-year-old West Australian University student causes something of a stir. 'These are extraordinary poems for an eighteen-year-old,' writes editor Clem Christesen. 'All the poems sent in by Jael Paris show a distinctive poetic talent.'

I sit in the Women's Common Room, or curled up on the window seat at Ridge Street staring out at the distant river, self-absorbed, writing my poems about flame-tree women, red moons rising over stable roofs, architects suiciding from the university tower, unaware of anything else, even the progress of the Second World War.

I am a poet. I have my vocation, and I have a secret lover.

Diary: March 1941
I first saw you when I was a schoolgirl. I don't even know what year it was, or why I always remembered it. It was nothing, just a boy with a big head passing on a bike. But I never forgot it. It was like one little picture. I must have been in school uniform. I know I felt dark, and my hair must have been long and fair and my face pale. You came riding round the corner suddenly with your head bent over the handlebars. I remember your face was very pale and it floated over your body. Your head seemed something entirely apart from the rest of you. I can't remember anything except your head ...
your fair straight hair and the extraordinarily sullen mouth and eyes. It was by that wattle on the edge of the street. I think it had been raining because the road seemed to be very blue and wet.

We fall in love on the back verandah one moonlit night in late summer and very soon we are inseparable. We meet in the evenings at the university and take off our clothes to lie in each other's arms, naked, on the white strip of sand along the river bank smoking our Camels, till he dinks me home on his bike about two miles over the Causeway to South Perth.

I talk him out of using Brylcreem and give him a copy of *Wuthering Heights* for his birthday inscribed 'To my Heathcliffe/from your Cathy'. We talk about spending our whole lives together on a deserted, tropical island with our two children, Michael and Karen.

One night, lying out under the pines on the university oval, I lose my virginity at last, but so briefly and quickly, with no pain, I hardly know it has happened. I hold him shaking in my arms. The wind blows the boughs across the open space. The scent of the pine needles, crushed under the weight of our bodies, fills the night air. To be joined to another human being seems to me the ultimate mystery.

We tell each other everything and he absorbs me so completely that I can't stay away from him, but it is as if I live two lives – one life at the university, where I am developing a reputation as a bohemian poet, and another down by the river with my lover, where I can be completely myself. I love his big muscular body. It seems so absolutely clean and straight. My own soft breasts and wide hips, with the moist hole between my legs, disgusts me. 'Don't say that,' he says roughly, pulling me into his arms. 'You're totally beautiful.'

My 'intellectual friends' look askance and wonder what I see in him, but to me he is my secret lover, my other self. When he comes back from working in the wheatbelt that first summer, he is peculiarly undemonstrative. At last he admits that he thinks he has fallen in love with a country girl who 'doesn't expect too much of me and isn't complicated like you'.

After a few days he tells me it has all been a mistake but once, as I walk with him in the city, a brown girl passes, laughing, with strong, square teeth, and he stiffens.

'Who's that?' I ask him.

'That's her,' he says, and I see him watching the swing of her blue skirt until she disappears into the crowd.

My mother tolerates him until she reads my diary. In it I describe exactly how I feel about him and the time we once spent together in his single bed in the sleepout while his parents were out visiting.

There is a terrible row and from then on we are allowed to see each other only if my parents are present. It is a nightmare sitting there on the sofa with those gimlet eyes watching every move. We can't even talk any more.

'I can't stand it,' he mutters between his teeth.

'Don't leave me, please don't leave me,' I whisper.

Of course I meet him in secret, until the inevitable happens. One night my father discovers our meeting place (God knows how) and when I arrive the street is deserted. I wait for an hour. A damp mist is rolling in across the Chinaman's gardens. I run all the way to his house and stand by the garage, calling to him softly until he comes out into the back garden. He is shaken and angry. 'It's all your fault. Why did you leave your bloody diary around for her to read? Don't you see how impossible it is? They're making it impossible. They hate me.'

I cling around his neck. 'Don't leave me. Don't let them destroy us. I love you.'

Our Idyll is destroyed. When he turns eighteen he joins the air force and is sent to a training camp overseas, but one afternoon before he leaves with the draft he lets me into the garage. 'We'll have to hurry,' he says. 'They'll be home soon.'

I stare into the dim recesses of the garage, biting my lips, feeling nothing. When he is finished, he gets up awkwardly. He never looks at me once. 'Goodbye,' I say bitterly. His father calls from the house. He bends and kisses me clumsily. 'I'll have to go now,' he says. 'Take care of yourself.' He never writes and I don't see him again until 1945 when the war is over.

I walk out of the back gate and decide to be a whore. I'll pay him back. I'll pay them all back. There is no such thing as love, only sex. I am nineteen-and-a-half years old. Men, I think, are the great deceivers. I write a vengeful poem to him about taking me to bed and finding he is holding a skeleton in his arms:

> Bury your face and dream
> Of her you loved
> And spit her name in prayers.

I still have a lock of his straight blond hair in an old exercise book.

CHAPTER

8
♥

I had failed as a university student, I had failed in love; to succeed as an amateur whore seemed even more unlikely. Maybe the Psychology Department had been right after all.

My career as a whore gets off to a bad start, when I am called into the Australian Broadcasting Corporation to rehearse for a leading role in a radio play. The ABC Director of Drama is a gross sixty-year-old who looks like a bullfrog and is nearly ready for retirement. After the first rehearsal he calls me back for 'coaching', locks the door of his office and makes a grab at my breasts. 'Unlock the door or I'll scream,' I say.

As I flee into the corridor, shaking, I see a familiar face waiting outside. It is the same young woman who had submitted to the fumbling in the back of the Repertory Club bus on the army camp tour three years before. She has quite a lot of leading roles in ABC radio that year, but I am never cast for anything again.

I have joined the Communist Party, recruited by a Jewish university student whose name I can't even remember. Sitting on the stone seat carved with 'Verily it is by beauty we come to wisdom', she tells me about this exciting group of people who meet clandestinely and want to change the world.

Although Hitler invaded the Soviet Union in June 1941, the Australian Communist Party has been illegal ever since the Soviet–German Non-Aggression Pact in 1939.

I go to my first cottage meeting in an ice-blue taffeta 'ballerina' with high-heeled slingback shoes. I have no idea what a 'cottage meeting' is, but soon realize I have made a serious error of judgement. Everybody else wears slacks and jumpers and is terribly serious. Someone gives a talk on Communism and there is a discussion afterwards, with wine and cheese. I understand very little of what is going on, but they are all friendly and dedicated to the Revolution and social justice. There is a drawing of Lenin with a quote underneath it about the shining red star of Communism. I discover afterwards that Lenin never even wrote it. I think it is all marvellous. Gregor McLeod is delighted and tells me that Lloyd Davies has joined the Party.

Gregor, Lloyd and Mary Bell have all enlisted to save Australia. Singapore has fallen to the Japanese and the 8th Division of the Australian Imperial Forces are imprisoned in Changi.

'Our honeymoon is finished,' says Labor Prime Minister John Curtin in the *West Australian*. Reversing all the old ties of Empire, he calls on the Americans for assistance. Four days later the Japanese bomb Darwin. Against the wishes of Churchill and Roosevelt, the 6th, 7th and 9th Divisions of the AIF come home from the Middle East to fight in New Guinea. There is rationing; sandbags and air-raid shelters stand in the Perth streets. My father joins the Home Guard and drills on the golf links in the weekends. He goes to a gunnery school in Fremantle and is trained by Gregor McLeod and Lloyd Davies. I decide to join the WAAF, but as I am under age and my parents won't sign the enlistment papers, it all comes to nothing.

In May the Yanks and the Australians win the Coral Sea battle and in June Sydney and Newcastle are attacked by midget Japanese submarines. In the same month the US Navy defeats the Japanese at Midway Islands and turns the tide of the war in the Pacific.

I am working three days a week as a junior reporter on the *Daily News*. With so many male journalists enlisted as war correspondents, it is easier for women to get part-time jobs on the local papers.

I am sent mainly to cover the run-of-the-mill cases in the lower courts: a man charged with having intercourse with a cow; platinum-haired madams in big black Garbo hats charged with keeping unlicensed premises for the purpose of prostitution (the licensed brothels are across the railway line in Rowe Street); a pallid-looking woman suing for separation in the Married Women's Court on the grounds of 'unnatural sexual practices'. I have no idea what that is.

Maybe it was the Children's Court that helped me into the Communist Party, although if you were 'a rebel in thought and deed', there was nowhere else much to go. The Children's Court is presided over by a sanctimonious white-haired Salvation Army chaplain, who delivers his sermons to the lost children of Western Australia: long-haired wild boys absconded from Reform School who lived out in the bush, rough and starving, undersized fifteen-year-olds skiting about the jobs they'd pulled, encouraged by matey, plain-clothes detectives with their ever-ready notebooks; a fourteen-year-old Yugoslav girl with an odd, sad smile, charged with having a lesbian relationship with a twenty-two-year-old, in court with her fiancée. The case is dismissed when the lawyer reveals that the woman is getting married in a fortnight, but the girl is packed off to a home for delinquents. A sixteen-year-old who was at Modern School with my sister is sent to Reform School because of her love affair with an American. A grim, corseted mother in a toque gives evidence that her daughter 'is likely to lapse into a life of vice and crime'. I shiver, remembering Ralph Lang.

The hypocrisy sickens me. Cynically, I sit next to the teenage reporter from the yellow press *Mirror* and help him invent alliterative headlines for his lurid stories. Then I rush back to the reporters' room, type out 'my story' with two fingers on slips of copy paper, yell 'Boy!' and send it off to its fate with the sub-editors.

Once I got into serious trouble for mixing up the dates and reporting that all the current tea coupons would be called in the following morning. I had frantic women queuing up all over Perth, the telephones ran hot and the Chief of Staff was furious. I cried in his office and got out of it, but my reporter's career was short-lived and inglorious. The three days shrank to two, then one, and gradually they dropped me altogether.

I am attached to the Victoria Park Branch of the Party in a working-class suburb and made Branch secretary on the first night. The Branch meeting always begins with a study class in which we are bombarded with weird names like 'Mensheviks' from *The History of the Communist Party of the Soviet Union,* by J. V. Stalin. On Sundays I am taken round by an experienced cadre to sell the local *Workers' Star* and a glossy magazine called *The Soviet Union* canvassing from door to door.

My mother rages. My father is sarcastic but philosophical. He seems to think that it is all part of the process of growing up. Finally I decide I'm not good or selfless enough to be a Communist, so when the romance of it wears off I just drift away. They don't try to keep me.

The only thing I managed to salvage from my first Communist Party membership was a black kitten. Two boys were trying to push her under the Victoria Park tram, so I took her to the Branch meeting. 'You want to get rid of that cat,' said the chairman's wife, who had five small children. I called the kitten Ooloo and she sat on my shoulder while I typed and patted me while I lay in the bath.

My career in promiscuity had begun with a medical student who said, 'You don't expect it from a girl you could take anywhere.'

Two soldiers, Barry Bastow and Bill Woodlands, have followed me home, to be taken in, fed and made much of by my mother. She washes, irons and mends their uniforms – maybe they are the surrogate sons she never had; maybe she fancies them.

Barry Bastow is a mad Irishman with a broken nose and a winning Irish accent who claims to be descended from Roger Casement. He also claims to be writing a novel and carries around a pile of exercise books full of indecipherable gobbledegook. Once we make love on the golf links, but he is so consumed with guilt it never happens again. He wants me to run away with him, to sail the seven seas in a fishing lugger. The romance of it all is very suborning, but one night, sitting on the empty wharf waiting for the last ferry, I confess that I am in love with someone else. He leans forward, squeezing his fingers around my windpipe. 'If I can't have you, nobody else will,' he hisses.

Gasping for breath, I struggle under his hands. Is he actually going to strangle me? Then his fingers loosen and he starts to cry. I put my arms around him trying to comfort him, but coldly somewhere a warning voice is saying: 'Keep away from this man. He's dangerous.'

When he finally catches the troop train back to Sydney, his wife sends my mother a letter thanking her for her hospitality, 'on behalf of myself and the children'. He had never mentioned that he was married.

After the war a policeman comes to the door of my flat, trying to serve a summons for maintenance on Barry Bastow. He carries a photograph with him of a bearded Barry dressed in duffel coat and beanie, propped up on crutches on Sydney wharf. 'We think he's changed his name and probably disguised himself,' says the copper.

Bill Woodlands is the son of a Sydney washerwoman. He gives me 'knee-trembles' at the front door before my father puts out the milk bottles. He is obsessed with sex. We wander beside the river for hours, and because the only contraceptive we use is withdrawal I leave my stained knickers abandoned under the tea-trees. Sometimes he only has to touch me and I 'come', but because there is no love in it, only raw sex, I can't bear for him to enter me afterwards.

'You selfish bitch,' he sobs, furious and unsatisfied.

Once, when we are kissing and drinking beer on the Esplanade, two Vice Squad detectives flash their torches in our faces.

'How old are you?'

'Twenty-one'.

'She doesn't look twenty-one, does she?'

'It's okay,' the second one mutters. He has recognized me as the *Daily News* reporter in the Children's Court.

Eventually I grow tired of Bill Woodlands and brutally tell him so. One night, when I have made a date with Wally Thomas, he follows me to the bus stop. Twisting my arm up my back, he frog-marches me up the Terrace to Kings Park. I am too embarrassed to call for help.

'Go on,' he says, 'go on, why don't you scream?' Throwing me down on the grass, he ineffectually tries to rape me.

'You low bastard!' I hiss. 'But what can you expect, with your background? You're just trash. What makes you think I could ever care for an ignorant bully like you?'

He bursts into tears and I feel ashamed at my snobbery. He is only eighteen. My mother keeps on washing and pressing and sewing on his buttons for the war effort. She is not a good judge of character. My father looks sardonic. He has been a soldier himself. The truth is I don't really care much about any of them. They are only the means to an end, and the end is revenge on my parents, revenge on my idealized concept of the perfect love – Heathcliff and Cathy, and the sentimental love songs on the radio that still brings tears to my eyes.

But the most important thing that happened to me that year was meeting Bill Hart-Smith. Clem Christesen sent me a letter asking me to look Bill up. He was sick and lonely in an army hospital in Midland. Excited, I caught the train. I was going to meet my first live poet. He was in a psychiatric ward suffering from blinding headaches, later diagnosed as the first of several cerebral haemorrhages.

Bill Hart-Smith was a handsome thirty-two-year-old from Sydney, with a wonderful speaking voice, who looked like Ray Milland. He came to the house on weekend leave and we walked along the river talking about poetry and poets. He criticized my poems for their adolescent lushness. 'You've got to work at them,' he said. 'Hone them down. Don't just let it all gush out.'

I listened and I learned, but I knew Bill's way wasn't mine. He wrote imagist poems, brief, spare and controlled. I had to find my own style – and it wouldn't be Bill Hart-Smith's. He told me marvellous stories about the bohemian life in Sydney's Kings Cross, where he'd worked as a radio announcer and analysed handwriting for a living. He had married, not for love but for companionship, on the rebound from a failed affair. He warned me about Barry Bastow and Bill Woodlands. 'What are you hanging round with them for?' he said. 'They can't give you anything you need.' I knew he was right. 'I distrust love,' he said. 'It's a destructive emotion.'

I missed him when he had gone. I suppose I had really wanted him to love *me*. Fired by his stories, I wrote my first musical, with predictable duets on park benches and dance routines through the crowded streets of Sydney under the flashing neon lights of a mythical Kings Cross, borrowing the techniques I'd learnt from Busby Berkeley and the Hollywood musical.

> There's a blond on the corner,
>
> A redhead at the door,
>
> Is it any wonder that I do get sore,
>
> But I'm just crying for more, more, more,
>
> Of that no-good guy.

♥

At the end of 1943 we spend the holidays at Cottesloe, staying in a green two-storey boarding house, at the beach all day while our mother, dressed in her dark clothes and gunmetal stockings, sits like a duenna beside us. It is certainly not my idea of a good time.

I escape into Perth on some pretext and meet Peter Foulkes in the Esplanade Hotel. He is a friend of Lloyd Davies, 'an older man' I've met at somebody's party. I consider him ultra-sophisticated, sitting there in his white ducks in the saloon bar. Drinking schooner for schooner with the hard-drinking Peter, I am trying terribly hard to be as sophisticated as he is. This is easy, I think, but then the floor starts heaving. Desperately, I make for the glass doors. They are doubling and trebling like a mirage. Outside I get rid of Peter with some lame excuse and, running into the nearest building, am systematically sick on every landing in every drum of sand, placed there as part of the air-raid precautions. Afterwards I lie on the Esplanade for hours with my face buried in the grass, until I feel well enough to catch the bus back to Cottesloe. My favourite white sharkskin dress is ruined with grass stains and vomit, so I hide it in the rubbish bin. 'That Dorothy Hewett,' says Peter Foulkes, 'can drink like a fish.'

I go to the Modern School break-up party with Lesley. She has been head girl this year and now, with a brilliant leaving, she is going to university to enrol in first-year Science.

I look around at the party. They are all at least two years younger than I am, but there are a couple of interesting-looking boys; Colin Brindall, with his hooked nose and blond hair, who would join the navy and that thin, long-waisted, wild-looking boy with a schooner in one hand, who is he? Wally Thomas -- the best friend of Frank Lynn, Lesley's boyfriend. Together they share a passion for surfing and traditional jazz. That night Wally Thomas and I finish up under a bush in the garden in each other's arms. At an open-air dance at the Cottesloe Lido, I ditch Colin Brindall and disappear with Wally along the beach. We come back hours later to find Colin standing in front of the deserted dance floor, white with anger. I feel ashamed and we both apologize. In spite of it all, Colin and I stay friends, but Wally Thomas is my new lover. For the first time since I walked away from the garage under the wattle tree, I feel involved.

North Cottesloe is the fashionable surfing beach. We lie sunbaking for hours in the blazing heat, our bodies touching, kissing under our beach towels, and then fling ourselves into the surf to cool off. We walk for miles until we find a secluded spot in the shadow of the rocks, making love while the sand rasps under our bathers. We jitterbug all night at the Surf Club dances and when university starts again, skip classes and wander around the second-hand record shops, picking up Chicago cool jazz and New Orleans blues; fantastic trumpet and sax solos, Bix Beiderbecke, Jelly Roll Morton, Mugsy Spanier, Charlie Parker, Lester Young and old Fats Waller and Bessie Smith classics.

It is the era of 'the big bands', Lena Horne singing 'Stormy Weather' and Cab Calloway in his zoot suit singing 'Minnie the Moocher'. 'Caaab!', the Negro soldiers breathe ecstatically from the back row of the stalls.

As we lie on the floor in the dark in his parents' house, making love to 'The Creole Love Call', Wally and I never talk about any future. We make no promises and no commitments. Somehow it is a relief just to be with him. He is another working-class boy, the youngest of a big family of older brothers and the only one to make it to university.

Occasionally he borrows his father's car and takes me to the university dances, getting drunk and driving home like a maniac. Nobody owned cars at university then, except the son of Michaelaides, the millionaire tobacco manufacturer, and the son of an Indian Rajah, his fingers glittering with rings, who kept a blonde mistress like a bruised white camellia.

Wally and I climb up Jacob's ladder into Kings Park and lie out under the pines. He is the most extraordinary lover. He gives me my first experience of orgasm, but I am frightened and don't know what it is. Strangely enough, neither does he. I think there must be something wrong with me. I have experienced love, excitement and pleasure but never before this shaking, physical annihilation of the self. I ask the medical student. He is astonished at my ignorance, but explains it quite clinically. 'I can't believe this is your first experience of orgasm,' he says. He seems to be a bit piqued at his failure.

Wally was a chronic asthmatic and after any excitement he'd often sit gasping for breath with his head between his knees until I was frightened he'd choke to death. I was determined I would never be left alone again, so I kept on seeing all my other boyfriends. There was safety in numbers, I thought.

They come and go on leave. If things get too difficult, I remember *Belinda* in her hammock and go into a decline, entertaining them all around my cane lounge under the jacaranda tree on the back lawn. It isn't entirely make-believe. In between bouts of frantic activity – dancing, writing, acting, making love, staying up three nights running to finish my long-overdue Psychology assignments – I suffer these strange bouts of febrile exhaustion when I can hardly drag myself out of bed. In a benign mood, my mother says I am living on my nerves. In a temper, she says I remind her of a bitch on heat. All most of these young men want to do is strip me off to the waist while they gaze at or, at most, fondle my bare breasts. My reputation soars, but there is more smoke than fire. Years later Lloyd Davies told me I was notorious as 'the university bike', but you didn't really have to be too outrageous to upset the Grundies of Perth in the early 1940s.

The pattern is repeating itself – again I have two lives: the serious life with my 'intellectual' university friends, who are involved in literature, art and the theatre, and the hedonist life with Wally Thomas – wandering the beaches all summer, jitterbugging to 'The Dark Town Strutters Ball', listening to 'The Beale Street Blues', making love in the Undercroft and all those secret groves we discover in the university grounds.

Ron Strahan, Connie Spurway and I have started the University Dramatic Society. Amongst the new intake of Freshers there is lots of talent and we sit for hours in the refectory, arguing, planning, drinking cup after cup of black coffee, our faces floating in a haze of cigarette smoke – tall, red-headed, intense Philip Parsons, eyes and hair blazing, incubating his marvellous plan to direct Douglas Stewart's new poetic drama, *Ned Kelly*; statuesque, classically beautiful Pat Skevington, her long blonde hair in a smooth coil on the back of her head; Jeff Craig, drifting like a gazelle, drawing and painting the round rock hills and ancient blackboys of his native York, and Strahan, that *joli laid* young man, walking with long strides, his face twisted and arrogant under a crushed dark-blue porkpie hat.

Of all the old crowd only gigantic Mick Wright is left, and he is soon to join the air force and spend part of the war in an Australian military prison – Mick Wright, ugly as Caliban, with his monumental benders and his translations from Verlaine and Rimbaud, walking beside me reciting:

> Walking in rain in winter
> and in summer drinking by the sea
> grudge me not then this somewhat
> for no one knows as well as I
> how small it is.

The last I heard of him he had married an archaeologist in Beirut.

While the local Repertory Club are performing innocuous comedies by Clemence Dane, we are erecting the trestle stage in the refectory and playing Eugene O'Neill's *Where the Cross is Made* with Strahan in the lead, William Saroyan's *Across the Board* and *Tomorrow Morning*, Clifford Odet's *Waiting for Lefty* and Wilde's *Salome* with a Herod wearing long, purple, thrillingly decadent fingernails.

Both on and off stage we see ourselves as born actors, creating our vision of a little cultured avant-garde at the ends of the earth, but of all of us only Skev (or 'the beautiful Miss Skevington', as she is always called) becomes a well-known Perth actress.

Philip Parsons, with his wife, the drama critic Katherine Brisbane, pioneers Currency Press and the publication of Australian plays, but at the time all we manage to do is to send the University Dramatic Society flat broke. Jeff Craig paints in Paris, designs textiles in New York, becomes a *Vogue* photographer and burns to death in a house in Soho. Strahan becomes head of Taronga Park Zoo and writes books on small Australian mammals.

Impersonating a fallen angel in my mother's wedding dress, I stand on the trestle stage in the refectory reciting:

Have I indeed come downwards all this way
And in so short a time?

Afterwards, whenever he thought I was playing at the naive romantic, Strahan would tease me. 'Have I indeed come downwards all this way . . .' he would mock, with his sardonic smile. Strahan and I discovered our affinity one night after a rehearsal, sitting by the university pool watching the lights double in the dark water.

In spite of the sex manual, we have never experimented with sex. 'I don't want to be one of your sex objects,' he tells me. Once we almost make love in Albany, lying on the little single bed in the weatherboard cottage with the flywire door snibbed, but my mother comes back early from shopping, her face dark with rage and suspicion, while Ron disappears into the Katanning Reserve.

He is putting himself through university by working as a lab boy and has a chip on his shoulder about his lower-middle-class parents – a father in the naval stores who drinks too much and a mother who keeps a little grocer's shop in Victoria Park and has ambitions for her two clever sons.

When he invites me home to tea, I wear an embroidered peasant blouse, a red skirt, and strings and strings of looped, coloured beads. The meal is strained. His mother obviously doesn't approve of me at all. I try to be on my best behaviour, but it doesn't help when I spill a big blob of beetroot on her snowy linen tablecloth.

When Strahan joined the army he gave me his rare, battered copy of Dante's 'Inferno' with the famous Doré engravings. I wrote poems to him and he wrote me long letters from camp addressed to 'Dearest Dreamgirl'.

For the first and last time, my father tried to talk to me about sex.

We were driving home from the Regal Theatre, where I worked on Saturday nights handing out passouts to the audience for extra pocket money. 'I've been young myself,' he said. 'I know what men think about girls who make themselves cheap. You've got to have some discrimination, some sense of your own worth.'

It was sad and embarrassing. 'Things have changed, Dad,' I told him.

'They haven't changed that much,' he said.

Maybe he was right.

'The world tastes like blood in my mouth,' I cry dramatically. Lesley looks alarmed and my mother is horrified. I am rather pleased with the effect. They both go off to interview the head psychiatrist at Claremont Mental Hospital. 'Girls often go through a disturbed period in adolescence,' he tells them.

Lesley has missed out on the quota for Melbourne University Medical School. Modern School banned girls from the Chemistry and Physics classes, so she has tried to catch up with night classes at Technical College, but the odds are impossible. As long as I can remember she has wanted to be a doctor and now it looks as if she will never make it. Undaunted, she has enrolled in a double major in Psychology and Biology. Boiling up frogs on the gas stove in the kitchen, getting distinctions in all her subjects, carrying on her love affair with Frank Lynn with no fuss, she never ceases to amaze me. She seems to have her whole life so beautifully organized. She is 'the good girl' of the family and I am the bad seed. It is almost as if we have switched roles – she is the responsible older sister and I am the younger, difficult one. 'What do you want to do with your life?' Philip Parsons asks her. 'Do good deeds,' she tells him.

Years later, sitting on her front verandah in Victoria Park, we talk about that old, lost relationship with our parents.

'How did you manage it?' I say. 'I was always in trouble and you just went on doing exactly what you wanted.'

'You never learned to shut up,' she says. 'You were always so confronting.'

I think about that for a while.

'Anyway, don't you know why?' she says. 'It's because you were the precious one, the one they loved the most. They were always trying to protect you. They never cared that much about me.'

I stare at her in astonishment. This is a totally new interpretation, and I am still thinking about it.

9
♠

MY mother is demented, inspecting my clothes every night for 'semen stains'. When she throws my fur fabric coat down in front of me as evidence, I pitch a shoe at her head and miss. 'Tom, Tom,' she screams. 'She's trying to kill me.' My father rushes in, white faced, with blazing eyes, throws me down on the floor, kicks me, and calls me 'a filthy slut'. The second time he tries it, I slap his face as hard as I can, pack a small suitcase and prepare to leave home. My mother pulls all my clothes out again. 'They're all mine,' she screams.

With a copy of D. H. Lawrence's poems, a spare pair of pants and no money, I walk out, my mother still screeching behind me. But there is really nothing they can do. I am an adult. I have just turned twenty-one. Mary Vetter takes me in and I stay with her parents in the big house on the river foreshore, meeting Wally in the rushes and swearing I'll never go home again. 'It's all my fault,' he gasps, going into another asthma attack.

There are frantic phone calls and long talks with Mary's mother. My parents are mortified at the publicity. At last, with my log of claims clasped firmly, I go back for a peace conference. I seem to hold all the trump cards, so they sign submissively and I move back home to the sleepout where my father sleeps in his iron bedstead beside the door.

Now I can't even remember what I demanded, but it all had to do with freedom – freedom to see whoever I liked, to stay out as late as I liked with no questions asked, no more opened letters and diaries read in secret, no more telephone receivers stuck down with chewing gum so I can't hear the phone ringing.

Wally Thomas breathes a sigh of relief, joins the air force and goes off to a training camp at Victor Harbour. I am alone. The war has swallowed up all my boyfriends. Safety in numbers has failed. It is time to make a commitment. I decide that I really love Wally Thomas and write him dozens of passionate love letters, as I masturbate myself into an orgasm on the edge of the wooden chair. His replies sound half-hearted, but that is probably 'because of the censor'.

When the university lose patience at last and throw me out I am devastated, but I must have seen it coming. I take a job in Albert's Bookshop, but it lasts only a few months. The assistant manager, who has halitosis, says I don't smile enough at the customers and lends me a copy of *How to Win Friends and Influence People*. The manager is carrying out his own time-and-motion study from the balcony. Eventually I am sacked for reading the books, particularly *The Psychology of Sex* by Havelock Ellis.

I enrol at the Kindergarten Training College, where I make a toy wooden train, cover art folios with wall paper and spend three days a week as an assistant trainee at the Lady Gowrie Child Centre. They say I have a natural ability with children, but after a large four-year-old knocks me down in the playground and screams out the colour of my pants, I'm not so sure. The Duchess of Gloucester comes to inspect the kindergarten. As the eldest student I have to present her with the bouquet, but I refuse to curtsy. At the end of the year I poison my foot with the red dye out of my high-heeled court shoes and can't sit for the exams, which is just as well as I would never have passed any of them.

A letter arrives from Wally Thomas. He has fallen in love with another girl at Victor Harbour. It has happened again. Desolate, I wander the beaches and the banks of the river. Strangely enough I have never written a single poem to Wally Thomas, and I don't now. Instead I write a long narrative in blank verse commemorating the memory of Lilla Harper, my first lover and the farm:

> These have I lost, being too much beloved,
> And having for their virtue only this –
> That I have loved them.

A miracle happens. 'Testament' wins first prize in the ABC Poetry Competition. I have arrived. I am interviewed on the ABC, my poems are broadcast on the Young Artists' programme, my photograph is in the ABC Programme Guide.

On a winter's afternoon my father is sitting and talking by the gas fire with Miss Wilkins, a retired high school teacher who has become a friend of the family. I come into the room without them noticing me.

'Do you realize she might become very famous one day?' says Miss Wilkins.

'She might,' says my father dubiously. 'I don't understand a word of it. I can't read poetry. God knows where she gets it from.'

A telegram comes from the *Reader's Digest* offering me twenty-five pounds to publish 'Testament'. Breaking all the rules of the poetry fraternity, without even understanding what they are, I agree. When Clem Christesen's telegram of congratulations arrives, asking for permission to print in *Meanjin*, I have to say no. The *Reader's Digest* instead of *Meanjin*! Dimly, I realize I have damned myself as a money-grubbing philistine.

The telephone rings. It is Strahan on leave. Will I meet him on the golf links? He has something to ask me. Excited, I race down the hill to the tram stop. He is standing there by the white stile, and hand in hand we walk over the green towards the river. 'Will you marry me?' he says.

I am flabbergasted. Marriage? I've never thought of marriage. I don't believe in it. It's a bourgeois convention, and what about Fairhaven and the Red Resting Room? 'You know I don't believe in marriage,' I say. 'I believe in free love. Why can't we be free and happy? Why can't we be lovers?'

But it is an ultimatum – marriage or nothing. I go home and agonize over it all night. 'I am going to marry Ron Strahan,' I tell my mother. She looks astounded.

I have decided to capitulate. I can't stand being alone any more. I ring him and arrange to meet at the university pool at midnight. It seems the right setting for the grand sacrifice. He is standing in his army greatcoat by the dark water with his back turned towards me. I hum a few bars of Stravinsky's *Rite of Spring*, which has always been our signal, and put my arms around him. 'I'll marry you,' I whisper.

But he has changed his mind. I've convinced him it won't work. I'm not the marrying kind. I argue and argue. 'How can you change your mind *that* quickly?' I ask him. But I have come up against the cold, stubborn, contradictory streak I have always known existed in Strahan. In desperation I pull him down beside me on the chilly grass. Perhaps I can seduce him. He wraps me in his greatcoat. We begin to kiss. We are making love at last, when suddenly he leaps up and turns away, leaving me lying there, alone. I can't believe it.

'What's the matter?'

'It's no use. It won't work,' he says.

We catch the last trolley bus into town and part coldly.

'Well?' my mother asks.

'It's all off. He doesn't want to marry me now.'

She is outraged. 'How dare he? I'll *make* him marry you. I'll offer him a thousand pounds. He won't refuse *that*.'

I look at her wearily. 'You'll offer him nothing. You'll just mind your own business and shut up and leave me alone.'

'It's his loss,' she says. 'He won't ever find anybody else as good as you.'

I stare at her in amazement. Does my mother actually admire me?

♠

I decide to do something positive. I'll consult a gynaecologist about the period pains that have plagued my life since I was eleven years old.

'You don't mind a bit of discomfort, do you?' he says. 'You do have an infantile womb, but everything will be fine once you get married.'

'I'm not thinking of getting married,' I say coldly.

'But when you do, your husband will expect you to be – intact.'

'It's a bit late for that,' I tell him, and his handsome jaw drops.

So I have a simple curette at The Mount Hospital and never suffer again. Home once more, I lie raging in the sleepout, thinking about all those years of pain and gin, of staggering home from school, lying on the sofa for days every month, a procession of fatherly, middle-aged doctors mouthing, 'She'll be perfectly all right once she's married.' All for the sake of this male conspiracy about virginity.

One morning I wake up with palpitations of the heart. It goes on and on, this strange, frantic beating in my ears. It lasts for weeks, then my glands swell up and start to throb. I have mumps at twenty-two. My face and head feel like a football. A nervous, well-known voice on the telephone wants to come and see me. I wait for Wally Thomas in the darkened sitting room, trying to hide my swollen face.

'Are you still with this girl?'

'Of course. I couldn't do this to you unless I was serious.'

'And all the time I was writing to you, it was going on?'

'Not *all* the time – I didn't know how to tell you. I didn't want to hurt you.'

'So you wait and wait and end up hurting me twice as much?' I rage and cry. I do everything I swore I wouldn't do. 'How can you do this to me? Don't you remember anything?'

'I'm going to stay with her. I've got to stay with her. Otherwise I couldn't live with myself.'

'Why did you come at all?' I cry.

'I had to see you. I couldn't just leave it at that.'

'Just go,' I whisper, 'and don't come back.'

He leaves me, weeping. I weep for days. I weep everywhere. I am hunched in front of the gas fire . . . weeping. I can't sleep. My head is splitting. 'For God's sake!' my father shouts, 'haven't you got any pride?'

Pride . . . what's that? I don't even know who I am. I'm nothing. I'm unloved. I'm totally unloveable. I'm sick with pain. I can't stand it any more. All I want is to obliterate *me*. I make up my mind. I stare at the river. It's like sheet metal reflecting the fitful sunlight.

'Strange grows the river on a sunless evening,' I murmur over and over from the *Oxford Book of Modern Verse*. I'm looking at it for the last time. Surreptitiously, I rummage through the kitchen cupboards. There is a bottle marked Poison in red letters. I hide the Lysol, pushing it under the mattress. Alone in my mother's bedroom, I pick up the poison bottle and take a swallow, but I'm not prepared for the result. It burns like fire. I scream and choke. When my mother rushes in I have fallen across the bed, grabbing at my throat.

'What is it?' she is shaking me.

I point to the bottle.

'Tom, Tom,' she screams, 'she's taken poison!'

He is holding me and sobbing. I've never seen my father cry before. 'What have you done? Oh! My little girl, what have you done?'

With all the force of her powerful personality, my mother is willing me to live. 'You won't die,' she grinds between her teeth, pouring salt and water down my throat. I am in the back seat of the car, dressed in my red woollen suit, and my mother is supporting me. I am in some sort of shock. 'Hold on,' she says.

Doctors are questioning me in the hospital ward. Did you actually swallow anything? How much did you swallow? They are forcing a stomach pump down my throat. Nurses are holding me down . . . my head, my legs, my arms. I am arching in convulsions. I am choking to death. I am vomiting and vomiting salt and water into a bedpan.

I am in constant pain. The skin peels off my burnt throat like tissue paper. I can't eat, sleep or even speak. I can only whisper. There are raw sores around my mouth. A plain-clothes policewoman is standing beside my bed with a notebook, questioning me. I realize my parents have cooked up some story about 'an unfortunate mistake in medicine bottles'.

'Didn't you read the label?'

I smile sourly. It hurts to smile. 'Let's cut the nonsense,' I whisper.

'A young girl like you,' she says indignantly, 'with everything to live for. It's wicked. You're a wicked girl.' She is furious. 'Next time you do it, you won't get away with it.' I smile again.

In the bed next to me, an old woman keeps ringing for a bedpan. When nobody comes she gets out and pisses on the floor. It runs over the lino. Further down the ward, a woman with a bandage covering an operation for brain tumour screams all night. The drunks are dragged in late, yelling abuse up and down the corridors. It's like a scene from Dante's 'Inferno'.

Visiting hours – I look up. There is a thin shadow in air force uniform against the glass door. It's Wally Thomas. He sits beside the bed, holding my hand and crying.

109
♠

'How did you know?' I whisper.

'It was in all the papers. Why did you do it?'

I say nothing.

'My parents blame me. They want to know what I've been up to.' Miserably, he touches my scarred mouth. 'Will it be all right?'

I nod my head and press his hand. I feel sorry for him, but I am too tired. I close my eyes. When I open them, he's gone.

A young intern, who looks like a movie star, comes to talk to me. 'We thought you were just a kid when you came in. We very nearly put you in the kids' ward. Your throat'll be okay but you could have destroyed your vocal cords. Look, I think you should try to get back into university, find some sense of purpose again. Everything isn't over. You might think it is, but it isn't.'

My parents shift me out of the Royal Perth into a private room in The Mount Hospital and I sit up on the verandah reciting over and over from Eliot's *Ash Wednesday*.

Teach me to feel
And not to feel
Teach me to sit still . . .

If I say them often enough, surely they will save my life. Mick Wright brings me books to read and is totally and blessedly pragmatic about suicide. Wally Thomas comes again and I walk with him like a stranger in the garden, wearing my aquamarine chenille dressing-gown.

'Don't come any more,' I tell him wearily. 'I look at you and I don't feel anything. I've burnt you out of my brain.'

Nothing seems to touch me. I am like a sleepwalker, a chrysalis in a cocoon. When the actress Lyndall Barbour reads my prize-winning poem over the ABC, my parents bring in a little mantel radio, and I lie there in the hospital bed listening while the 'on' light glows in the half-dark.

And I have loved
An old house lying silent in the summer
Haunted by children, flowers and orchards,
Days that seemed a dim and golden
Heritage of dream; then all the years
Moved in a liquid sunlight on the grass.
We never knew that time went slowly, only
The moving shadow on the orchard plough
Was a kind of time-piece . . .

Something breaks, something leaps up, the ego comes back. It's rough in parts, and the cadence is Edith Sitwell out of *Colonel Fantock*, but maybe this is a real poem at last. I am a poet and I have forgotten my responsibilities. I will have to remake my life.

A few days later Lloyd Davies arrives on leave from Darwin, smiling behind a huge bunch of poinsettias, and Strahan writes after a long silence to say he has read a poem I have published in the *Black Swan*:

> When Gershwin plays on summer afternoons
> 'An American in Paris', 'Porgy and Bess'
> I think of you and see you walking in the rain,
> with your face crinkled under your blue felt hat,
> your tall body bent sideways under streets
> and steeples, and the golden light
> falling across your hands.

Perhaps, he says, he has made a mistake and we should get married after all.

One stormy night in Cottesloe I walk up and down for hours under an avenue of wet black pines agonizing over Strahan, but he can't save me. He will only exacerbate my problems. Driving along Riverside Drive in his mother's little car, Lloyd suggests we get married 'after the war', but it's 'now or never', I tell him. 'If we don't do it now I won't be here when you get back.'

Lloyd's mother is horrified. After the war she is planning to take him on a world cruise, my parents are 'in trade' and he needs to finish his law degree before he can even think about marriage. He comes to bring me the news while I wait in a crimson crepe de Chine dress with rows of red beads under the London Court clock in The Terrace.

'Mother says we can't get married,' he tells me.

I am outraged. 'What's Mother got to do with it?' I say.

Days pass. I refuse to see him again. When we finally kneel on that tatty velvet hassock in front of the altar, his leave is almost over. The Registry Office has refused to marry us at such short notice, so we are left with a special licence and a stuttering parson in a run-down Anglican church in Belmont. I think he believes he is conducting an under-age and probably 'shotgun' wedding. The witnesses are Lilla Harper and Lloyd's friend, the Rhodes scholar Sam Clarke. The wedding guests are my parents and Lesley.

Our wedding night is haunted by different memories. Lloyd has left a note confessing all to his mother. I am consumed with guilt because I know I have pushed him into this marriage and am not at all sure I'm up to it. Trying once again to keep up with the hard drinkers in the ladies' lounge in the Hotel Bohemia, I spend a great deal of that night vomiting. He sits hunched in the bedroom window, staring out over the city. I think he is crying. 'Poor little bitch,' he murmurs tenderly as he pushes me under the freezing shower in the ladies' bathroom.

Next morning at dawn he leaves for Darwin and another year in army education. Waking alone, I hear a voice calling from the corridor. 'Mrs Davies wanted on the phone downstairs.'

It takes me minutes to realize that this is actually me. Turning my wedding ring round and round on my finger I think about the past, but that seems counterproductive. I have asked myself all the questions and I have made my decision. Lloyd and I are friends and lovers. We share the same politics. He believes in the importance of Art, as I do. We are temperamentally very different but the differences seem complementary. A joyful person with a wonderful eccentric sense of humour, he believes in happiness and the new world – the socialist future.

But it is a strange wedding. Here I am going back home again to my parents' house when at least one of my reasons for getting married is to escape from my mother. I know I have come to the end of an era. The bohemian life is unliveable. It has ended in destruction – attempted suicide. Looking for some viable alternative to promiscuity, I have become a wife.

When Bill Hart-Smith sends me a telegram saying that his marriage is over and he is flying to Perth to see me, I telegraph back: 'Too late'.

Only once in those weeks do I falter when my mother says, 'We were going to send you to England, to drama school, after the war if you hadn't decided to get married.'

A few weeks later Joan Thomas rings. She has left the *Daily News* and is editing the Communist Party weekly newspaper the *Workers' Star*. They need an extra reporter urgently. Am I interested? I report for work to the third floor of London Court, that glitzy parody of a Tudor mall where the West Australian branch of the Communist Party has its headquarters.

So my salvation will be politics and marriage, in that order. Politics first, because that commitment will last for twenty-three years. I need order in my life. I need a pattern, a systematic view of the world – and Marxism will give it to me.

Lloyd has introduced me to a whole new circle of intelligent, dedicated Communists who live in a two-storeyed wooden house in Cottesloe called 'The Kremlin'. Through those winter nights of his last leave we sat by the fire drinking claret, talking and singing songs like 'Joe Hill' and 'Harry was a Bolshie' with Grahame and Joy Alcorn, the two New Zealanders who will become our closest friends. Grahame is a tall angular Zoology graduate who has published a poem on Lorca in *Meanjin*. Joy is a long-legged, warm-hearted schoolteacher who writes a column for servicemen called 'Dear Bill' in the *Workers' Star*. It was Joy who nicknamed me Toddy, a name that stuck for thirteen years or so and helped to legitimize my new personality.

'The Kremlin' was a collection of flatettes run by a tough old Cockney woman called Fossie, who kept advising Joy Alcorn to give her baby Jane a rag dipped in whisky to suck when she cried. All the flatettes were rented out to Communists: Leah Healy, the Party chairwoman; Barbara Boyd, the secretary; Molly Thorpe, who worked as a reporter on the *Workers' Star*. The Party was a matriarchy while the men were away at the war. Now I would become part of this network, taking Jane for walks and swimming with Joy at Cottesloe. I was happy on the *Workers' Star*. I cut, pasted and rewrote articles from the *Sydney Tribune* and Communist international newspapers and journals. I wrote my own column, 'A Woman Says', and occasionally reviewed a book or a film. I was reading poets I'd never heard of before, like Mayakovsky, Nazim Hikmet and Pablo Neruda, books like *The Ragged Trousered Philanthropists*, *Ten Days That Shook the World*, *The Grapes of Wrath*, *Quiet Flows the Don* and *USA* by Dos Passos. But still I didn't rejoin the Communist Party. This time I wanted to be absolutely sure of what I was doing.

I attended a State Conference, blasted by the furious J. B. Miles, the general secretary from Sydney, who lambasted sections of the State Committee for their 'Browderism'. Earle Browder, the general secretary of the American Communist Party, was responsible for 'the peaceful transition to socialism', a theory which had been brought back to Australia by Ernie Thornton, the powerful secretary of the Federated Ironworkers' Union. Later Earle Browder became an anti-Communist, which only goes to prove how pernicious his theories are.

I attend a Party school and am lectured by Grahame Alcorn on Dialectical Materialism, Political Economy and the Theory of Surplus Value. For the first time in my life I have found a philosophy that seems to make sense of the world and promises a positive future. I am like a shy convert to a new religion, but I am still divided in my allegiances, and my literary preferences are deeply suspect. I admire *Drift*, the West Australian Peter Cowan's new book of Modernist short stories. I delight in Eve Langley's poetic novel *The Pea Pickers*. My favourite poet is T. S. Eliot, who has just published his magnificent religious allegory *Four Quartets*. My favourite poem is *The Wasteland*. I admire the Imagists and read Ezra Pound, the controversial American poet and polemicist who has been imprisoned for treason.

The Angry Penguins, an avant-garde literary magazine edited by

Max Harris from Adelaide, has introduced me to the Australian artists Nolan, Tucker, Vassilieff, Gleeson, Arthur Boyd, John Percival and the European Dadaists. They have been responsible for my first overseas publication – a poem, 'Australian Sunset', in Harry Roselenko's magazine *Chicago*. They have published new work by Dylan Thomas and Rimbaud in translation, so that I can actually read him. When vague rumours of a Melbourne struggle between the avant-garde, led by John and Sunday Reed, and the Marxist artists, led by Noel Counihan, drift across the Nullarbor, all my natural sympathies have been with the Modernists rather than the Socialist Realists.

Then, one drunken night in Sydney, two young conservative Australian poets, James McAuley and Harold Stewart, invent the posthumous poems and tragic biography of Ern Malley. They send the poems to *The Angry Penguins*, where they are published with much acclaim as a new Modernist voice in Australian poetry. When McAuley and Stewart – defending, they maintain, the cause of true poetry against the philistines – tell the story of their hoax to the newspapers, the Angry Penguins are held up to ridicule, and the cause of Modernism in Australia is set back two decades. When Max Harris, charged with obscenity in an Adelaide court, is fined £5 with £21 costs for publishing the Ern Malley poems in *The Angry Penguins*, I am scathing against the philistines. But after I join the Party it isn't long before I am attacking the Angry Penguins and Ezra Pound in the *Workers' Star*. Like any good convert who needs to nail her new colours to the mast, my conversion has become absolute.

> *Dorothy Hewett sums up . . . Ezra Pound and his Australian Godchildren*
> I used to think that a man of genius could be excused many things. I know now that a man of genius can be excused far less than any ordinary man. He can be such a power on the side of good or evil. There can be no doubt that Ezra Pound was a genius who ran off the rails. Brought to the United States by plane last month, poet Ezra Pound, awaiting trial in Washington for broadcasting Axis propaganda from Rome, was freshly indicted for nineteen overt acts of treason.
>
> He helped to found a new school of poetry in 1913; they called themselves The Imagists, and based their theory on the fact that all moral, intellectual and aesthetic values were uncertain, only sense impressions or images could be relied on and could be described exactly. That theory led Ezra Pound to Fascism and to a charge of treason in 1945. His life is an indictment against escapism.
>
> It is probably more luck than anything else that many of the young poets of his generation don't stand beside collaborator Ezra Pound today, the man who exercised one of the greatest influences on them.
>
> The Angry Penguins, emotional godchildren of Ezra Pound, have

let forth another long strident squawk, consisting of 179 pages, proving once again that it is possible for Penguins to have infantile regressions.

How could this have happened so suddenly? Had I abdicated my conscience? The answer was that I wanted so desperately to believe, and was so afraid of backsliding. I had to attack what I had most loved and admired to make my conversion complete.

On VE Day, we danced in the streets and a Cockney sailor, draped with streamers, said, 'Now we'll get rid of that booger Churchill.' When night fell, the amorous good humour got out of hand and girls fled screaming from 'the drunken soldiery'.

In the *West Australian* there was a blurred photograph of Mussolini and his mistress hanging upside down like dead meat in a street in Milan, savaged by Italian Partisans. Three months later, when the Americans dropped the atom bomb on Hiroshima and Nagasaki, nobody seemed to realize the enormity of it. I celebrated VJ Day in the lounge of the Ocean Beach Hotel in Cottesloe. An Australian soldier punched a Yank through the plate-glass window. Afterwards we went swimming in the nude at North Cottesloe and I broke my wedding vows with the medical student amongst the sandhills.

Emaciated men with Atebrin-yellow skin appeared in the streets of Perth, back from the Burma Road and the Thailand Railway. On a visit to the farm that summer, I went with the Sartoris to the Returned Services League hall in Yealering and saw the first newsreels of the corpses piled up in Buchenwald and Belsen, the survivors like living skeletons clinging to the concentration-camp wire. Tony Sartori took his women and walked out, denouncing it all as propaganda.

Staying at the Alcorns' flat while Grahame and Joy were away at a Party school, I made love to a red-headed psychologist, a Communist from a working-class family, who was engaged to a Catholic girl who didn't believe in sex before marriage. 'You middle-class girls who join the Party are all the same,' he said. 'Full of bullshit!'

The war was over. Goodbye blackouts and bride ships in Fremantle Harbour, padded shoulders, victory rolls, runny leg make-up and Sheepskins for Russia.

A year had almost passed, and I was beginning to be afraid. What had happened to commitment? What had happened to all my good intentions? Was I hopelessly promiscuous after all? It was hard to imagine I had ever been married and now everything was changing again – soon they would all be home, all my old flames – they would all pass me in the Perth streets as if the war had never happened. Only Gregor McLeod would not be there. He had crashed in a plane, giving up his parachute in a last heroic, quixotic gesture.

WHEN I walked into that hot little kitchen that summer evening after the war and saw my secret lover of three years ago sitting there at the end of the table in his air force uniform with the light on his hair, it was as if those lost years had never even happened. We left together and spent the rest of the summer walking hand in hand through the city streets, making love wherever and whenever we could: in the Alcorns' flat; on the beach at Cottesloe; and once, secretly, in his parents' house, naked in the front room in the darkness.

I told him about everything – my promiscuity, my attempted suicide, my marriage. For the first time it all seemed to fall into place. I could see the pattern. I could see where it had begun. I had loved him all the time, I had never stopped loving him. My marriage, even the Communist Party – they were all part of a gigantic trick I had played against myself. Yet we never talked about any future. As I lay in his arms in the sandhills, listening to the surf heaving on the beach, he told me how shocked he had been when his mother wrote and told him I was married.

'How could you marry anyone else,' he said, 'when you belonged to me?'

I sat up, staring at the sea. 'No letters, not a word in all those years . . . what did you expect – I'd still be here waiting for you to come back to me?'

'Yes,' he said simply.

On the night I told him I was pregnant, he pulled away. I wanted him to say let's run away together, nothing else matters, but he said, 'We thought we were so smart. We thought we could get away with anything. Well, you can't break the rules.'

When I found out the name of a famous Perth abortionist, I sent him a telegram and we met late at night in the empty streets, walking side by side, not touching, under the street lights, his face turned away. 'My mother said, "What are you doing getting telegrams from a married woman?",' he told me.

He borrowed his father's ute and drove me to the abortionist's.

There were two chipped marble cupids by two stone urns in a thorny garden. The abortionist had a soft Irish brogue. In the darkness I never saw his face. 'Relax,' he said, masturbating my clitoris and inserting the thin rubber tubing, until I felt violated. 'Remove it in three days,' he told me, and I came out into the sunlight already bleeding.

Joan Thomas had offered to put me up until it was all over so I kissed him goodbye and watched the ute disappear into the dusk down the highway. I felt as if my life had ended. For three days I lay in the little back bedroom with a raging temperature. There was no word from him, but my mother kept ringing up suspiciously to ask why I hadn't come home. I'd stagger to the phone and make some lame excuse. 'What's the matter with you?' she said. 'You sound very strange.'

On the third day, when I took out the rubber tubing, I was so ill I could hardly balance on the china chamber pot. I thought I was probably dying. Joan was so worried that she managed to get hold of a new wonder drug called sulphanilamide from a Communist army doctor who was too frightened to examine me. He said I probably had septicaemia. Towards dawn on the fifth day, the fever broke and I lay weakly staring through the window at the last stars, realizing that I wasn't going to die after all. The sulphur drugs had saved my life. I went home to my bed in the corner of the sleepout, but I kept having bouts of such excruciating pain I knew something was wrong. Joan found me a sympathetic young gynaecologist who asked no questions, but put me straight into The Mount Hospital for a curette. My mother kept ringing him up to ask what was wrong with me but, true to his Hippocratic oath, he was calmly evasive.

One day, as I lay in my hospital bed, I looked up to see Lloyd smiling in the doorway.

'Has anyone told you what's wrong with me?' I asked him brutally.

Nobody had.

'Cowards!' and I told him everything.

'Cuckolded, by Gad,' he quipped, then his face twisted and he took me in his arms. As far as I knew, he had forgiven me. He had proved how superior he was to other men. He had saved me once again and I was grateful.

For our second honeymoon I bought a cream satin nightgown, my father and Lesley vacated the sleepout and my mother presented me with a Dutch cap and a copy of Marie Stopes's *Married Love*.

Marie Stopes said that the way to seduce your husband was to lie in a bath filled with mauve bath salts and invite him in for a look. The healthiest babies, she said, were conceived in the fresh air, preferably on the beach. Well, I'd proved that worked.

Mrs Davies told my mother she had worried because I'd been seen with a man in air force uniform while Lloyd was in Darwin. My mother told her it was probably Mick Wright, so everybody was satisfied. I wept for the dead baby. Sometimes I fantasized that I would pack my satin nightgown and run off, disappearing for ever up some tropical river, to anchor at a lost island.

Lloyd and I were victims of the post-war housing shortage. We moved from a bug-ridden room to a communal kitchen so crowded you couldn't cook your dinner until nine o'clock. The other women laughed at me when I forgot to wash the potatoes and peeled them with the eyes left in. I could not cook, sew or iron. I had never washed clothes in my life. Lloyd, on the other hand, was a good cook and quite a domestic treasure. Finally we finished up in a dingy, run-down flat in Milligan Street, in the inner city. A bevy of prostitutes lived in a row of tiny rooms like rabbit hutches in the concreted back yard. We threw out, or disguised, the worst of the landlady's furniture, bought some long red curtains and white sheepskin rugs.

Lloyd went back to the university to finish his law course under the post-war Commonwealth Reconstruction Training Scheme. I was allowed to re-enrol part-time, although Alec King told me he had decided I was one of those people who did better outside a university. I was still working full-time at the *Workers' Star* for £2 a week, when there was any money to pay me. We were poor enough but we had lots of parties where everybody 'brought their own', got drunk, pissed in the garden and sang bawdy student ballads – 'It Was on the Good Ship *Venus*', 'Mister Winkelstein', and 'The Ball of Carrimoor'. Lloyd's favourite party piece was 'The British Workman's Grave'. He was tone deaf, but his enthusiasm always made up for his lack of tune.

Sometimes, in the early morning, there was a knock at the door and I'd let in Ron Strahan, drunk, incoherent, unhappy, and make him a shakedown on the sitting-room floor, waiting up with him until Lloyd called from the next room, 'Toddy, for Christ's sake come to bed!'

Ron Strahan seemed to have lost his way in the post-war world. He kept on asking every woman he met to marry him and talked wildly about sleazy nights in somebody's 'shaggin' wagon'. It was all so unlike the real Strahan who had walked with me in rain and sun through the streets of Perth, his porkpie hat shading his ugly, intelligent face. 'If you ever split up,' he told Lloyd, 'I'm the next in line to marry her.' Finally his visits just ended.

The first chill breath of the Cold War was beginning to blow. In

March 1946 Churchill had given his Fulton speech attacking the USSR and Billy Snedden arrived drunk at the university dances, with his lawyer mates in tow, yelling 'Get the bloody Coms' and threw me across the refectory floor. Billy, a widow's son from Victoria Park, just out of air force uniform, was being groomed for stardom by the local Liberals.

Much the same thing happened at a friendly party in Applecross. Our 'best man', Sam Clarke, who called himself a Trotskyite, was punched in the head by a young Communist engineer for a similar act of bravado. We all left the party in disgrace, while Peter Foulkes smiled satirically from the sidelines.

Looking more than ever like a character out of a Noël Coward drawing-room comedy, Peter had turned up again from Sydney. Famous for his exploits during the war, when he successfully feigned madness for months in an army psychiatric hospital, Peter was as urbane and sophisticated as ever. He invited me out for dinner and drinks and told me the story of his marriage. According to him, he had married his wife on the advice of a Catholic priest because she threatened suicide if he didn't. Not surprisingly, it hadn't worked out.

I discover that without asking me he has booked a double room in a third-rate pub across the Horseshoe Bridge. Fascinated at his effrontery, but always willing to play with fire, I find myself confronting him in a bleak room with lino on the floor and the usual centrepiece of cotton-quilted double bed. The whole set-up makes me feel like a whore. I apologize but refuse to get undressed. I thought I could go through with it, but I can't. He pleads with me. Don't I realize he has always been mad about me? What is a beautiful, talented woman like me doing in a boring backwater like Perth? Working for a pathetic rag like the *Workers' Star*? What has happened to all my ambitions? He'll take me to Sydney, where I should have gone years ago. He's making pots of money writing 'soapies' for commercial radio. He knows all the influential theatre people. With his backing and my talent, I'll be famous in no time.

'But I am a Communist.'

Do I really believe in all this naive rubbish?

'Yes I really believe – and I'm married to Lloyd.'

'You don't love him. You're just grateful to him because you think he saved you from yourself.'

'He trusts me. I owe him some loyalty.'

'Is that all? What man wants gratitude from a woman?'

'It's more than gratitude.'

Peter looks at me with one eyebrow raised. 'He's really got you,

hasn't he?' he says, and rings a cab. 'You'll be sorry about this one day.
We could have been a marvellous team.'

I leave alone, with his last words echoing all the way across the
bridge . . . 'It won't last, you know.'

'The clever bastard!' says Lloyd indignantly. 'He really knew how
to get at you, didn't he?'

'It didn't work,' I tell him, but I don't forget the encounter.
I know enough about myself to recognize the Devil's advocate when
I hear him. Years later, I learn that Peter Foulkes has committed
suicide in Sydney.

I have a weakness for sexual adventures and one night, waiting
for a tram, I accept a lift from a stranger in a shiny, expensive-looking
car. The driver is a young Greek with saturnine eyebrows who speeds
off to Cottesloe beach and tries to take me by force. I get out of it by
talking like a blue streak. Amused and apparently impressed by my
gift of the gab, he drives me back to the city and makes a date to meet
on the same corner a week later. I tell Lloyd about this too and against
all his advice and for reasons I can't explain, keep the appointment.
The Greek never turns up.

Somewhere, under the façade of the responsible Communist,
there is still a wild girl in the heart. But part of Lloyd's hold over me is
that he never issues ultimatums. I am free to make up my own mind,
to do what I have to do, and it works, diffusing every half-hearted
rebellion.

Once, at a university dance, I see Wally Thomas sitting with the
sweet-faced brunette he eventually marries (who didn't come from
Victor Harbour). As I whirl around the refectory dance floor in my
black satin pyjama trousers and a brief red bra, I see him glance at
me, but he never speaks or gives any sign that we've known each
other.

I stay at university only long enough to play Crystal, the husband-
stealing bitch in Clare Booth Luce's *The Women*. Dressed in Gabrielle
Cunningham's skin-tight silver lamé or stripped to flesh-coloured bra
and briefs, I play Crystal opposite Pat Skevington, who is the good
wife, Mary. It is my last stage performance and my mother says
I couldn't have been that convincing unless there was a lot of Crystal
in me.

My only other successful *coup* is to edit the notorious red *Black
Swan*, which causes such a furore that it is banned from distribution to
any other Australian university. Determined to keep it 'politically
pure', I have written most of it myself under various *noms de plume*.

Lloyd and I manage one idyllic holiday at Rottnest, where we sleep illegally on the beach, cooking crabs for our breakfast on an open fire.

Sometimes, with Mick Wright, we catch the train to the ranges and wander amongst the streams and rocky hillsides singing 'Soviet Land So Dear to Every Toiler' (much to Mick's disgust). Coming home in the evening, we stand on the observation platform while the bright sparks from the engine roll back across the valleys. Once, we share a holiday hut with the Alcorns under the lighthouse at Cape Naturalist. The railway carriage to Busselton is crowded. We sit up all night arguing with a returned soldier who spent most of the war in a German prison camp and regales us with tales of the glories of the Third Reich and how much Hitler has done for the ordinary German people. In Busselton I brave the public bar for rum and milk, but the barman flatly refuses to serve 'a woman'. We swim nude in a sparkling sea and watch the seals tumble down a swift-running tidal estuary into the Indian Ocean. Grahame is embarrassed at taking his clothes off in case he has an erection, and Joy is angry at the stretch marks on her ample belly. She envies my slim, unmarked body, but time will take care of that.

When I decide we are paying too high a rent for the Milligan Street flat and complain to the Fair Rents Board, I discover that my mother and Lloyd have a secret agreement. She has been paying part of the rent for us ever since we moved in. I rage at him, accusing him of double-dealing behind my back.

The landlady gets the Health Inspector round and tries to have us thrown out for holding wild parties and keeping filthy premises, but it doesn't work.

Now that I am a married woman, my father offers to hand over the properties he has listed in my name. I can collect the rents and augment our meagre income. I agonize over the morality of this for weeks and finally take the problem to Grahame Alcorn. 'Collect the rents,' he says, 'but demand to inspect all the properties in case there is anything substandard about them. If you feel unhappy about it, you can always donate the money to the Party.'

When I deliver this ultimatum to my father, he is furious. I can accept the rentals from his hand or sign over all the property to Lesley. I sign over my capitalist birthright, feeling morally cleansed and totally justified.

My mother is worried about my grandmother. She is liable to wander off when my grandfather is out in the garden, her petticoat on over her dress, or disappear, perched up behind a horse and buggy with the Jehovah's Witnesses who deliver religious pamphlets

to her door. My mother is certain they are only after my grandmother's money.

One day, when my grandfather is burning off leaves in the
garden, she wanders into the bonfire. He drags her out unhurt, but
his own ulcerated leg is so badly burnt he has to be rushed off to
hospital for a skin graft. It is a small private hospital and when he
develops pneumonia, nobody seems to notice how ill he is. He lies
there with his cheeks bright and sunken while they trundle the
oxygen tank up the stairs and my mother tries to ring the doctor on
the public phone in the foyer.

Before the oxygen tank or the doctor reaches him, he has two
major strokes one after the other, his eyes bewildered and bulging, his
mouth slipped sideways. 'You couldn't kill me with an axe,' he's always
boasted, but he dies there clinging to my hand, while my mother sobs
hysterically in the corridor. The Sister closes his terrible eyes and
I watch his face, under the crest of silver hair, sink into the calm
anonymity of death.

'It's better this way,' the Sister says. 'A stroke like that, he couldn't
have made a recovery. He's at rest now.'

I turn on her savagely. 'He hated rest and he loved life. He was
the most alive human being I've ever known.'

I fly out of the hospital. Lloyd is in the grounds with his arm
round my weeping mother. When the tears come, I weep on and on
for hours. I have lost my beloved grandfather, my other self, the gay,
blond, tender, blustery companion of my childhood. In the last few
years a rift has developed between us. He never understood why
I had joined the Communist Party. To him it represented the Anti-
christ, the enemy who would take all his hard-won wealth away from
him and give it to the no-hopers, who couldn't even keep 'a billet'.

It is my first experience of death. 'Cathay' is rented out and my
grandmother moves into the second-best bedroom in Ridge Street,
where she wanders the rooms in her nightie, occasionally asking for
Ted. When Lloyd and I stay overnight, she demands to know what
Dorothy is doing sleeping on the floor in the sitting room with 'that
strange man'. It isn't long before she is totally bedridden and incontinent, her thick little fingers continually pleating and unpleating the
sheets in a fantasy of ball dresses for Melbourne ladies. Most of the
time she doesn't even recognize us, but she still has a roguish eye for
my father. She always recognizes Tom, that handsome young man
who took her fancy when he rode through the streets of Corrigin on
his prancing black horse.

◆

I have stopped writing poetry. These days I write only political articles for the *Workers' Star*. Lloyd says it's because I am always too busy working for the Party. You have to have leisure to create. But I know that isn't the real reason. I have turned myself into a political creature and dried up. I can't write poems like 'My Glorious Soviet Passport' or 'The Railsplitters Awake', so I write nothing. Everything is politically suspect and I burn the only copy of my novel *Daylight* because I consider it might have Fascist undertones.

Joan Thomas has married the poet Vic Williams, a former schoolteacher who has deliberately proletarianized himself by taking a job on the Fremantle wharf. A dark, saturnine proselytizer, son of a Kalgoorlie gold miner, Vic argues Marxist theories of literature for hours and keeps us all strictly in line. His first book, *Harvest Time*, has been published by the Jindyworobaks, but after that he roneos his own books like pamphlets, giving them titles like *Hammers and Seagulls* and *The Golden Giants*, and sells them at the pick-up to the wharfies. Secretly, I much prefer Judith Wright's *The Moving Image*, which bursts on me like a bombshell. For the first time I have discovered an Australian poet who creates unselfconscious symbols out of the landscape I grew up in.

Pete Thomas, Joan's former husband, writes leader articles for the *West Australian* and is an undercover member of the State Committee of the Party. He is delegated to tell me, in the nicest possible way, that J. B. Miles, the feared 'old man' of the Party, has complained about my hair. I wear it long and loose, past my shoulders, but this is apparently too bohemian for the general secretary, so I roll it up reluctantly and make jokes about it behind Communist backs.

The Party is trying to clean up its image for the new struggles ahead, making itself super-respectable to fit in with its idealized view of the Australian working class. There was always a great mistrust of intellectuals, bohemians, anarchists and the unorganized lumpenproletariat amongst the Australian Communists. No one was going to accuse them of free love, extra-marital affairs, wild and reckless behaviour or wearing the wrong clothes or the wrong hairstyles. The dictatorship of the proletariat referred only to a certain kind of worker, one who punched the bundy without fail, brought home his pay packet to his wife and kids and mowed the lawn in a white singlet on Sunday morning.

Now all I feel are the constrictions, and I resent them. What business is it of theirs, the way I wear my hair? Why can't I write any more? What is happening to me? Does this mean that I am hopelessly bourgeoise and can never espouse the values of the sacred proletariat? Will I ever learn this new language of Socialist Realism; or do

I have to remain dumb for ever? Where is the rebellious girl with the hooped earrings and the black velvet beret, who wouldn't be seen dead with her hair in a victory roll? In burying her, have I fragmented my personality so drastically that I have killed the poet in me, traded the gift of tongues for the dream of a Marxist Utopia? All these questions are buzzing in my head when one evening, at the Alcorns' fireside, we meet an astonishing man from Port Hedland called Don McLeod.

A well-sinker and wharfie, he has worked around the North-West stations with an old lawman and songmaker called Kitchener. Together, by the light of a hurricane lantern, they have read *The Marxist Classics* and dreamed of a great strike of Aborigines in the Pilbara. The first meeting of Aborigines, which led eventually to the strike, was held at Skull Springs on the Davis River in 1942. Two hundred Aborigines and senior lawmen came from a thousand miles away to attend this traditional meeting, which took place every fifty years or so. The meeting lasted six weeks and sixteen interpreters were needed for the twenty-three language groups represented.

On 1 May 1946 the Aboriginal stockmen in the Pilbara walked off the stations and gathered at Mooleyalla and the Twelve Mile, old Aborigine camping spots outside Port Hedland. They knew the date because of the calendars delivered quietly to the station camps with 1 May circled in red crayon. They struck for thirty-five bob a week and their keep. The police were sent out to round up the leaders, throwing McLeod and the Aborigines, Clancy McKenna and Dooley BinBin, in the Port Hedland jail. Questions were asked in the United Nations. The young men, marching through the streets of Hedland to demand the release of Don McLeod, put the fear of Christ into the white inhabitants. The strike escalated. An Anglican parson called Peter Hodge, secretary of the Committee for the Defence of Native Rights in Perth, was jailed under an old ordinance which forbade any citizen the right to be found within five chains of a congregation of natives, without written permission. More uproar. A ban of almost total silence descended on the West Australian press, but in the *Workers' Star* we were printing Don McLeod's dispatches from the Nor'-West as if they came from the revolutionary front.

And here he is, bearded, intense, with deep-set eyes hidden under a protruding brow, sitting by the Alcorns' fire in 'The Kremlin', calling on us to take up the cause and send revolutionary cadres to the Pilbara. We feel as if we are on trial.

Don McLeod was only briefly a member of the Communist Party. What he wanted the communists to do in that winter of 1946 they were totally unable to deliver, but listening to him that night I am fired with a new project. I will go to Port Hedland and write the story

of the strike. This will be my contribution to the epic struggle going
on unheard, unsung, on the great spinifex plains of the Pilbara.

Lloyd and I took a month off and caught the plane, landing on
the lonely sizzling tarmac in early December 1946. We were nervous,
wary and excited. We knew we had to be extremely careful. It would
be useless to end up in the Port Hedland lock up or run out of town –
a town still seething and bitter from the events of the past year. Race
hatred simmered under the quiet surface of reefs, mangrove swamps
and tropical bungalows. Strange faces from 'down South' were
regarded with deep suspicion.

We put up at the Esplanade Hotel facing the harbour where,
early in the mornings, we saw the Aboriginal women picking the reef
for oysters and bêche-de-mer. The licensee was an ex-wife of the
famous Australian airman Kingsford Smith. Cautiously, Lloyd set
about trying to contact McLeod through the wharfies in the bar. We
knew that Don had been in real fear of his life, hunted by the
squatters' men, hiding out under a railway culvert, but now he had
been given temporary shelter in a fettlers' shed by one of the sympathetic railway workers. Once we actually saw the back of him, just at
dusk, walking out of the town with his stores, dressed in a pair of
ragged khaki shorts, his hair and beard wild as an Old Testament
prophet, but we didn't dare contact him directly. It was frustrating,
but as the days went by we built up our cover as two young Perth
tourists interested in everything but with no axes to grind. At last,
through a surreptitious contact in the bar, Lloyd managed to send
Don a message and get a reply. That evening we set out towards the
edge of the town, strolling casually as if we had no particular destina-
tion in mind.

The sun is sinking in a great red ball, trembling over the scrub, as
we make our way along the deserted railway line. Here is the shed.
We knock, a voice calls 'Come in', and there is Don sitting smoking
and grinning at us by the light of a hurricane lantern. He is taking us
to meet 'the mob'. As we walk further down the line, I look up. On the
top of the embankment, the sentinels stand silhouetted in a silent line,
the first great blazing desert stars behind them. The air is full of the
delicate scent of the white native rose bushes blooming in the darkness. We come to a clearing of pale grass and sit down to wait. There
is no sound except the crickets clicking and the occasional cry of an
unknown night bird.

But when we look up we are surrounded. Hundreds of Aborigines are standing in the circle of moonlight. 'The mob' has come so
silently we have heard nothing. Clancy McKenna steps out from the

crowd and shakes hands. Handsome, over six foot tall, son of a
Scottish squatter and a full-blood Aboriginal woman, he introduces us
quite formally to the Twelve Mile People. Many of them can't speak
English, but they all clasp our hands. There is total acceptance. We
are the friends Don has told them about who have come from down
South to speak for them. We are invited to a special corroboree at the
Twelve Mile, two nights later. They will arrange for one of their
relatives in the half-caste shanty town to take us out in his ute. Don
won't be there. He is forbidden to go anywhere near the Twelve Mile
or 'the mob' on threat of instant arrest.

Two nights later we are bumping over the causeway in an old ute,
driven by a drunken part-Aborigine. I sit in the front seat with him
and his wife; Lloyd is in the back. The driver keeps dropping lighted
cigarettes into the gears and under foot while his wife grumbles and
stamps them out again. Once, when he stops to grab another bottle
from the back, Lloyd puts his head through the window and whispers
to me, 'He's got a whole stack of grog here under the tarp.' We know
how dangerous this is. It is unlawful to bring any alcohol on to an
Aboriginal reserve. If we are caught, all hell will break loose for all of
us. When we reach the 'Twelve Mile', Lloyd has a quiet word with
some of the responsible men. Magically, the grog disappears and our
loud-mouthed driver is whisked off somewhere before he has a
chance to distribute his largesse.

We sit in a firelit circle. As the didgeridoos begin to drone and the
women beat their sticks into the dust, chanting, an extraordinary
elongated, dehumanized figure, decorated like a stylized dragonfly,
flits from the darkness. His body is composed of the thorax and
segments of an insect. He thrums and leaps and hovers like transparent gauze.

Our drunken driver moves in behind me, grabs my waist and
fumblingly tries to kiss me. There is a quiet scuffle and two men lead
him away without a word. It is time for the next performance.

Silence – only the night crickets chirping and far out across the
black plain the bones are dancing, coming closer and closer in the
dance of Death. The women circle and shuffle around him. His skull
grins as he stalks and grabs at them, and they scatter and shriek,
throwing dust in his eyes. The didgeridoos drone higher, the sticks
beat louder. Turning, the women drive him out of the circle, laughing
and jeering with defiance. As he disappears with great, high-stepping
leaps back into the darkness, dwindling like a tiny white image on the
plain, the whole camp dissolves into relieved laughter. Once more
Death has been defeated. It is the comical resolution of an ancient

terror and we have been privileged to see a great artist perform that night.

When we visited the 'Twelve Mile' once more in daylight, driving out one blazing day with a sympathetic council worker, we met the dancer – a strange, ingratiating, bony giant with an oblique eye. He made us a cup of tea in his hut and proudly showed us the photographs of the squatter's family he had worked for all his life – smiling groups of white women in shady hats and little girls in spotless white dresses. Later we heard that he had been driven out of the camp, accused of being a police informer.

Clancy McKenna led his wife out to meet us, an old woman with eyes milky-blind from trachoma. 'Her sight gone,' Clancy said, 'from the smoke of too many camp fires.' Tommy Sampey was in charge of the children. Mission-educated, Tommy was a strict disciplinarian. His children washed morning and evening in drums of cold water. They wore clean khaki shorts and shirts to school, they used knives and forks and were taught table manners. Later, there was conflict between Tommy's ideas and the old law, and he left the co-operative. Clancy and Don McLeod clashed over questions of leadership and Clancy pulled out, driving away in his ute to take his chances somewhere else. In his book *How the West Was Lost*, Don McLeod describes the fate of Clancy McKenna:

> McKenna was threatened, bribed and tricked by unscrupulous bureaucrats, squatters and priests until he eventually lost the will to live. He believed it when they told him he could be a citizen and the equal of a white man. When he found out this was not so, he was left with no secure identity and threw in the towel. His mighty frame literally shrank and shrivelled under the effects of alcohol and social degradation. He died in 1980. They say he dropped dead under the drunks' tree in Marble Bar.

We never met the fabled desert lawman Dooley BinBin. He was a wanted man, riding round the country on a bicycle organizing for the strike, his horse hamstrung by the squatters' men.

Triumphantly, the women brought us Normie, a shy little blond boy with a pale yellow skin. They had saved him from the Protector of Aborigines, the local copper, who periodically raided the camp to round up all the half-white children, dragging them away from their screaming mothers into mission 'homes' to be trained as stockmen and servants, removed for ever from the pernicious influence of their black relatives. 'The people' had hidden Normie in the creek bed, smeared with mud so he could 'pass', and the policeman had ridden by, unnoticing.

The Twelve Mile people were justifiably proud of their camp – the neat huts, the site swept spotlessly clean. They were on display and they knew it. One slip and they'd be hounded off and the camp would be condemned as 'insanitary'. Against threats, intimidation and violence they hung on there, going cheerfully about their business, hunting kangaroo and wild goat and collecting the buffalo-grass seed.

The strike continued on and off for years. In a sense it has never really ended. Eventually the Aboriginal stockmen got their minimum wage and in 1960 the strikers set up their own co-operative mining company, Pindan Pty Ltd, mining the rich mineral deposits of the Pilbara they had always known about, long before the Lang Hancocks and the big multinationals moved in. When the mining boom came to the North, the co-operative split. McLeod resigned from Pindan and at least half the original group walked out with him. Goldsworthy Mining Ltd took over the Pindan leases, the blackfellows lost an income of around half a million dollars annually and control of large areas of pastoral lease. The Pindan group were offered a share of the mineral boom, but that promise was never fulfilled.

McLeod, Dooley and the hard core of 'the mob' formed Nomads Incorporated and moved across the ancient plains yandying the rich outcrops of minerals which were there for their sharp-eyed, careful sifting. In 1971 they purchased Strelley station, forty miles south-east of Port Hedland, but that was twenty-five years later, after decades of being 'jailed, flogged, neck-ironed, robbed, and kicked from one rough piece of ground to another all over the north-west'.

But that day when we were driven out of the Twelve Mile in an ancient old jalopy held together with wire and hope, 'the mob' were only at the beginning of their long struggle for some kind of self-determination.

The jalopy has no radiator cap and is liable to conk out any minute, leaving us stranded amongst the miles of spinifex and mirage. Like all young men these are amateur mechanics, and all the way into Hedland one of them sits laughing on the bonnet, balancing a drum, pouring an eternal stream of water into the tank. Coughing and spluttering, we make it to the edge of town and there, with a few careless apologies, they have to leave us. It is the way of the world. The car will go no further.

Thirsty and hot, we walk up the white road through the shanty town and decide to call in for a drink of water. A big, motherly, brown woman insists on making us tea in a huge chipped enamel tea-pot.

The walls are papered with blurred photographs of the Royal Family out of the illustrated weeklies. Two mongrel dogs thump lazy tails under the kitchen table, while the King and Queen and the two Princesses gaze smiling over the dirt floor and the corrugated-iron walls dancing with heat.

Back in the town we visit the local priest, a canny Irishman with a glib tongue who can talk the leg off an iron pot, but all the time he is quizzing us with his suspicious eyes. What are we there for? We show him our letters of introduction from West Australian writers. We are interested in the Nor'-West and he is an old-timer. We are particularly interested in the Aborigines. Why is this? We mean no harm. We are not 'troublemakers or do-gooders'. We are on an expedition for 'local colour'. He takes us to the Aboriginal Lock Hospital run by a thin, tight-lipped white woman who kowtows to 'the Father'.

'And how is Dora getting on?' she asks him.

'She's happy with the nuns,' he says.

She turns to us. 'We had a hard time bringing Dora in. She was half-white, you see, but her mother hid her in the mangrove swamp and it was weeks before the constable found her. He had to ride them both down and carry off the child. The gin was shrieking like a wild thing. You'd almost think she had feelings like the rest of us. But they're only animals really.'

The Lock Hospital is more like a compound than a hospital. Men and women are segregated behind tall cyclone fences. The wards are like prisons.

'We have to lock them up,' she said. 'They've nearly all got VD, so they have to be kept apart, but they won't stay in the wards. They prefer it out in the yard in the dirt and the heat. It's what they're used to.'

Silently we leave the hospital. When we look back, we see the Aboriginal girls like thin black she-oaks standing under a gunya they've constructed in the desolate yard, their eyes fixed on the distant horizon.

'The only way you can teach a nigger is with a big stick,' says the cool-drinks manufacturer in the pub dining room that night.

He is making a killing, gathering up all the old Coca-Cola bottles left over from the Yank invasion and filling them up with his own concoction. Someone tells us he's already outlived two wives. 'He had a farm once,' they say, 'but he went broke in the Depression and they had to live off the rabbits. The wife starved to death.'

We decide to take the trip out in the mailman's truck to the Ninety Mile Beach, mile after mile of spinifex and great, dry river beds that can be crossed only by laying cyclone wire over the sand.

Our first stop was the DeGrey Station, where a fat, sad-eyed station manager, with a few tufts of white hair sprouting over his ears, made us welcome. An ice-cold rainwater shower under the tank stand and then his wife, a sallow woman with an anguished mouth, served afternoon tea from a silver tea service in the cool verandahed sitting room. She was getting ready to go south. She always went south just before the wet. Beautiful Aboriginal girls in loose bright cotton dresses padded in and out. It was comfortable and civilized, but there was something sinister and secretive, something strained and not quite right in the atmosphere.

The mailman winked and told us the story. 'Notice all them good-lookers? Hand-picked by the ol' feller. He's a well-known combo in the North, got a real harem there. He's only waitin' for the missus to get out of the way, then he'll be inter it. Happens every year. Reckon it takes him six months to get over it.'

Crossing the dry bed of the DeGrey, I remembered Clancy's story: 'The bones of my people are lyin' out there, massacred by the station owners in the old days. When the floods come down you can see the skeletons.'

The petrol fumes in the front cabin had driven me out to ride on the back of the truck, high up on the load, climbing down to open the endless gates that barred our way. In spite of the searing heat there was fresh air outside; towards evening the desert breeze sprang up and when night fell, I slept under the wheeling stars of the Southern Cross.

We stopped at a kangaroo shooters' camp and had a drink of black tea with a grizzled, bleary-eyed 'roo shooter reefing his pants up over his belly with binder twine. While his dogs whined and pissed on the truck tyres, we filled the water drums. 'Will you give the missus a ride on the back?' he said. 'She wants ter visit 'er old people further out.'

'The missus', a thin, barefooted Aboriginal girl, climbed up on the load with her swag. Through mile after mile of daylight and darkness she wouldn't speak, but kept her eyes turned towards the low line of mulga scrub in the distance. One evening she slipped silently off the load and was gone. 'Her people'll be out there somewhere,' the mailman said. 'They sense it, God knows how. She's awlright with ol' Fred. He treats her well, but they get homesick – like most of us.'

When we reached the station on the beach, I was so ill with the heat, the motion of the truck and the drinking water laced with petrol from the steel drum, I fell thankfully on to a real bed under a mosquito net and slept for hours.

When I woke next morning there was a big breakfast waiting in the flywired patio laced with creepers, a sprinkler system spraying the roof all day. Aborigines were sweeping the yard, taking in the dishes and bringing out new ones. The two young daughters were home from college for the holidays. It was like a movie of the deep South, a paternal and benevolent mini-world, too good to be true. The station owner looked like the epitome of the big, cheerful, red-faced Nor'wester; his wife was an ex-nurse, brisk and spectacled, a thin line of black moustache on her upper lip. They lived in a beautiful old stone homestead, the double walls insulated with dried seaweed, set not far from the shore, where Aboriginal boys rode the turtles, laughing into the sea.

'I've told the boys to get into the dam and pull my pony out,' said the eldest daughter, angrily tapping her riding boot with her stock-whip. 'But they won't do it. You've got to make them, Daddy.'

'I wouldn't ask a dog to pull that carcass out,' her father said. 'It's been there for over a week, rotting in this heat. You've got to be reasonable, darling.'

'I don't care, I want him buried,' she wailed.

Back in Port Hedland the heatwaves dance and the sandflies hit the town. Every day is 116 degrees in the shade. In old utes and trucks the Aborigines flee to the desert, leaving us to carry the white man's burden. Every fan in the town is commandeered. I lie in the saltwater bath until the landlady bangs on the door, then I move across to the showers where giant cockroaches drop from the rafters on to unprotected flesh. There is a shortage of fresh water in Port Hedland. It is carted in from outside the town by the Lord Mayor, who has the only franchise. In spite of the warnings, we go swimming in the harbour. None of the locals swim there. It is alive with sharks and the shark net has gaping holes ripped in it. I hang my bathers up to dry on the verandah rail, but in the morning there are only a few shreds of red wool left. The cockroaches have eaten them.

People are taken off to the hospital with sandfly fever. In the room next door Reg, the bulldozer driver, and his wife Rene drink and battle all night, finally spilling out on the landing to throw each other savagely down the stairs. Rene is a faded blonde with no teeth, covered in sandfly sores.

'I remember when I was down souf,' she says dreamily, scratching her bites. 'We usta go swimmin' at Norf Cott in the nuddie. Wisht I was there now. Maybe – next year we'll make it.'

The Dream of Down South – they would come in from the stations, where they worked for six months getting together a cheque, and blow it all in a week on the booze. 'Next time we'll get down south,' they'd say.

I am feeling sick all day now. 'I can't understand it,' I tell a couple of commercial travellers innocently. 'I'm sick as soon as I wake up in the mornings and yet I'm always hungry. I don't know what's the matter with me.'

'There's only one cure for that sickness,' they say, and snicker behind their hands.

I look at them puzzled, then light dawns. In all the excitement I've forgotten. We've been a month in Hedland and a month before that – of course I am pregnant.

As the airport bus pulls out I have my last look at the town – a black man in white shirt and trousers stands under a poinciana tree, blazing against the lime-white road. It looks like a picturesque post-card and not sinister at all. It is all in the eye of the beholder. We fly back to Perth, but already I have relinquished my dream of the book I'd planned to write. I've lost my self-confidence.

'How could you possibly learn enough in one month to write a book about it?' says Grahame Alcorn. He is probably right but, looking back, I wish I'd done it. Instead I go to bed with the flu and write a ballad called 'Clancy and Dooley and Don McLeod' which becomes famous over the years amongst the Australian lefties and folkies.

Clancy and Dooley and Don McLeod
Walked by the wurlies when the wind was loud,
And their voice was new as the fresh sap running
And we keep on fighting and we keep on coming.
Don McLeod beat at a mulga bush
And a lot of queer things came out in a rush,
Like mongrel dogs with their flattened tail,
They sneaked him off to the Hedland Jail.

Vic Williams is delighted. 'It just shows,' says Lloyd, 'that Toddy has to get sick to find time to write these days.'

Years later in Sydney somebody asked me, 'Are you the Dorothy Hewett who wrote "Clancy and Dooley"?'

'Yes,' I said.

'Good God! I thought you'd be dead or else a real old woman.'

CHAPTER

11
♣

1947 and the Cold War – the Truman doctrine has recast American foreign policy. From now on the United States will be principally engaged in containing Soviet power. The British, bankrupted by the war, have lost their Asian colonies and can no longer afford their foreign aid programme. India, Burma and Ceylon are all independent. Europe faces economic ruin, and the unconditional surrender of Germany and Japan has left a world of two powers, facing each other with increasing hostility. On 5 June the Marshall Plan outlines America's new global strategy.

University friends lend me Koestler's *Darkness at Noon* and Orwell's *Animal Farm*, but this is not the time for asking awkward questions. This is a time to close ranks. The heroes of Stalingrad have been renamed 'the enemy' in the capitalist press, and anti-Soviet stories about Stalin's death camps are obviously only *Reader's Digest* propaganda. Refugees from Eastern Europe gather on the Esplanade to disrupt the Party platform, sometimes with violence.

My breasts swell up and, resentfully, I have to wear a bra for the first time. I have all-day morning sickness, but I won't give up. I go to work in bright patterned smocks and a huge green hat woven out of dyed reeds I buy from a craft shop in London Court. Defiantly I take off my wedding ring, and enjoy the scandalized stares at my swollen belly.

When Joan Williams and Molly Thorpe both go off to have their babies, I take over the *Workers' Star* single-handed. Joan works until the last possible moment. Molly has to go to bed and stay there, or else lose her baby. Lloyd wants to give up his law course and work as a journalist on the *Star*, but the Party needs a qualified lawyer so, reluctantly, he abandons this particular dream. He is a totally gregarious human being, but when I stagger home late from work, I am in no mood for a flat full of carousing students and, like a virago, order them outside the door. We have had these confrontations before. Once outside the Palace Hotel I smash two beer bottles poking out of his coat pocket. Lloyd is amused at my fury. 'What a terrible waste, darling,' he says, gazing ruefully into the gutter.

I write articles, paste up, choose typefaces, and work long hours on the printer's stone, putting the paper to bed. The first issues have black oversized typefaces for the leading stories, and look absurd, but gradually I learn to be more professional.

Eventually Grahame Alcorn is made editor and takes over the political responsibility, but he is even less technically experienced than I am. Somehow the paper comes out. We never miss an issue. In these last months I have so much energy I feel as if I could bring out an issue every day.

Two weeks before the baby is born, Mrs Davies goes on holiday and Lloyd and I move into her house in Peppermint Grove. I have been accepted at last. I am the bearer of the new twig on the family tree, framed above the fireplace. It is a breathing space, an idyllic time for both of us.

Looking back, the green garden is always bathed in a stream of light. The old cockatoo swears away in his cage beside Lloyd's water-lily ponds. 'L'Après-midi d'un faune' seems to be playing over and over on the gramophone. I lie like a bursting pod on the green lawns while Lloyd, slant-eyed as a faun, gambols through the spring days.

The bedroom is mauve, with a purple eiderdown that smells faintly of cat's piss. When the idyll ends, I cling to the curtains, astonished by pain. Nothing has prepared me for this. My body has been taken over, struck down by a huge alien force, leaving me totally helpless. Afterwards, when I try to remember the birth in detail, it has become a blur. Even if I keep on saying to myself over and over, 'Remember this', all I have at the end of it is a vague memory. They say this is nature's way of making sure the race survives. If I could really remember such pain I would never do it again. But I feel cheated. This is a tremendous, agonizing experience and yet I can't retain it.

When they put the chloroform mask over my face, I am certain that the doctor is a Fascist torturer planted in the King Edward Maternity Hospital to kill me. When I wake up I have a nine-and-a-half-pound boy. We call him Clancy, after Clancy McKenna. I sit up in bed with a flat stomach and no stitches, drinking champagne. Lloyd calls it 'wetting the baby's head'.

But when we take the baby back to Milligan Street, I feel drained and helpless; obsessively scrubbing out the baby's room with disinfect-ant every day, boiling up the endless nappies in the wood copper in the back yard. The responsibility is terrifying. I am haunted by the possibility that something may happen to him and it will be all my fault. My milk begins to dry up. Nobody warned me that this could happen. The Sister at the clinic treats me like a criminal because the baby is not putting on weight. I am ordered to drink six bottles of water a day, massage my breasts after every feed and drink a glass of stout with every meal. The baby cries louder. I walk him up and down. Lloyd walks him up and down. My baby is starving and neither of us is getting any sleep. Everything revolves around this screaming morsel of our own flesh who cries and cries.

'Put him in the room and close the door,' says Joan Williams, but I can't stand to hear him crying.

'Give him some dill water,' says Joy Alcorn. 'He's probably got two-month colic.'

I feed him his dill water and read and reread Truby King on babycare. The world has shrunk to the four walls of this dingy flat. Lloyd is away at university all day and I am imprisoned with a screaming child. I touch the soft spot on the top of his skull and weep with him.

At last I give in and we pack up and go home to my mother. Abrogating all my responsibilities, I fall asleep. My mother is always at her best in a crisis. She is in her element. Now she has not only me to look after, but the baby as well. What a relief it is, at first, to sink back again into my own childhood. The comfortable domesticity of the middle-class household folds itself around us. The meals are cooked and on the table, the nappy service is paid for and delivered to the door. I take the baby for long walks in his pram every afternoon along the river foreshores.

He is the centre of the family. Everybody dotes on him. With his golden hair and his eyes as dark brown and velvet as pansies, he sits in the garden like a fat baby Buddha, happily chewing up earth and snails, while I struggle on, trying to produce enough milk to satisfy him. The glasses of stout are beginning to make me fat. 'Better be careful or you'll have a weight problem,' says the gynaecologist at the post-natal examination.

I am horrified. I have always been the same size – small-breasted, with a twenty-three-inch waist, hourglass hips and heavy thighs. Now I feel like a milch cow. My sister's friends treat me as if I had joined another generation overnight. I am in bed every night at nine o'clock. I can never go out because I have to feed the baby. Lloyd and I have no private life any more. If he comes home happy and garrulous after a few too many beers at Steve's, the university pub, the atmosphere is icy.

Everyone is going somewhere or changing their lives. Mary Vetter comes to see me before she leaves for London. She is married to an English historian and has a small daughter. Ron Strahan calls in. I put on a black dress to disguise my figure, but he tells me I look

Wearing my Mary Pickford curls for the gala opening of the family's new Regal cinema in Subiaco, Perth, 1938.

At sixteen, 'I am the resident genius of 5B'. Photo: Betty Picken

'I sit on One Tree Hill amongst the blonde grass while Betty Picken takes my photograph with a box-brownie.' Myself, aged sixteen on the school geology expedition to Gingin, Western Australia, in 1940.

'There was only one beauty in our family and that was her downfall,' says my father. Myself, aged twenty-two, just after winning the ABC National Poetry Prize for narrative verse, 1945. Photo: Betty Picken

'20 Ridge Street, South Perth, the house of my adolescence, a monument to the thirties.' Photo: René Hewett

A photo of Lilla Harper on the lawn at Perth College, 1949, and inscribed: 'To Dorothy – you asked for it. Lilla'.

Bathing Belles of the 1940s. Myself and Lesley posing for our mother's camera on the sandhills at Middleton beach, Albany, Western Australia.

'Seek Wisdom'. Freshers at the University of Western Australia in 1941. I am fifth on the right in the front row, wearing red tartan under an academic gown. On my right is Mary Vetter, next to her is Julia Drake-Brockman, Henrietta's daughter.

Myself and Clancy in South Perth, 1948.

'The house in the hills outside the city is the first house I will ever own.

It looks like a real house now, a pergola out front, embowered in the full grown trees and shrubs we once planted long ago.' The house at Darlington, Western Australia. Photo: Merv Lilley, 1987

matronly, and after that we have nothing to say to each other. Jeff Craig has gone to East Sydney Tech. Pat Skevington has married dashing David Roe in the fashionable wedding of the year. Heir to one of the oldest West Australian families, he already has a drinking problem. Pat goes off to live amongst the family vineyards at Sandalford and her own particular Gethsemane. Lesley, engaged to our fourth cousin Noel Dougan, is working as a psychologist in a clinic for deaf children, and filling up her hope chest. Soon she too will be transferred to Sydney. But here everything revolves around the baby. He is like a monster in the house, beautiful and implacable. My mother is obsessive. I should have no other life but my child. She is chained to a dying animal – the old incontinent woman in the back bedroom she has always disliked and resented.

A district nurse comes twice a day to wash my grandmother and change her catheter. 'Without me draining her legs, she would have died long ago,' she says proudly.

'For God's sake!' I say. 'Why don't you just let her die?'

A bossy woman with a big jaw and a bottom like a huge white shelf, the nurse is scandalized. 'What an unnatural girl she is,' she tells my mother, who privately confesses that she thinks I am right.

'It isn't as if you ever even liked her,' I tell my mother. 'Why don't you find a well-run, expensive nursing home and put her in it? She can afford it.'

But my mother won't do that. It is her duty to look after Nana, and besides, the Tindales put Aunty Eva in a home and when she went to rescue her, she found her neglected and terrorized by shock treatments in a smelly ward amongst a lot of old, bed-wetting women. They'd even taken her own silk stockings away from her.

My mother has found Aunty Eva a home in the hills with two elderly nurse companions who are kind to her and don't let her wander away. Sometimes, when we take Aunty Eva out for a drive, she tries to leap out of the car door and finish it all. I think she has a point. 'You can put me in a home when I get old and gaga.' my mother says. 'I wouldn't want anybody to be tied to me like this.'

We escape to Rottnest with the Alcorns and while I am there I put Clancy on the bottle. 'I knew you'd do that as soon as you got out of my sight,' my mother says.

Clancy is less than a year old when I discover I am pregnant again. I am hysterical at the thought of having another baby, so once more I line up in the long queue of girls and women by the crumbling cupids in the neglected garden of Perth's leading abortionist. When Lloyd takes me back home, I have two haemorrhages and pass out in the bedroom. 'I don't know how you can do it,' my mother says, getting rid of the bloody newspapers. 'I saw a perfect miniature baby lying there.' She makes me feel like a murderer.

When we find the little house in the ranges, it is like an escape into Paradise. Leaving Clancy with my mother, we go up at the weekends, sleeping in the single iron bedstead on the front porch. The night is full of crickets and strange bird noises. The stars are large and glittering, the moonlight streams across the valley. A sharp, acrid, dewy smell tingles our noses. In the mornings we wake with the frost on our blankets and a row of kookaburras sitting on the top of the cement wall waiting to be fed. If we sleep too late, one old man kookaburra taps with his beak on my forehead and I wake to see his glittering eye.

When we shift into the house, it is transformed. My father and my husband have gone up at weekends, carpentering and painting. We have bought an old army hut from Disposals and added it to the dwarf's cottage. The front room of the cottage is now a small kitchen. It drops down through a little wooden gate to a cement-floored dining room with an old whitewashed fireplace and a picture window framing the valley. In winter, the stone room is a washout. It has no damp course, so everything we put into it goes mildewed and mouldy, but in the summer its thick walls cut off the blazing heat and it becomes a refuge.

The large main room of the army hut becomes our living room. An old bricklayer builds us a huge fireplace and Lloyd faces it with stone, lugging the golden blocks up from the wall and setting them in place, learning as he goes. There is a big window that takes in the whole sweep of distant blue ridges, clumps of jarrah and homesteads hidden amongst groves of trees.

At night he builds roaring whitegum fires and we sit staring into the heart of the coals, the flames dancing on the white walls, reflected in the big glass window. Outside the bush leans to listen. Great red moons rise over the valley, lifting and paling to a white globe. Frogs and crickets sing in the moonlight together. But everything is not always a country idyll.

The army hut is surrounded by verandahs with sliding asbestos panels – no glass – partitioned off into our bedrooms and the baby's room. At first we have no bathroom, and wash in an enamel dish in front of the kitchen fire, our skins tingling, alternating from frost to flame. Later on, in a walkway between the old house and the new, my father builds us a corrugated-iron bathroom with a chip heater and an old bath. Our water comes from two big rainwater tanks at the side of the house, crystal clear and icy, summer and winter. At first we have no refrigerator. I climb down and put the milk and butter in a shady overhang in the creek where a trickle of water flows over the gravel bottom.

Sometimes, when I am alone at night, the ceiling overhead is alive with bush rats. I sit clasping the baby in terror as they squeak and scuttle, transported into the world of 'The Pit and the Pendulum'. One night I hear the sound of thumping in the dry grass and look up – a huge rat is approaching me fearlessly down the slope. We stare at each other. I throw a stick at it and, hissing, it disappears into the night. I shut the doors and windows and sit there trembling until my husband comes singing home through the bush at the back of the house. Sometimes the heat hits us like a solid wall and we gasp, listening to the hot wind cracking off the iron roof and the metallic gums. The baby cries and cries. We have no car and catch a little bush train from the station about three miles away – two miles if we walk through the timber. Once that timber catches fire and the flames sweep crackling down the slope to be stopped, just in time, by the stone wall.

We leave the billy at the front gate and our milk is delivered by the local dairy. Sometimes, putting the baby in his pram, we walk to the dairy in the evening and stand amongst the cows, their breath filling the starry night, to chat with the dairy farmer and his sons – round-cheeked, taciturn men in gumboots with red veins broken on noses and cheekbones. Sometimes we walk on further to the nursery and buy shrubs and trees for our stony hillside from a little, dark, lame-legged Welshman, who lives with his old mother in a tiny weatherboard cottage, a thin stream trickling past the front door. The old woman comes to the doorway, squinting against the light, and asks us in for a cup of tea.

In summer we go swimming in a deep hole in the creek about three miles from our house. Here the creek widens out between high banks and we swing out on a rope over the water to fall into the icy depths, or slide off a granite boulder under a huge fallen gum root to be swept along in a torrent of foam to the glassy pool on the other side.

Lloyd plants a vegetable garden at the back of the house and a strawberry patch by the stone wall under a few spindly fruit trees. The frost glistens on the cabbage leaves and the strawberries wink in the moonlight. He builds us a stone lavatory with an endearing crooked wall. Looking out through the window, we see the valleys unroll, mile after mile of blurred blue scrub and misty distances – the loveliest view in the world. Inside we have books and paintings: Monet's 'Summer' in the kitchen, Van Gogh's 'Portrait of a Young

Man' in the sitting room, above the fireplace the Elizabeth Durack oil painting of a young Aboriginal woman with exaggeratedly big feet perched on a rock.

Lloyd is articled to a law firm in the city and I am alone all day until late in the evening, when the little steam train brings him slowly home again. 'Let's go to Sydney after your articles,' I beg him. 'You can easily get a job with a left-wing lawyer.' He writes a letter, but there are no jobs and anyway, he has a duty to the West Australian Party.

'I could have joined the New Theatre,' I tell him. I am twenty-five. Time is passing and all my dreams are dissolving in dust. Soon it will be too late. I sit on the front step with Clancy, watching the lights come out across the valley, feeling intolerably lonely and isolated. Obviously I am not cut out to be a full-time mother. We decide to share the house with Joan Williams's young sister Laurie and her new husband. Laurie will look after the baby and I will go back to the *Workers' Star* for three days a week. I am reprieved.

Sam Aarons has come from Sydney to take over as Party secretary. He is a black-haired, handsome Jew in his early fifties, an ex-Spanish brigadier who has left Sydney under something of a political cloud because of a love affair with a young married woman. Annette arrives eventually to join him. Years ago I had seen her play in *Precious Bane* at the local Patch theatre. She comes from a middle-class West Australian family and has been sent to Sydney to recover from a disastrous affair with a man old enough to be her father. A Party marriage is 'arranged', but it is never successful. She makes me a present of her old blue wedding dress because she 'can't stand the sight of it'.

The Aarons clan are like a Communist Royal Family – one sister runs the Sydney New Theatre; another is married to the secretary of the Sydney District Committee; Laurie Aarons, Sam's eldest son, will one day take over as Party chairman, and his younger son Eric is a well-known Marxist theoretician. Sam introduces a new style into the West Australian Party. He is a dramatic speaker and a political autocrat; the old leadership can't work with him and one by one they leave for the Eastern states. I find him totally irresistible – a passionate, highly intelligent, charismatic man with a glamorous history.

At a political meeting in Midland, when someone in the raging crowd shies a broken brick straight at Katharine Prichard's head, Sam leaps off the back of the truck and knocks him down. 'We need women like you,' he tells me. 'Forget about writing. You've got a great future ahead of you as a Party organizer.'

He is teaching me how to be a public speaker. 'Don't be afraid of using gestures,' he tells me. 'Be dramatic. Australians are frightened of gestures, terrified of showing their feelings.'

I stand up shaking on the Party platform on the Esplanade for the first time. The white-headed stalwart who has spoken there since time immemorial holds up a patriarchal hand to quell the crowd: 'Give the little lady a go. She's only a woman.'

When Sam kisses me in the back of a car on the way home from a party, I find myself responding. I am, I think, in love with Sam Aarons. What I actually do have is a bad case of hero worship and besides, Sam has a most uncanny resemblance to my own father. He bends me back on the desk in his office, but before we can consummate our affair we are interrupted by the old Party caretaker, locking up for the night.

'If anyone finds out,' Sam says, 'my political career will be over – and you're just the sort of woman who'd go home and tell her husband. Sharkey has already told me if there's any more gossip about me and other women, I'll be on the outer. He's had it in for me ever since I stole his girlfriend in Spain.' (Lance Sharkey is the new general secretary of the Communist Party.)

Sam's stories about Spain fascinate me – the ragged, starving, lice-ridden brigade stumbling towards the sea coast, defeated and half-drunk on Spanish wine.

While Katharine Prichard is overseas, Sam and Annette are living in her weatherboard house on the old York Road in Greenmount – a romantic house with a patio covered in bougainvillea. As a special favour, Sam asks me to stay and help Annette with their new baby. It's a cruel thing to do but, feeling like a hypocrite, I endure it for his sake. We all sleep on the creeper-clad jarrah verandah: Lloyd and I down one end, Sam and Annette on the other. Sam and I never have a chance to be alone; once or twice a hurried embrace against his leather jacket before he leaves for the city. 'I do appreciate what you are doing for me,' he whispers. 'I know it's rough on you, but I can't ask anyone else. Anyway, I know how strong you are. You're the strongest woman I've ever known.'

When he leaves for the Central Committee meeting in Sydney, I am there at the airport bus to see him off. He takes my face in his hands. 'Look at you,' he groans. 'Christ! You're younger than my youngest son. Don't forget about me while I'm away,' but by the time he comes back, I am making love to Les Flood – in the back of his old Humber Snipe, in his room at the Railway Hotel or in a dark deserted part of the Esplanade after we've both been to a Party meeting – and it is too late for Sam to do anything about it.

My first meeting with Les Flood is at a Party picnic by the river at Point Walter. I am sitting with Clancy on my knees and when I look up, he is standing there grinning at me and someone is saying, 'This is a comrade from Sydney.' What did I think of him at that fateful meeting? Brash, round-faced, with a thatch of reddish hair and pale-blue prominent eyes, he looked me up and down appraisingly until I felt as if I had been stripped in public – and found wanting. A Sydney boilermaker, he has driven across the Nullarbor from Whyalla with two English seamen who have jumped ship in Australia.

Our second meeting is at a Party school tutored by Ernie Campbell from the Central Committee, who has written *The History of the Australian Labour Movement*. I stay in the Alcorns' flat, going off to the pub most nights with the young unattached men, arguing Marxist theory and whether Bertrand Russell has sold out to the imperialists. Over pots of Swan lager in the ladies' lounge, my eyes meet the strange reckless eyes of Les Flood, who is never afraid to disagree with Ernie Campbell and say so, both in the school and out of it. The school lasts a fortnight and at the end of it I feel as if across the heady talk and argument, the Communist Party texts and smeary pub tables, invisible sexual threads are pulling us tighter and tighter.

'Socialism in three years,' Ernie Campbell has predicted and I believe every word of it, working like someone possessed – selling the *Workers' Star* on the Fremantle wharves and outside the Midland Railway workshops, coming home on the last train from endless meetings in Perth, missing the connecting bus and hitch-hiking to Greenmount Hill to be picked up by the wheat trucks revving for the climb. The drivers are always kind and courteous, dropping me at the turn-off to walk the four miles home through the bush. I am running away from, or towards, some catastrophe, and I am not sure what it is.

One night, after a meeting in London Court, Les Flood stops me at the lift and offers me a ride home. It's not out of his way. He works at the Midland Railway Workshops and lives in the Railway Hotel. He pulls up outside Katharine's house, where we are still staying with Annette.

'I know you want to get off with me.'

I hesitate, but one bald truth deserves another. 'Yes.'

'Then why don't you do it?'

'Because it would be a disaster.'

'How do you know?'

'I just know.'

'You've been watching me for weeks, thinking about it.'

'So have you.'

He laughs. 'Well, why don't we do something about it then? What's wrong with that?'

'Everything's wrong with it.'

'Bourgeois morality!' he says. 'It's no use feeling guilty. If you've thought about it, you might as well do it.'

I get out of the car and open the door into the back seat. 'Okay,' I say, and he laughs again, but I know I've astonished him.

We make love that night as I haven't made love in years. He touches my face gently: 'Now you won't ever be able to get rid of me,' and I know it's true, but when I leave the car I am already almost hating him. He has awakened me from my long domestic sleep. Work and the Party, husband and child, friends, family – everything I have shored up against my ruin. I run inside, determined never to be alone with him again.

Back in Darlington, hunched up miserably on the back step with my first attack of cystitis, I tell Lloyd all about it and promise him it will never happen again, but in less than a week I am rolling over naked in Les Flood's bed in the Railway Hotel to read the luminous dial on his little travelling clock.

When Sam comes home from Sydney he calls me into his office, staring at me from behind his desk with those hooded eyes.

'My spies tell me you've been seeing someone else while I've been away.'

'You don't need your spies. I'll tell you anything you want to know. I've been making love to Les Flood.'

Sam's face freezes. 'Well, that's brutally honest,' he says. 'Why? Was it all bullshit? Didn't you care about me at all?'

'Yes, but it's hopeless, you and me. You're living with Annette, you've got a new baby and you're terrified of being found out.' I can hear the beginnings of contempt in my voice.

'I'm sorry,' he says, 'I know it's been hard on you.'

'It's been impossible. How can I work side by side with you in the same office after all this has happened?'

'I'll try to make it easier,' he says, 'but this Flood isn't any good to you. He's a lightweight. Promise me you won't see him again.'

'I can't promise you that.'

'You are the most bloody-minded woman,' he says. 'You're so fucking honest, you always speak the unvarnished truth and it's not necessarily a virtue.'

I move towards the door.

'If you go on with this,' he says, 'I'll be forced to try and put a stop to it.'

'Try then,' I tell him, throwing down the gauntlet.

♣

Very early one Sunday morning in Western Australia the Criminal Investigation Branch swoop down on hundreds of Communist households and carry off crates of books, notes and anything else that looks suspicious to their simplistic minds. When they arrive in Darlington, Lloyd and I aren't there. I have left with Les for the Holiday Inn at Yanchep, a few miles up the coast, and Lloyd has taken Clancy and gone home to his mother.

In the empty hotel sitting room, Les is playing 'The Rustle of Spring' by ear, on an out-of-tune piano, while I try to recover from the decision I have finally made. I have moved through these last weeks like a sleepwalker, never still, travelling on buses and trains, with my head splitting and Clancy tight in my arms, unable to make up my mind. I have given myself strange ultimatums – if I am elected to the State Committee I will stay with Lloyd, but I am not elected to the State Committee.

Les tells me that we can't go on like this. He is leaving for Sydney.

'Will you write to me?'

'No, once it's over, it's over.'

I try to imagine never seeing him again, but even the thought is impossible.

Together we have stormed the Council meeting at the Midland Town Hall. Bursting through the closed doors into the sacred Council chamber with hundreds of furious citizens demanding a hospital in the district. A child has died of snakebite during the long trip by ambulance into the city. The councillors sit stunned, speechless with indignation at this affront to their dignity. Doctor Alec Jolley, the only Communist member, is sitting back grinning at us and drumming his fingers on the table. Outside, the rest of the Party Branch are still on the stairs exhorting the masses to elect a deputation and behave in a more disciplined fashion. The Lord Mayor's flabby face is pallid with fright.

'Doctor Jolley, do you know anything about this outrage?'

'No, Mr Mayor.'

'Can't you control your people?'

'They're not *my* people, Mr Mayor, they're the citizens of this municipality and they have got a legitimate grievance.'

I look across at Les in his boiler suit, with his pale hair catching the electric light, and see him as the personification of the working-class hero. Three years the Revolution, I think jubilantly, as we leave with the promise of a new district hospital.

Lloyd tells me he has gone to Sam for advice. The situation is so ludicrous I can hardly believe it.

'You went to Sam about our private life – and what did *he* say?'

'He said I could either ignore this and wait for it to burn itself out, or else issue an ultimatum.'

'The bloody hypocrite! Don't you know that Sam and I have been having an affair for months?'

Lloyd stares at me. 'You don't leave me with anything, do you?' he says bitterly.

Finally, without ever consciously planning it, I manoeuvre us all into a situation from which there can be only one result. For the first time, I take Les home to Darlington. Coming back from a meeting, Lloyd finds us sitting together on the floor staring into the fire in the sitting room. There is a fight in the moonlit back yard, stumbling over cabbages, and when I try to intervene, Les throws me down hard on the ground and orders me to 'keep the fuck out of it'.

I leave next morning dressed for the occasion in my old black slack suit and velvet beret. When we come back from Yanchep, we stay in a cheap room across the Horseshoe Bridge in 'Little Italy' and Les buys me a wedding ring in a second-hand shop.

'With this ring I thee wed,' he says, 'in true Communist fashion.' In bed at night he tells me he is beginning to smell like a woman.

Sam calls me into his office and warns me he has reason to believe that Les is a police agent who manoeuvred me away from Perth while the CIB carried out a police raid on the Party. I laugh in his face.

'Your political career is finished,' he says. 'I'll see to it that you'll never get a position of responsibility in the Party again.'

I demand a meeting with the State Committee so that I can put my case, but he refuses. 'I suppose you think I'm doing all this out of jealousy?' he says.

I go to work at the *Star* day after day and sit there in almost total silence. Nearly everybody has sent me to Coventry. Grahame Alcorn equates me with his own personal tragedy. Joy has left him and taken Jane to Sydney. 'We were too soft on both of them,' he tells Lloyd bitterly. Outside the Chinese café I see Ron Strahan standing with a group of university students. He cuts me dead. I have left it to Lloyd to tell my parents. Mrs Davies pays my mother a visit and tells her that God will punish me. 'But I don't want God to punish her,' wails my poor mother. My father is adamant. 'She ought to be horsewhipped.' Lesley, back from Melbourne, her engagement broken, is roped in as the family go-between. She makes an appointment to see Les and offers him £3,000 to leave me and go back to Sydney.

'Make a better offer,' he says. 'Is that all she's worth?'

I spend an afternoon with Clancy down by the river below the university where I used to meet my lost lover. We sit under a weeping peppermint by a little wooden fishing boat turned turtle on the sand. 'Down she came and found a boat,/Among the willows left afloat,/And round about the prow she wrote,/The Lady of Shalott,' I recite to him, while he digs in the sand.

Have I made the wrong decision, underestimated the terrible primitive pull between mother and child? I will have to get away by myself somewhere and think it all out again. I book into a room alone in a cheap pub in Wellington Street opposite the Hotel Bohemia. It is a bleak room: four empty single beds with white cotton covers. I stand out on the balcony for hours trying to will myself to jump, but I haven't got the courage. At two o'clock in the morning, tears streaming down my face, I run back across the bridge, burst into the room I have shared with Les, find him lying on the bed smoking and staring into the dark, and throw myself sobbing beside him.

'We'll go back to the big smoke,' he says. 'It's obvious that we can't stay in Western Australia. There's no possible future here for us.'

I see Clancy only once more before I leave. The family have removed themselves from Ridge Street for the day, leaving Lesley in charge. She is about to fulfil her life's ambition. She has been accepted into the medical faculty at Melbourne University. It had never occurred to me that if I left Lloyd, Clancy wouldn't go with me. 'Take everything,' Lloyd had said. 'Leave me with nothing, no wife, no child, nothing.'

So, consumed with guilt, I had agreed to let him take Clancy, but when I tried to open up negotiations again, he was adamant, he told me, and I knew enough about the law to realize that as the absconding wife and mother I'd never stand a chance. But in these last wild moments I have all kinds of secret plans to grab Clancy and run away where none of them will ever find us. Instead I kiss him and turn quickly and walk out of the front gate, believing that I will probably never set eyes on him again. Twenty years later, my sister asks me have I ever regretted that choice. 'I'd never leave a child for any man again,' I tell her.

Only Vic Williams comes to see us off at the station. 'She wants to join the New Theatre,' Les says. 'Tell her she'd do better to stick with the working class.' He makes me feel like a failed bourgeoise girl. 'Good luck!' Vic waves, as the train pulls out.

I stand on the observation platform with a middle-aged Yank tourist, looking back at the city. I can see the silver tower of the Dingo Flour Mill glittering, a black sickle painted on the side.

'Look at that,' says the Yank businessman. 'The Commies are taking over the country.'

But I am looking back like Lot's wife, past the silver silo and the black sickle. I am standing outside London Court wearing the New Look, laughing with Sam Aarons in the rain. He leans across and flicks the gilt spider pinned to my lapel.

'Very appropriate,' he says. 'The female spider always eats her mate.'

My red flannel skirt whirls as I turn and see Strahan smiling at me over the heads of the crowd. The clock whirrs and strikes the hour. The rain falls. The medieval knights perambulate around the painted face, their lances tilted.

A child is calling, 'Mummy, Mummy!' all the way up the hill to the Darlington train, a ute is driving into the dusk and distance while I stand bleeding at Joan Williams's gate, Lilla in her school uniform is coming towards me through the Guildford grass, my grandmother's dying breath fills the back room like a bellows, the wind in the unripened wheat flows in a green sea to the foot of Rock Hill.

PART III

I woke up in the darkest night,
knew all the world had caught alight
The surf was pounding in the weather,
And Moncur Street was mine forever.
The little bat upon the stair
came out and flapped: it wasn't there,
the snapshot album turned and turned,
the stew caught fire, the budgie burned,
the pensioners at draughts and dreams
picked bugs between their trouser seams
And Sammy Smiles (that lovely man!)
and Aime and Alf and little Fay,
and Beat and Bert and betting slips,
The man I love, the child I bore,
have all gone under Bondi's hills,
And will return here never more
   in Moncur Street
   in Moncur Street.
          'In Moncur Street'

PART III

SIXTY-FIVE Marriott Street, Redfern, in the Cold War fifties – my very own Wigan Pier. This is a card house with a difference. Dying asparagus ferns, dead pot plants and chamber pots, hanging baskets draping a dismal curtain, three stands of rusty barbed wire looped along the front fence, it is a fitting memorial to Miss Donithorne and her maggot. The maggot is love, both spiritual and carnal. I have embraced the working class, and the symbol is this decrepit brick corner house where we squat one dark night with our two pink blankets, amongst the chocolate boxes, scent bottles, rice-coloured face powder and laddered silk stockings. The newspapers under the balding lino date back to the thirties. We are pulling up the giant weeds, throwing out the cracked chamber pots, the wire baskets and the mountains of buried tins.

A thin man, with no teeth, in a beanie, two muzzled whippets straining at the leash, stops by the front fence. 'There's six dorgs buried in that front yard,' he tells us mournfully. This is the Red Belt, where house-proud working-class housewives sweep the pavements, blacken the front doorsteps and polish the brass doorknockers until they glitter, but the poor, the old, the homeless, the mad, the alcoholic, the subnormal, the disabled, the petty crims and the Aborigines exist behind tattered blinds, boarded-up shop fronts and two-storey terraces with the staircases burnt up for firewood.

The air is breathless with soot and smog. The knock-off whistles from the brewery, the print factory and the glassworks punctuate the day. Up on the hill, in towering blocks of concrete, the rehoused look sadly down on us from their Housing Commission flats.

The two front rooms are large, with an autumn leaf dado. The kitchen is painted a dreary railway fawn. An ancient Early Kooka stove, with one burner and a missing leg, lists drunkenly in the corner. There is no sink, so we wash up in the pitted cement tubs in the wash house; an old bath in one corner and a bricked-up wood copper in the other. The second bedroom has abstract wet blue patterns crisscrossing the wall, furred with mould in the winter. The kitchen looks like a giant spider web. We have so many electric cords running off the central bulb that we are always blowing the power lines. The man from the electricity department turns up, scratches his head and laughs.

'What's this, mate?' he says.

'Bunnerong!' (Bunnerong is the main Sydney power station.)

Richardson and Wrench, the housing agents, send round a lard-faced, heavy-jowled man in a grey double-breasted suit to bang on the front door, yelling, 'I know you're in there,' while I huddle in the hall or slip out the back to wander the streets till the coast is clear.

When winter comes we wade in the freezing streams in National Park to collect the coal that washes down the hills from the mines. When we burn it in the little black grate in the front room it spits out clinker, frightening the stray black cattle dog that has come to live with us.

Under the autumn leaf dado we type up the stencils, and print hundreds of illegal leaflets on the flatbed out in the shed. We are 'the centre' for the South Sydney section of the Australian Communist Party. There are no books or paintings in our house until we start a lending library of what we call 'working-class classics' – *The Ragged Trousered Philanthropists*, the novels of Howard Fast, Eleanor Dark and Katharine Prichard, *The Socialist Sixth of the World* by the Red Dean of Canterbury.

Dark figures knock on our front door late at night, picking up their copies of *Tribune* (the Communist newspaper) for sale at branches and factory gates. I have a *de facto* and a new baby, but we hardly spend any time alone. Our lives are devoted to the betterment of the row on row of little semis surrounding us, whose inhabitants neither know nor care.

The people next door hold a wild party every Saturday night. When the piano belts out 'The Old Piano Roll Blues', it is a signal for a punch-up – yells, broken glass and crockery, bodies thudding against the common wall. Once, passing the house, I see smoke and flames pouring from their car parked outside and run in to warn them. A week later, a skinny-faced man with crossed eyes sidles up to me in the lane and passes me a bolt of dress fabric, mumbling toothlessly out of the corner of his mouth, 'For your trouble, Missus.'

Across the street live a bevy of beauties, ageless, black-haired and lithe – grandmother, mother and several grown-up daughters. They swan around the front porch or hang over the front fence like birds of paradise. The father, a tall, silent seaman on the Suva run, comes home occasionally, bringing exotic silken kimonos 'for the women-folk', who all have lovers. Their parties are legendary – bottles whizz down the front hall, shadowy figures skid out on to the pavement, pulling up the wooden fence posts and belabouring each other across the skull. The sounds of broken glass shatter the night. Next morning they leave for a week or a fortnight, coming back when the coast is clear with lowered heads and subdued voices, until they have built up their reputations again. Further along the street a toothless father, mother and subnormal daughter live in a boarded-up shop front. As I pass, pushing the baby in the pram, I hear the bed springs creak. 'My turn now,' shrieks the old woman.

Our back room is packed full of illegal literature, and when the referendum to ban the Communist Party looks as if it will be won, we realize we will probably go to jail. We spend hours burning the dangerous stuff in the back yard. Ash floats over the roofs of Redfern. Nobody takes any notice. By the afternoon, when most of it has gone up in smoke, the referendum is lost and we breathe again. But when the news breaks that the Section secretary has gambled all the secret funds away at Thommo's Two-up School and the Labor Party representative on the Referendum Committee has stolen all the profits from the grog sold at the referendum party, the Redfern Communists are under something of a moral cloud. We have always been regarded as anarchists, or worse, by the Centre – Marx House – in the heart of the city. Everybody knows about the Redfern comrades in the Council elections who vote several times, trying on the shoes of all the dead still left on the electoral rolls.

Snowy has done time in Long Bay jail; Carol Jackson, her black bodice stuck full of pins, is the local dressmaker. Her son Eddy, covered neck to buttocks in lurid tattoos that rock seductively as he walks, is a genius. He taught a Party class on political economy when he was only twelve. Pat Gale is a Party sympathizer. She lives with her son Red Siddy in a battered semi under a loquat tree with Frankie Laine belting out 'I must go where the wild goose goes' on the record-player and a whippet dog they race at Harold Park 'for an interest'. Her twinnies smile like street-wise cherubs from the sideboard, their naval caps cocked provocatively over one ear. 'I've spent nights in Hyde Park in the Depression wrapped in newspapers against the cold, Red Siddy at the breast,' she tells me.

Joe the anarchist is an ex-American seaman, blackballed on the San Francisco coast. Bill is a tall, balding ironmoulder who sits in the kitchen drinking endless cups of Lipton's tea. Harried from town to town by the cops in the Depression, jumping the rattler, he has never settled long enough to marry. Now he has been put out to grass with a job in a peanut factory. 'It's no job for a man,' he tells me bitterly.

My friend Gwen met her husband Jimmy Shipton in the orphan-age. They have a star boarder in the back room. One night, in a drunken confessional, he is unmasked as Gwen's lover and the father of the two children Jimmy Shipton always thought were his. Both men dump her to fend for herself with the two unwanted children. When I protest, Pat Dale grows philosophical: 'No man wants to be lumbered with another man's kids,' she says, turning up 'Mule Train' on the record-player.

Sometimes I wake early to the baby's cry and lie for a moment watching the sunlight flush the fronts of the little semis along Marriott Street. In the evening in the sitting room, when the dust motes dance in that last luminous Sydney light before the sun goes down, I sit repainting the walls in pale pastels, hang up paintings, build bookshelves full of books in the wide alcoves beside the fireplace. 'If we do it up, they'll put up the rent,' says Les.

I have opened my house up to the world and invited them all in – the homeless, the runaways, the bludgers, the users and the dreamers all sleep on our floor and then move on. They flock to me like homing pigeons. 'It's like a bloody dosshouse,' Les Flood rages. 'Why don't you go out into the street and drag them all in?'

But I cannot get enough of them. Typewriters clatter, voices murmur into the early hours over the spitting coal, the kettle boils itself dry and is filled again. I'm obsessed. I want the front door to be permanently open, I want to invite them in and fill the house with noise. I want the talk never to stop. I am a soft touch. I am the Florence Nightingale of South Sydney. 'Give me your poor and your homeless – I am the Statue of Liberty, I have built a giant card house that can swell to accommodate the universe.

'Let none go by while this house lives'. In the old days the bagmen used to mark the front gate of any farms that were good for a handout.

When my grandmother dies and leaves me some money in her will, we buy a house in Rosebery. The Redfern comrades are disgusted. 'You'll never come back,' says Snowy. 'You've deserted the working class.'

He is right, in a way. We will never see any of this again. But the house will go on. It will be a Party house, the key passing from hand to hand for years, until a sheetmetal worker from the 'Glassie' buys it, puts up a new tapestried brick front fence, waxes the pine floors and fills the rooms with fleshy tropical pot plants. But now, the steps still unblacked, the brass knocker still unpolished, I shut the front door for the last time.

'Get a bitta leg opener into y',' calls Madge O'Grady, the felt flowers bouncing on her home-made hat. She is the champion *Tribune* seller in the South Sydney section.

Street after street of ugly, liver-brick tradesmen's cottages built in the 1930s, Rosebery is a respectable, working-class suburb, further out. Gabled and liver-bricked like the rest, with a stiff dwarf pine on either side of the front porch and a blue plumbago hedge, our house is built opposite the wire factory, working day and night shift, blaring noise and light into our front bedroom.

Textured walls and autumn tonings, a gas fire in the sitting room, wall-to-wall floral carpets, cream lace and brocade curtains hanging heavily at all the windows, blocking off the air – but there is a back garden with a lawn and two peach trees with fruit fly. A line of cypresses with a resident possum marks the back fence. We buy two white leghorns and I hang a print of Van Gogh's 'Cypresses' on the dining-room wall. To our two-year-old son it is such a miracle that he buries his face in the grass on the first day and sings.

Next door lives a skinny deserted Catholic with a bevy of little boys in hand-me-down trousers, too long for the youngest. They swarm in the crepe myrtle over the garage roof. When evening falls our son comes screaming into the house, his ears full of tales of the Devil and the bogeyman who waits in the dark.

On the other side, a surly retired policeman turned night-watchman never speaks. At night we lie in bed listening to the wire factory. A drunken shadow coming off night shift snarls, 'Dirty Commos!' In the winter mornings before the first light, a flower-seller shambles past calling, 'Paaps, iced paaps.'

Rosebery is a lonely, pursed-mouth sort of place with wide empty streets, the doors shut tight on their secrets, the dusty squares of front lawn carefully mowed on the weekends. Threatening anonymous letters are pushed into our letter box warning us about the black cattle dog we have brought with us from Redfern, until one day he disappears altogether.

I wish I had never taken my grandmother's money to buy a stranger's house full of tasteless furniture. I hate the cut moquette lounge suite, the polished veneer sideboard, the inevitable chrome smoker's stand. I miss Redfern, I miss the life and the talk and the easy friendliness. Times are hard, but there is nobody here to care or bring you a plate of soup if you are starving. Les has lost his job, the gas and the electricity are about to be cut off, and I am pregnant again. We fight bitterly, sell the house and part.

But by the end of the winter we are back together again, with a new baby, in Railway Parade, Rockdale, an old weatherboard riddled with white ants and borers, facing the railway line on the flight path to Mascot Aerodrome. From the front verandah the horizon stretches away towards the flat, dull waters of Botany Bay. The thin plume of the Bunnerong smokestack hangs motionless in the air. A plane glints and turns on its approach to the runway. The electric trains rush by carrying the packed commuters towards Central. The steam trains rock the rails in a smother of smoke and fury. The redwood house shakes and trembles in a continual ague. When the wind blows off the bay, a huge coconut palm in the front yard makes a melancholy scraping in the gutters.

We decide to renovate, pulling down interior walls, prising up rotten floorboards, throwing out the borer-ridden but rather beautiful remnants of the original Victorian furniture. For months I balance precariously on planks across gaping chasms, a baby on one hip; cook on a double-burner primus; hold up new Gyprock ceilings till my arms ache; shovel terrible mountains of wet concrete through windows from the Readymix truck in the driveway. The white ants click away in unison. Out in the back yard, a blunt-nosed grub bores holes in the yellow cassia.

Finally it is ready. The wind sweeps down the wide passageway where every wall is a 'feature' – mountain blue, deep red, the colours clash like the gaps in our lives. Unshaded light globes, uncurtained windows – the house screams with light. There is no place to hide. The furniture is strictly utilitarian: a Laminex kitchen table, chrome kitchen chairs, pine divan beds, pine and burnie-board wardrobes with sliding doors that stick and tear out our fingernails. The living-room chairs are constructed of welded pipes upholstered in red vinyl, a praying mantis light curving over each one.

On the front verandah, supported by bright yellow welded pipes, we watch the Queen and the Duke glide by like white dolls, waving from the front platform of the Royal train. Across the night sky Sputnik moves serenely amongst the stars. The Russian tanks roll into Hungary, Khrushchev exposes Stalin's crimes to the Twentieth Congress, I face the Petrov Commission as a ludicrous, suspected spy, pregnant again.

Two cats and a spotted, half fox-terrier, half cattle-dog pup adopt us. We live in that house for five years, skidding on the hard, bright surfaces until we crackle with madness. Next door, in the front garden, the neighbours are building a helicopter, but it never gets off the ground. On the other side a man in a white singlet mows the lawns every Saturday while a fat, desexed bitch runs up and down on an iron chain. The traffic rushes through Five Ways. The plastic banners snap in the wind over the crowded second-hand-car yards. The children careen down the hill on their toy cars and scooters, while their father paces the hall all night whispering in his two voices, 'Shall I kill her tonight or tomorrow?' I sit huddled on the front step under the shadow of the coconut palm in my balding fur fabric, seriously contemplating suicide again.

Down the slope from the railway station, the sunflowers flash gold against a crumbling wall and I know it is time to go. Secretly, I pick the children up from school. Les Flood lies unaware in the front bedroom behind the new Venetian blinds reading the *Sydney Morning Herald*. We leave in the clothes we stand up in, flying incognito along the Great Australian Bight, curling cobalt blue at the foot of the Nullarbor cliffs, all my card houses collapsing behind me.

Years later, I catch the train at Central ... Tempe, Cook's River, Arncliffe, Rockdale, the railway bridge, the slope running down beside the railway line. I close my eyes. If I open them, will I see him standing under the coconut palm, the half fox-terrier dog at his feet, the crazy house he built at his back?

I look up – a white block of concrete flats – and I am one of the anonymous faces in the train window passing by ... passing ...

And the house opposite the wire factory? I can't even remember the name of the street any more.

12

S0, in a brown corduroy slack suit, with cropped hair and a new name – Toddy Flood – I cross the continent to Sydney, the Big Smoke, the fabulous city. Carrying all my life in one battered suitcase, I stand mesmerized under the smeared dome of Central Station, clanging with timetable directions, the rush of electric trains, the echo of footsteps.

Playing pontoon and poker across the desert with a couple of travelling jackeroos, we had seen the Aborigines in filthy rags scavenging like dogs in the red dust for scraps of bread and meat thrown out by the Trans-train cook. We had stayed in a damp stone slum in Adelaide City Square with a violent Communist couple who staggered home drunk from the pub every night. We had sat at the foot of a giant blonde Queenslander's bed while she reminisced about her hero, Jack Henry, who had been one of the leaders in the 1935 cane cutters' strike in North Queensland. I remembered Jack Henry in the Party rooms in Perth guffawing over a parody of Jean Devanney's novel, *Sugar Heaven*. 'Would you like to come into the movement?' he'd said, doubling up with laughter.

As I read 'Arvie Aspinall' aloud from Henry Lawson's Short Stories, it dawned on me that this fortyish, six-foot blonde had been Les Flood's former mistress in Adelaide. I imagined him perched between the trunks of her legs like Jiminy Cricket and felt a fastidious revulsion.

'You never even bothered to say "Goodbye" or "Up your arse" before you shot through,' she said. 'Ah well. Take your little *Star* and go – and good luck.'

At the railway station, I was taken aside by a young journalist from the Adelaide Communist newspaper: 'Is it too late to go back?'

'Too late,' I said gaily.

'You poor little mug,' he said. 'You haven't got a clue what you're letting yourself in for, have you?'

In Melbourne, in agony from another cystitis attack, I called into the Medical School to see a sad and disapproving Lesley. 'It's named the "honeymooner's disease",' she told me.

And now the winter dusk is drawing in as we trudge, travel-weary, up Elizabeth Street, looking for a place to spend the night. Muffled figures pass on the pavement; trams clatter past with a conductor hanging perilously over the footboard; newsboys, with their strange flat guttural argot, dart in and out through streams of traffic, dingy shops, greasy cafés – can this be Bill Hart-Smith's city of my dreams?

We book a room in Mansion House from a shifty-eyed clerk under a green eyeshade. On the wall, facing the sagging double bed, somebody has drawn the crude outline of a nude with no head, but all the basic anatomical details of her sex marked by arrows. Next to it a sign says, 'Warning – keep this door bolted at all times', but the bolt has been forced long ago. The walls reach up only three-quarters of the way, the rest is netted in with wire, leaving the bare minimum of privacy.

We have a cheap, overcooked meal in the greasy café downstairs, where a big drunk with malevolent eyes lurches across our table and out the door. Les puts the salt and pepper shakers into his pocket. 'Might come in handy,' he grins.

That night he goes off to his union meeting to pick up news about the job situation. Our funds are dangerously low already. I sit in the ugly little room shivering while a drunk with the DTs and a cut-throat razor foams up and down the hall, threatening to do himself in, or anybody else who gets in the way. When I can't stand it any longer I creep out into the streets, trying to memorize the landmarks, window-shopping like any country bumpkin outside the big department stores.

A middle-aged man comes up behind me. 'Hello, dear, and how are you getting on these days?'

I turn and stare at him. 'I'm sorry . . .'

'Now where was it we met?' he says. 'I'm trying to remember . . .'

So am I, but without success. 'I just can't remember you at all,' I tell him apologetically.

'Where was it?' He seems genuinely puzzled.

'Perth?' I suggest, trying to be helpful.

'Perth – that was it.' He is delighted. 'And how do you like the bright lights?'

'I've just arrived tonight,' I say, 'off the Trans-train.'

'We'll have to take you out on the town, then, show you the sights.'

We are walking side by side, chatting amicably.

'Where are you staying?'

'Mansion House. You know, it's funny, I've got a good memory for faces but I can't place you.'

'Bill,' he says. 'You remember Bill?'

As we turn into Elizabeth Street, I decide to be hospitable. 'Would you like to come up for a coffee?'

His face lights up like a neon sign.

'My husband should be back from his union meeting by now,' I say. 'I'm sure he'd like to meet . . .' I stop. My new-found friend has melted into the shadows.

I climb upstairs and tell Les all about it. 'I don't understand it,' I say. 'He just disappeared.'

Les stares at me, incredulous and furious. 'I turn my back for two minutes and you're out on the make,' he says bitterly, getting into bed and turning his face to the wall.

I cry and cry until he turns back again.

'Listen,' he says. 'Wake up to yourself. Nobody can be as green as all that and survive in a big city.'

'I thought he really must know me,' I whisper miserably.

Next day we report to Marx House and I stand outside gazing up in awe at the many-storeyed office building with the hammer and sickle displayed prominently on the side. 'Communism in three years,' echoes the voice of Ernie Campbell, and my heart lifts and sings. Maybe the Yank tourist had been right; maybe the Commies *are* taking over Australia.

Len Donald, a thin dyspeptic-looking man in his mid forties with sucked-in cheeks and nicotine-stained fingers, greets us affably in the office of the Sydney District Committee. It is a good sign. He is married to Sam Aarons's sister. Perhaps, then, Sam hasn't carried out his threat to blacken my name in the party all over Australia.

'I want to work in the worst factory in Sydney,' I tell Len Donald earnestly.

He gives me a sardonic smile. I think he believes I must be pulling his leg. 'Why?' he says.

'I want to go where the conditions are really bad, so that I can do something about them.'

'Ever worked in a factory before, Comrade?'

'No, never.'

'So you're totally unskilled?'

'Yes, I am.'

'I believe there's always jobs going at the Alexandria Spinning Mills. You could try there, but I've heard it's a pretty tough place.'

'That's what I want,' I say, the feather bobbing on my green velvet cap.

He watches me thoughtfully from his desk with a puzzled frown as I go triumphantly down in the lift, a lamb to the slaughter. The new life is beginning. I will proletarianize myself. I will be a heroine of the Marxist Revolution, I will be rehabilitated in the eyes of the Party and the working class.

'He seemed a nice sort of a bloke,' I say.

'He couldn't keep his eyes off you,' Les grumbles. 'They don't get many girls who look like that comin' in here.'

Next day we shift into a tiny room, two narrow single beds and no space to swing a cat, seven storeys up with no lift, in Kings Cross. Les gets a start as a boilermaker/welder at Cockatoo Docks in Balmain and I become a trainee rover in the Alexandria Spinning Mills, a black hellhole of flying wool dust and grinding metal. For two days I am apprenticed to old Bet, a fat fiftyish spinster in a filthy overall with a face like a good-humoured currant bun, then the coal strike paralyses Sydney and we are both locked out – and almost penniless.

One night we pack our bags again and catch the train to Rockdale.

'Ma'll give us a shakedown until we get on our feet again,' Les says. He knocks on the front door of a prim little brick semi with a square of lawn out front. A small, neat woman in curlers and a pastel cardigan stands in the square of light from the hall. 'Goodday, Ma,' he says. There is no embrace.

'The police have been here looking for you,' she says. 'I told them you were interstate.'

'Good,' he grins. 'Ma's been well trained,' he tells me.

Clarice Flood lives with her unmarried daughter, Claire, in the house the whole family has scrimped and saved to buy for her; so squeaky clean it is intimidating. 'A place for everything and everything in its place,' she says, her mouth pinned tight against her soft oval face, her mousy, greying hair confined under a fine hairnet. It is a typical, respectable working-class house with a Cosy stove, a day bed, Venetian blinds and a strip of floral carpet. We take over Les's adopted brother's bed, leaving him to grumble on the day bed in the lounge, and every night, naked in each other's arms, have to muffle our cries against the censorious ears.

I know they don't approve of me. I am something absolutely outside their range of experience. Claire, in her pastel twinsets and tweed skirts, works as a clerk in the city; Clarice in the carpet factory at Mark Foy's Department Store. The adopted brother, Paul, is apprenticed to a furniture factory. I think they believe they might be stuck with us, feckless and broke, forever. 'We don't use each other's flannels and face towels in this house,' Clarice says. 'If you don't have your own things, you only have to say.'

We try to keep out of the way as much as we can. Every morning we have Bonox for breakfast and then catch the train into Redfern to the Henry Lawson Memorial Hall, where the South Sydney Coal Strike Committee has its headquarters. We lunch at the same soup kitchen that has been set up to feed the unemployed. At night we either have dinner with a charitable comrade or sometimes go without. I can remember going down the stairs past a hamburger bar, faint with hunger at the smell of onions and mince. Because I can type, after a fashion, I have been given the job of typing the stencils for the Party leaflets on an ancient Remington set up in a sympathizers' house close by. The sympathizers are an old illiterate couple with a slow-learner, hunchbacked son and a screeching white cockatoo. It is like a low-life scene out of a Dickens novel. Day after day I sit there typing, sucking a lemon to settle my queasy stomach, while the hunchback capers and the bobbing cockatoo screams 'Dance, cocky dance' in my ear. I am pregnant again. The usual all-day morning sickness is just beginning, and I have mixed feelings about a baby. What will happen to us in Sydney with no job, no money, and nowhere to live?

Sometimes, for a change, I go out on the soup truck or wood delivery. It is a bitter Sydney winter and most of the workforce are locked out of the factories. There is a fuel shortage and anyway, nobody has any money to buy wood or coke. Redfern always lives pretty close to the poverty line. It only needs a coal strike to tip it over the edge.

We pull up at the end of the street, and women and children come out with basins and billies held out for food like the hunger queues in the Depression. I have never seen anything like it. As the weeks go by, apathy gives way to real anger. When we speak about the strike from the back of the truck, calling on Redfern to show its solidarity with the miners, women scream at us, throw basins of water from upstairs windows and ring cowbells to drown out our voices.

As I go from door to door, putting leaflets in the letter boxes, a huge woman with meaty arms chases me down the street screaming, 'Red bitch! Red bitch!' At weekends I sit out in the thin winter sunlight in the back yard at Rockdale and read *The Poor Man's Orange*, Ruth Park's novel about slum life in Surry Hills, serialized in the *Sydney Morning Herald*. Sometimes we make golden-syrup sandwiches and wander along the foreshores of Botany Bay, hand in hand, sitting on the cold strip of sand listening to the bay water lapping at our feet.

We are called in for an interview at Marx House with the head of the Party Control Commission, Wally Clayton, who will later became notorious in the newspaper headlines as the mysterious Comrade X in the Petrov Spy Trials. After that he disappeared into political oblivion and became a fisherman at Nambucca Heads, but now, here he is staring at me coldly over his bifocals, dismissing me with a few contemptuous words. It is obvious that he has Sam Aarons's report open on the desk in front of him. He calls Les back for some good advice. 'You can't possibly believe she'll stay with you, Comrade, a bourgeoise woman like that, who's deserted her husband and child. She's just a flash in the pan.'

From then on Les often calls me 'Flash'. 'I love the way you stick by me,' he says. But he doesn't know about my secret temptations, and I can't bear to tell him. I have never seen myself as a particularly maternal woman. I have opted for lover rather than child, but I have forgotten to take my own female biology into account. Every time I see a child in the street or a baby in a pram, I turn my eyes away. My mother writes to tell me how Clancy has run after a blonde girl in the street calling out, 'Mummy! Mummy!'

Maybe, also, I am finding the going too tough. I am pregnant and hungry and sick with longing for Clancy. Who is this man who wraps his body around mine every night in a borrowed single bed? Passionate, but without tenderness, love for him is always something for the dark. 'Tell me something nice,' I beg him, and he answers 'chocolates and ice cream' or 'words are cheap' or 'love is a fuck'.

Who can I really talk to? He is like a member of another tribe. There are no trimmings, there is no time for gentleness. He doesn't read books, only Marxist paperbacks. He knows no poetry, nothing about painting or the theatre. He has a marvellously quick intelligence but he left school at thirteen, and was apprenticed as a boiler-maker during the Depression. His father, a member of International Workers of the World, gassed himself in his early twenties, leaving Clarice to survive on the widow's pension with four small children to support. How can I live in this world? Perhaps Wally Clayton is right and I am only a flash in the pan. Yet it is only one moment that tips the balance. As we sit under the pines at Manly Beach, a small blond boy races across the sand, laughing under a dark sky, and the tears rain down my face.

That night I write to Lesley telling her I can't live without Clancy and I will have to go home to Perth. My family doesn't hesitate. Within days my mother and Lesley are at the Metropole Hotel in Sydney, my air fare ready and waiting. I confess to Les. I explain everything and he is extraordinarily supportive. We've tried and we've failed. If I can't live without the child, if I have to go, then that's it.

Miserably, I pack my bag. 'What's going to happen to our baby?' he says.

I stare out at the dreary street. I can't look at him. 'I suppose I'll have an abortion.'

'I'll call you a cab from the box on the corner,' he says, 'then I won't be here to see you go. There are some things I *can't* stand.'

I cling to him. 'I love you, I'll always love you.'

He tears his mouth away, turns and walks out.

'Les,' I call after him.

He looks back.

'Don't forget me.'

'That's not likely,' he says. Then he moves his hand in a half salute and is gone through the lace curtains.

I watch him walk away, squaring his shoulders. I want to call him back, but it's no use. Stiffly, I sit down on the edge of the bed. I feel cold. In a little while the cab driver will blow his horn. I climb into the cab and catch the train at Rockdale station. As it draws away I see him walking with a group of other men along the road beside the railway line, the wintry sunlight catching the bright thatch of his hair.

Toorak was another country, a million miles from Redfern, where my parents had rented a luxurious house in a Melbourne garden full of English trees and cherry blossom. After my grandmother died they had moved from Perth to Melbourne, to provide a home for Lesley while she studied for her medical degree at Melbourne University.

I lived in that house, amongst the heavy antique furniture, like an invalid, treated with tact and kindness, going for long solitary walks in the rain, trying to come to terms with the wreckage of my life. Taking the plunge before I lost my courage, I had rung Lloyd on the night I arrived from Sydney, asking him could I come home again, but he had been – understandably – less than enthusiastic. He was not prepared to take up our life together again. As I walked through the Melbourne drizzle, I was trying to decide – would I go back to Perth, have Les's baby, face all the scandal and see Clancy when and where I could? Would I have an abortion? Would I stay in Melbourne? As I came in through the French doors in a swirl of muddy white petals, a heavy blow struck me in the middle of my spine, forcing me to my knees. My mother found me there on the carpet, bleeding, and called the ambulance.

I lie in the Queen Victoria Hospital next to a pudgy teenager who has swallowed pills, jumped off walls, stabbed herself with knitting needles – anything to get rid of an unwanted pregnancy. Now she is trapped, brought in by ambulance, compelled to stay in the hospital ward until her baby is born. Perversely, now that I am losing my child all I want is to keep it. It is as if I am losing the last positive thing I can salvage from the ruins, the last thing nobody can take away from me.

'I wish all our mothers felt like you do,' says the woman doctor, 'but the fetus was really only a lump of gristle, dear, not much bigger than a blood clot. It could never have developed.'

This seems even more unbearable – the only residue from our passionate love affair is a deformed lump of dead tissue.

I try to talk to my father about it all. 'Promise me you won't do anything without telling me first,' he says.

I promise, but almost immediately I am using a boyfriend of the girl in the next bed to send an urgent telegram to Les: 'Lost baby in Queen Victoria Hospital. Please come. All my love, Toddy' . . . and miraculously, within a day, there he is walking down the ward, laughing, holding me in his arms. He has borrowed the money from his brother and flown straight to Melbourne.

I left the hospital with Les, feeling fragile but determined. We spent the night in a Melbourne hotel, the lobby twittering with delegates to a Country Women's Association Conference. Amongst that respectable, concerted throng, I felt like a scarlet woman. Giggling, our arms tightly round each other, we raced upstairs. 'You've grown so little,' he whispered, hugging me naked in bed.

I had to go back next morning and face the family. My father, furiously disappointed, refused to speak to me. 'He thinks you broke your word,' my mother said. 'You promised you'd do nothing until you'd discussed it with him.'

A telegram arrived from Lloyd. He'd changed his mind and wanted me to come home. 'Too late,' I wired back. It was all too late. There could be no turning back now, even for a lost child. For better or worse I had finally burnt my boats. I was no flash in the pan.

In my moss-green velvet suit with the green Robin Hood cap, the feather on it almost touching the roof of the plane, I flew back to Sydney. Spring was in the air and the factories were open again. Prime Minister Ben Chifley, the pipe-smoking ex-engine driver, had frozen the union funds, brought out the troops and smashed the coal strike.

And so we came to Moncur Street to live on the second floor, back with Aime and Alf and Ollie Tilley and Mr Smitherson, the lodger who shot through without paying but left his ration coupons behind. He was soon replaced by Olga, the blonde New Australian who farewelled her lovers on the landing in the dawn and wrestled with Alf in the back yard on the way to the outside toilet.

It's twenty years ago and more
since first I came to Moncur Street,
and lived with Aime and Alf among
the boarders on the second floor.
The stew was burnt, the budgie sang,
as Aime walked home the church-bells rang
she banged the pots, ring-ding-a-ding,
she'd lost at Housie in the spring.

Les went back to Cockatoo Docks and I got back my job at the mill, running down Oxford Street before the cold first light to catch Lowe's bus on the corner.

On Friday nights, when we met on the steps of the post office in Martin Place, he always bought me a bunch of violets and we strolled hand in hand through the city, admiring the window-dressers' displays in the big stores – Farmer's, David Jones, Mark Foy's. During the rest of the week I always got home before him, passing the old men playing draughts in the last of the thin spring sunshine in Centennial Square, flinging myself down exhausted on the double bed to wait for his step on the stair. Sometimes I would fall asleep to be wakened by his heavy shoulders and muscly body covering mine. Afterwards we would lie together in lazy contentment under the shadow of the crepe myrtle outside the open window until Aime called us down to dinner and we had to race under the shower, arriving at the table with glowing faces and lowered eyes, still smelling of love. If Aime was in a good mood, she would reminisce about her girlhood and bring out the snapshots and the family album: mythical figures in shady hats and muslin dresses, celluloid collars and high-crowned Akubra hats, standing dimly in the main street of *Sunny Corner*. But if she had lost at Housie, she banged the pots querulously and jabbed at Alf who, at seventy-two, still worked in a butcher's shop in Oxford Street.

'Alfie always goes to bed with the chooks,' Aime would say contemptuously, hinting darkly at the goings-on between her husband and Ollie Tilley. Ollie had come to stay uninvited and littered the lounge room with trunks full of ragged, beaded georgette dresses, rolled and laddered silk stockings and jazz garters from the twenties. She was the daughter of a bankrupt Chinese businessman who had known Alf in the old days. Her English mother had recently died in their rented house in Redfern and Ollie was too afraid to stay there alone.

'She's got a bad conscience,' said Aime. 'Everybody knows she starved her old mother to death in that house in Marriott Street. Mean as cat shit. No wonder she don't want to stay there on her own any more. It's poor old Mrs Tilley's ghost that's tapping on her winders. Now there was a real lady, but how she ever come to bring herself to marry that Chinaman . . . Ugh! He was an ugly old thing . . . and yeller, yeller as a sunflower.'

A travesty of a woman with a chiffon scarf draped over her bald head, Ollie was always threatening to throw herself over the Gap at Watson's Bay.

'Ah! She's a bad egg, that one, and she's always been keen on Alfie,' said Aime, her little plump body shaking with malicious mirth.

After dinner, Les and I would set off for the wilderness of

Centennial Park, the ponds overgrown with weed, the statues of Diana and Henry Parkes and Hercules, with their lost arms and verdigris stains, standing like ghosts under the Moreton Bay fig trees. It was a melancholy place in the evenings when the ducks rose whirring and crying from the reeds and old derros lay clasping their meths bottles in the shadows.

We would come back to our room, past the deserted kitchen with mosquito netting over the breakfast dishes and the cover over the budgies' cage, to lie in bed listening to Ollie Tilley's fingers, rustling like mice through her father's useless papers, and Alfie's home brew exploding under the stairs.

On Saturdays Aime's ex-star boarder Sammy Smiles, a retired policeman, arrived to sit smiling blandly in the kitchen, while her hard-bitten daughter Beat 'ran a book' and little Fay, the granddaughter, whined interminably in the stairwell. Escaping from Moncur Street, leaving them to argue over the relative merits of Sydney jockeys Georgie Moore and the immortal Darby Munro, we would buy a bag of bananas and a bag of chocolate roughs and walk miles to Watson's Bay, passing the lighthouse and the notorious Gap, the favourite suicide spot for Sydneysiders, with the Pacific foaming at the foot of the cliffs, and I would remember Christina Stead's *Seven Poor Men of Sydney*.

Sometimes we would thread our way through Darlinghurst, Wooloomooloo and Surry Hills, where foxy-faced men sat on the front step in their shirtsleeves reading the weekend papers and pale, dirty children bounced rubber balls through the rubbish blowing down the dismal streets. These were the slums of Sydney, and to me they represented a landscape of horror. The shabby terraces of Paddington and Woollahra were palaces compared to this mean, dingy wasteland that surrounded the inner city.

Once we went to the Tivoli to see the last of the fabled Mo, clown-faced and lascivious, still performing before an audience who loved him.

Les took me to visit his cousins, Betty and Rex Maguire, who lived with their new baby at Brighton-Le-Sands on the shores of Botany Bay. First cousins, who had married each other in spite of dire family predictions, they were struggling hard to own their own red-brick bungalow, with Venetian blinds at the windows and Feltex on the floors. Betty was a tall, good-humoured girl with prominent teeth and long marvellous legs, who never stopped talking. Rex, who had been in the Occupation Forces in Japan, was a rangy giant who drove a wheat truck for a living. Of all Les's relatives they were the only ones who became my friends, the only ones who ever made me feel welcome.

'She looks like Roma, Les,' said Betty, looking me up and down. 'Look, Rex, blonde hair and all, isn't she just like Roma? She even talks like her. She'll be good for you, Les.'

I'd heard about Roma, Les's favourite elder sister, who'd lived only long enough to take his hand in the public ward after a botched abortion. Eerily, Les had even brought me her old dresses and shoes to wear, but only the shoes fitted.

'Les and Roma, they were always together,' Betty told me. 'He was different with her. She made him laugh. She even taught him to dance. They were the smart ones in the family. We expected them to do great things. It broke his heart when she died and he never forgave Auntie Clarice for it.'

I had heard the whole novelettish story of Roma – how she had a good working-class boyfriend, but Clarice, who was always bitterly opposed to any of her children marrying, encouraged her to go out with this rich young man who abandoned her – pregnant. She told nobody, but after the abortion she was found bleeding to death in a cheap hotel room. Les, called home on compassionate leave from the air force in New Guinea, arrived in time to say goodbye.

His family history was full of these tragedies, beginning with George Blood, the radical leather worker who liked to sing music-hall songs in the pubs and wanted to call his sons Lenin and Trotsky, but Clarice rebelled, so he finally settled for Les (after Les Darcy, the famous Australian fighter) and Len (without the Lenin).

All Clarice's brothers, the Maguire clan, went off to the First World War, but George Blood was a member of International Workers of the World (the Wobblies), went to the Socialist Sunday School, and refused to fight in an imperialist war. Labelled 'shirker' and 'red ragger', he was given the white feather. Blackballed for his union activities, he set himself up in a leather goods shop in Oxford Street and made a Globite case to put on display in the front window.

The manufacturers sued him for breach of patent. Heavily insured, he set fire to the shop, the children escaping in their pyjamas over the rooftops. Les could remember his father helping them through the skylight, and how exciting it was with the sparks flying and the crowd in the street below. With the proceeds George rented a huge, run-down rooming house in Paddington and advertised 'Rooms to let for the working man', but it was the Depression, so nobody came. The rooms, denuded of the furniture seized by his creditors, echoed with a funereal emptiness. One night, coming home drunk from the pub, he laid himself out on the kitchen floor, spread-eagled, a child on each arm, a child on each leg. 'They have crucified me,' he said, and went up the stairs, crammed newspapers under the doors and windows, and turned on the gas jets. He was twenty-three years old. Les could remember him disappearing into the light at the top of the stairs.

Clarice had married him when she was pregnant with her first child. They had met in Centennial Park where George, resplendent in white flannels, played cricket every Sunday afternoon. 'Ma knew what he was going to do, but she didn't try to stop him,' Les said. He hadn't forgiven her for that either.

Clarice Maguire was an orphan, the youngest child of a large Catholic family with a dead mother and a father presumed dead, who had disappeared following the superphosphate trade to the Islands. The eldest brother and sister, still in their teens, took over the burden of raising the family. The Maguires had never approved of George Blood. He was a 'Wobbly' and they were followers of Jack Lang, the Labor Party demagogue, but they rallied round and shifted Clarice and the children to a cheaper house in Tempe. She fostered found-ling children and they all starved together on the foundlings' pittance and the widows' pension. Her elder, unmarried sister Ivy, who worked as a domestic, came to live with them and shared her meagre wages and any pickings from the houses of the rich. When the children started school, Clarice didn't like the way the other kids taunted them, calling them 'Bloody', so she changed their name to Flood. She had never set eyes on her husband's family since his suicide. Perhaps they blamed her for it.

Half the Maguires were Protestant and half were Catholic. Ivy shepherded the children off to Mass and they spent their school years seesawing between the convent and the state school until Ivy lost her faith and started buying the Communist *Tribune*. She married in her late forties, a night-watchman who had belonged to the Fascist New Guard in the Depression, and every week he used to burn her *Tribune* under the wood copper in the wash house.

Bloods, Floods, Maguires – all genuine, poverty-stricken Austral-ian working class of Irish descent, and I am the interloper amongst these pedigreed poor, condemned to pay penance for the sins of my birth, where the mills of Alexandria grind slow and exceeding small.

I work a forty-five-hour week – five hours' compulsory overtime – for £8; often not even that, because if I am five minutes late I am docked fifteen minutes by order of the bundy at the gate. As we eat our lunch, sitting out in the concrete yard, the cyclone-wire fence pressing its pattern into our shoulder blades, I try to raise the consciousness of my fellow workers. 'Get off your soapbox, Skin,' they call good-naturedly.

Since the coal strike and the lockout, the Communist Party isn't too popular in the mills. It's put them too far behind. Besides, the older hands remember the war years when waves of strikers were sold out by the Commos – patriots who were more interested in keeping up production levels for the war against Fascism than fighting for the mill workers' wages.

I have become the delegate on the job for a vicious, right-wing union who meet only once a year and if the rank and file are seen at the union meeting, immediately report them back to the boss.

I spend five days out of every week with the female lumpen-proletariat of Sydney, a group of workers unorganized and unknown to the cadres of the Communist Party. I roughen my accent ('Are you a Pommy or somethin'?'), disguise my handwriting ('You're very handy with the pen there, luv'), and discuss Bing Crosby, Frankie Sinatra, *True Love Stories*, sex, husbands, men, dirty postcards, comics, contraception, pregnancy, kids, dirty jokes, false teeth, the latest song hits, the ills of the flesh (female), and the old maid in Marrickville with the big Alsatian dog who gave birth to triplets with dog heads but it was all hushed up and they had to be quietly destroyed. Not much chance of masterminding the Revolution in the Alexandria Spinning Mills, nor of selling the *Tribune*, but I learn to know them all – old Bet, old Lil and Jessie, Julie, Shirl, Dawnie, Al, Beryl, Pattie, Jeannie, Gwennie, Val, Bonus Happy Maise, Curly the Horse, Greenie the leading hand, Dick the pannikin boss, Kenny his off-sider and Creeky the right-wing union organizer.

It is our fabulous year and I don't even recognize it.

'What do you and hubby do on the weekends, Skin?'

'Oh, we go walking.'

'Walking! Christ, you'll soon get over that caper when the first kid comes along.'

Australia seems to be going backwards. Menzies has invented a new name for the Conservatives, and his Liberal Party has defeated Labor in the December elections. But the Revolution is spreading throughout the world – the Chinese People's Republic has been proclaimed in Peking, the German Democratic Republic has split Germany in two. Only in Yugoslavia are there signs of dissension. The Yugoslavs have been expelled from the Cominform for hostility towards the USSR; Titoism is a dirty word. Remembering those hot summer days in Jandakot when Lloyd and I borrowed his mother's car and drove from vineyard to vineyard, sitting out under the vine trellises drinking red wine and toasting Stalin and Tito with the

Yugoslav vignerons, I wonder what has gone wrong. I don't recognize the first chill wind blowing across that pure, passionate Marxism of the forties. 'You're such a kid. What a pity it is that you have to grow up,' Les tells me.

In the summer holidays we escape to the South Coast, camping in a valley behind a beach under an overhang of black mountains. I am delighted to be two months pregnant, but the usual all-day nausea has begun. After a week of swimming in the surf I am cured. Les sets up our tent under the giant tree ferns and makes us a bed out of bush wood. The whipbirds crack overhead, at night the summer rain drums on the canvas and we wake to the chime of bellbirds, the whole valley steaming. It is like a short spell in Eden.

'You're starting to show, love,' say the girls back at the mill, as I sweat and strain over the spindles. Aime is worried. She doesn't want to be unkind, but she can't have another baby in the house. The young couple with the baby in the top flat are more than enough and *they* have a kitchenette, but her yard is always full of drying nappies and she can't get near her own copper. The housing shortage in Sydney is acute and nobody wants babies. 'Them Bondi sandhills,' mourns Alf, 'I could have bought them for a song.'

In the evenings we walk through the street, gazing in at the doors of lighted houses, so many of them. Surely there must be one somewhere in this teeming city to shelter us – but we can never find it. We catch the train to Redfern to see Jack Beasley, the red-headed district organizer. He knows about two top rooms in a half-ruined terrace. We might be able to move in there, but the stairs are out and you have to swarm up and down on a dangling rope. We all gaze dubiously at my swelling belly under the blue pleated maternity dress, and wordlessly decide it just isn't practical.

We wander along the ocean front at La Perouse gazing in at the homes of the cave dwellers cut out of the rock face, with geranium window boxes, and fantasize about moving in there, with a curtain of spray lashing outside the front door. But soon afterwards they are all moved out by order of the Council.

'Ol's got that house in Redfern still, lying there empty. You'll never go back there, will you, Ol? Worse luck!' says Aime bitterly over the dinner table. 'It's a crying shame.'

But Ollie is terrified of the landlord's No Subletting clause.

'If she's not willing to give it up she can go back there, and good riddance,' says Aime savagely. 'It's your job to tell her, Alf. She's *your* girlfriend.'

So Ollie is blackballed into surrendering the keys of the kingdom and Alf cracks open a bottle of home brew to celebrate. 'Les, Toddy, how about a noggin? Best brew I ever put up. Absolutely scarlet nonpareil. Aime, Ol, bottoms up!'

We moved into 165 Marriott Street, Redfern – four rooms and a lean-to scullery – one autumn evening under cover of darkness. We knew about Redfern's reputation – a ghetto for thieves, no-hopers and standover men. 'You can't live there,' said Clarice. 'Even in the worst times we never sank as low as Redfern. Why don't you look for something respectable in Newtown?'

'Don't open the door till I get home,' Les warns me. 'I'll give three knocks.'

He is working late on overtime at Cockatoo Docks. Night falls, the rain drips despondently off the slate roof into the weedy front garden. Three taps on the door and I fly to open it. A mumbling figure, sodden with booze and rain, stumbles across the threshold, reaching out for me. 'How y' goin', luv?' With one huge thrust of my belly I drive him skidding along the wet brick path, the momentum carrying him through the iron gate in Chaplinesque dance, to crumple up in a dishevelled heap in the gutter. 'Fuckin' lovely,' he mutters sadly, 'fuckin' lovely!' I slam the door, shoot the bolt and, leaning against the jamb, burst into tears.

A week later I see a shabby old alcoholic shambling past the house with red eyes averted. My night caller – who is he? 'Oh! him,' says May Webb, ex-Salvation Army lassie, now secretary of the Redfern Tenants' Protection Society. 'He's a poor harmless old thing, used to be the boyfriend of the woman who lived there – probably got drunk and forgot she'd moved away.'

Ollie Tilley's lover – who would ever have thought it? I feel ashamed. I should have asked the poor old bugger in for a cup of tea.

After this tragicomic interlude it seems ridiculous to feel frightened in Redfern. It is just another place, a network of sad, inner-suburban streets in a big city, but kinder than most, with a strange, fierce loyalty to itself, a real sense of community. We begin to fit in. We are accepted as Redfernites. We are safely buried amongst the masses who have nothing to lose but their chains. Thrown out with the rubbish in Aime's wash house in Moncur Street I had found an old paperback of Louis Stone's *Jonah*, and read it, enthralled, never having even heard of it before. I read Kylie Tennant, Eleanor Dark, and Ruth Park. I enter the comic world of Lennie Lower. I can recite whole sections of Slessor's *Five Bells* off by heart. Sydney is becoming once again for me the legendary city, but so different to the fantasy I had dreamt about in Western Australia.

I am creating another city for myself with its own geography and its own stories: a city of the poor and dispossessed, a city of struggle, with its smoky towers rising up through the harsh, discordant cries of paper boys, flower sellers, barrow men, and the murmuring voices of lovers.

'How do you know you'll always love me?'

'I know.'

'But how?'

'It's me form, that's all.'

But there is always a worm in the bud. 'I feel embarrassed walking down the street with you,' he says.

'Why?'

'I feel as if we've both got a sign on our backs a mile wide.'

'What kind of sign?'

'Yours says "I have been fucked" and mine says "I am the fucker".'

We buy a huge old Silver Anniversary Buick from the back yard of a second-hand-junk shop in Crown Street and christen it General Montgomery's Tank. In the crisp autumn mornings before the smog settles down, I run clumsily down the hill to catch Lowe's bus at the stop outside the Glassie, topple over and fall flat on the bitumen, knocking all the breath out of my body. I sit in the middle of the road, grizzling, nursing my grazed knee, trying to decide whether to take out another sickie. Les drives the Buick down Marriott Street, towards the Balmain dockyards, running on petrol, kerosene and hope, into an uncertain future.

CHAPTER

13

♠

I was sacked from the Alexandria Spinning Mills for being eight months pregnant, but before I left I managed two quixotic gestures. I stood up at the annual meeting of the Textile Workers' Union and demanded equal pay for women workers. There was a bit of a furore, they moved a point of order, and that was the end of it. I organized the Redfern branch of the Communist Party to Roneo and distribute a bulletin called 'Bobbin Up' outside the mill. The leading article began with Les Flood's immortal words: 'There's a name for a man who lives off women'.

At 6.30 in the morning Carol Jackson stood at the mill gates bundled up in her old overcoat with the ratty fur collar. Some of the women carried the bulletin into the mill, others dropped it in the gutter where they stood.

'What's goin' on?' said the gatekeeper, his long, furtive face with the bead of snot on the end of his nose always poking into everybody's business but his own. Amused and curious, the women ignored him, as usual.

'How did they know so much about us?'

'Wake up to y'self,' said Shirl. 'It's an inside job.' She sat on the washroom floor, her back propped against a toilet bowl, blowing perfect smoke rings, her pencilled eyebrows eternally surprised. 'Don't s'pose you had anything to do with this, Skin?'

I looked innocent and she laughed. 'Ah! Well, we all know you're a bit of a commo.'

The management sent the peggy round to confiscate whatever copies he could find, but a few of them no doubt found their way into bags, tucked into copies of *True Romance* or hidden in bras, to be read in the lunch hour and then forgotten. The bulletin didn't start a stay-in strike at the mill, as I wrote nine years later in my novel *Bobbin Up*. That was wish-fulfilment, sitting in front of my second-hand Olivetti portable at the Laminex kitchen table in Rockdale, learning to be a writer again.

The first-aid Sister complained about me to the pannikin boss. 'It's embarrassing seeing someone in her condition working in the mill,' she said. 'Some of these girls have got no shame.'

'They're frightened you'll fall in the machine and bugger it up, luv,' said Jessie, tipping a large turd left by the night-shift women into the toilet. 'I like a clean joke,' she printed laboriously, propping the sign up above the spindles.

I left the mill and never saw any of them again. Unless you lived in the same place all your days, life was like that, divided up into compartments, particularly if you were a woman. It was easy to take on the protective colouring of a different man, a different name, a different city, harder to hang on to any real sense of your own identity. And anyway, there was something oddly exhilarating about the fresh start, unburdened, homeless, with no ties or possessions and a change of name. To be someone else opened up such giddy possibilities.

I had deliberately kept away from any literary associations in Sydney, even in the Party. Once, after I had written an article for the *Tribune* under the byline 'Toddy Flood', one of the reporters had stopped me in the corridor in Marx House. 'You write a bit like that West Australian writer, Dorothy Hewett, who used to have a column in the *Workers' Star*.'

I said nothing. It was years before anybody put the two names together, probably not until *Bobbin Up* blew my cover. Why was I so obsessed with anonymity? What had happened to the girl who once wanted to be as famous as Edith Sitwell and Sarah Bernhardt, to live in a great mansion called 'Fairhaven' with a red resting room? It was the opposite end of the spectrum, that was all, and I was always an extremist.

Before the 'cult of the individual' became a Communist Party slogan, I was a devotee of the death of the ego. The ego stood for all the negatives – selfishness, vanity, corruption, bourgeois individualism – therefore it must be rooted out and replaced by this selfless servant of masses. T. S. Eliot's line 'a condition of complete simplicity costing no less than everything' always appealed to some deeper religious sense in me, for although I had long since changed from agnostic to atheist, pacifist to militant revolutionary, the mainspring of my political belief was a utopian faith rather than any philosophical, scientific Marxism. I actually believed that Communism had saved my life. 'Teach me to feel and not to feel,' I had recited on the balcony of Mount Street Hospital – and into my life had come the theory of scientific socialism. So Marxism for me was a conversion, an act of personal salvation. The only difference was that I believed in a purely earthly heaven, a secular heaven called the Union of Soviet Socialist Republics.

I was already well on the way to becoming that most dangerous and humourless of creatures, a martyr to a cause. I actually wanted to suffer in the cause of the working class. But I couldn't help lingering in front of shop windows, lusting after the latest fashions. Soon it would be too late and I would be too old to wear them. But then I would dismiss these thoughts as unworthy, the last twitch of a buried self. And because I had unerringly chosen the one man who would join enthusiastically in the destruction of my ego, I was in dangerous and vulnerable position. On the other hand, I was probably lucky – only *in extremis* did I discover that ego intact and indestructible: only by going to the edge was it possible for me to find myself again.

But now, heavily pregnant, I went to Canberra, on a deputation for price control. Driving back late at night, exhausted, through the fog, I spoke passionately to a standing ovation at a Communist Conference on Working Women. I distributed leaflets for hours in Oxford Street with a bandage around my varicosed leg and built up a big *Tribune* round as far afield as Surry Hills. I collected signatures on the peace petition against the atomic bomb, a cause that had only recently surfaced amongst Australian radicals. Remembering my pacifist girlhood and *All Quiet on the Western Front*, I could easily identify with such a cause.

As a founder member of the Union of Australian Women, a Communist front organization replacing the old Housewives' Association, I was in charge of women's work in South Sydney, harrying the Party members' wives to become politically aware and active. It made me highly unpopular with their husbands. Feminism and the equality of women were not causes dear to the hearts of working-class Australian men, nor were they particularly popular in the male-dominated hierarchy of the Communist Party. Oh, they gave it lip service occasionally – some of them even read Engels on *Women and Communism*, with his concept of the working-class woman as a 'slave of a slave' – but male supremacy was alive and well amongst the higher and lower echelons of the Party.

I belonged to the Redfern Tenants' Protection League and in my bumbling, proselytizing innocence immediately made a complete fool of myself and a few more enemies for the Party. Discovering two young Aboriginal girls and their numerous bare-bottomed babies living in an appalling shack in Kettle Street with no electricity, no stove, no toilet and no running water, I brought out the *Tribune* photographer and wrote up the story. I did a good job. The girls were immediately shifted out to a Housing Commission Settlement in the western suburbs, but when I went round to Kettle Street full of self-congratulation (so much for the death of the ego) I was met by silence and hostile stares. Prostitutes running their own amateur brothel, the girls had been exiled to the desert of the outer suburbs, losing their livelihood, their friends, their lovers, their customers and their black community. I remembered the young Aboriginal men glimpsed in the inner rooms sullenly pulling up their trousers, the rumpled beds and wary eyes. How could I have been so idiotically myopic? I told the story against myself and laughed.

It was the era of criticism and self-criticism. The Communist Party of China was already exercising a big influence on Australian Communists and would eventually replace the hegemony of the USSR. One day the two factions would actually split the Australian Communist Party. But now young Australian cadres were sent to 'study' in Peking and the writings of Liu Shao-ch'i, in particular, were taught in our Marxist study classes. Exotic terms like 'mountaintop-ism' replaced Lenin's 'Infantile Disorders of Left-Wing Communism'. Not that the Redfern comrades took much notice of any of this. As always they went their own way and practised the politics of day-to-day survival.

Joy Alcorn wrote to me. She had come to Sydney and fallen in love with a Communist tram driver. He had left his Catholic wife and six kids to move in with Joy, but it didn't last long. She was living alone in a single room in Bondi. Jane was a weekly boarder at a 'progressive school'. Joy had heard we had a house, perhaps even a spare room, where she and Jane could be together again. She sounded desperate and I wanted to say yes, but Les refused. Remembering how Joy had treated me like a loved younger sister, I felt like a traitor. But when Len Flood, his *de facto* Jean and Jean's young daughter Judith asked to share the house with us, Les insisted that we take them in. This was different, this was 'family'. I resented it, but in the end it seemed easier to agree and at first we all seemed to rub along well enough. We had to move out of the big lounge, which meant the end of the Party meetings. There was no place to sit any more except the small spare room at the back of the house, so we piled the grate up with coal and I sat there at night embroidering bibs for the new baby. It was a quiet, gentle time and maybe Les organized it on purpose. He was never exactly enthusiastic about being the Marx House of South Sydney.

And I wasn't unhappy; I even had hopes for the future. My mother had written that Clancy was probably coming to stay with her in Melbourne in the summer and she would bring him to Sydney to see me. Maybe, I thought, I could fix up the back room and he could come and stay with me for a few days, or even a week, maybe this could develop into a yearly meeting and eventually one day he might say to his father, 'I want to live with my mother.'

And then everything changed. I was about to start a new job, sorting at the printing works a few doors down the street. I had disguised my advanced pregnancy in a loose heavy coat, applied for the job and got it, when a letter arrived telling me that my mother was worried about Clancy. He had been taken out of kindergarten complaining of 'pains in his legs'. He seemed pale and listless and he didn't run or play any more. He'd had lots of tests but nobody could find anything wrong. One doctor thought he might have some form of infant rheumatism.

Immediately I sent an urgent telegram: 'What is wrong with Clancy?' Lloyd wired back, telling me it was nothing serious and he would 'keep me posted'. It was the beginning of a nightmare. Clancy's illness was eventually diagnosed as acute lymphatic leukaemia, a killer disease for which there was no known cure. I had never even heard of it before but, consumed with guilt and horror, I used money I didn't have to send urgent cables to children's clinics in the USSR and America. I rang and consulted dozens of Sydney child specialists. Each time the same answer came back, it tolled like a funeral bell. 'You must face the facts,' they said, 'that there is nothing to be done.' But I couldn't face it.

Only in action could I get any peace, and there was no more action to take. I even wrote to Arthur Calwell, the shadow Foreign Minister in the defeated Labor Party, whose twelve-year-old son had died of leukaemia. He sent a Commonwealth car round to Marriott Street with a parcel of his dead son's books for Clancy. I stood in the ugly room, touched almost in spite of myself, with the pile of books in my arms. In those days the Communist Party, echoing Stalin, saw the Labor Party as the main enemy. Social Democrats were traitors to the working class. They always sold out under pressure. Lenin had described the Australian Labor Party as a 'bourgeois reformist party'. But the simple humanity of a parcel of used books that had once belonged to a dead child cut through all the theories. I was conscious of Les staring out of the window as the car drove away, laughing grimly with his brother. 'That's an easy way to get a few votes,' he said.

When the news came that Mrs Davies had flown to Melbourne with Clancy for special treatment at a leukaemia clinic, I caught the train at Central. 'When will you be back?' Les said, but I couldn't tell him. I stood at the window as the train pulled out, watching him growing smaller and smaller on the cold platform. Then I turned back into the carriage. The middle-aged woman I was sharing it with complained about her bad heart and asked me to swap bunks with her. I didn't care. I dragged my bulk on to the top bunk and lay there listening to the train wheels racing over the dark miles, relieved to be moving, to be doing something again, no matter how useless.

The Menzies government had outlawed the Communist Party, but I had hardly noticed it.

When I reached Melbourne my mother, Lesley and Noel Dougan were there to meet me at Flinders Street station.

'Well, aren't you going to congratulate us?' Noel said.

I stared at him stupidly. 'Congratulate you for what?'

'We got married two weeks ago.'

I was flabbergasted. My sister had written to me from Melbourne telling me she had met Frank Lynn again and they were going to be married. What had happened to change all that?

'I wrote and told you all about it,' she said, but I'd never received the letter.

Later my mother told me Lesley had walked the house all night trying to decide which one to marry and had chosen Noel. He'd turned up again, saying he couldn't imagine her marrying anyone else but him. So now my parents, Lesley and Noel lived in an imposing, two-storey house behind a high yew hedge in Cape Street, Heidelberg, the stone steps flanked with blue hydrangeas, the garden fences smothered in yellow roses.

♠

Clancy is in the leukaemia ward at the Children's Hospital, being treated with a battery of new drugs. I stand in the corridor listening to him crying, but the Charge Sister won't let us in. 'They do better without the parents,' she says firmly.

When he comes home, the drugs and the blood transfusions improve him for a little while but he soon slips back again. His spleen swells up and the pain keeps him awake at night. The drugs make him so nauseous he scarcely eats at all, the slightest graze makes a huge blue bruise, his skin is the colour of tissue paper, his hip is twisted so badly that he drags one leg behind him. Yet in spite of his deformities, or maybe because of them, he has this strange, luminous transparency that tugs at the heart.

At first he doesn't know me at all, but in the way of children he soon accepts that I am 'Mummy' – and seeing us together it is impossible not to recognize our relationship. Except for the colour of the eyes, it is my face translated into this unearthly, dying beauty. 'When I was a little boy, Mummy, I could run, couldn't I?'

A month later Les arrives in the Silver Anniversary Buick with our home-made bed lashed to the roof and we shift into a bare, bleak house with a false attic in the working-class suburb of Northcote. It is typical of my father that rather than rent a house for us, he has insisted on buying one.

Clancy stares at Les suspiciously. 'Where are you going with that man, Mummy?'

'Did you see that?' Les says. 'They've already brainwashed him into thinking I'm the villian who's robbing him of his mother.'

For two months we live like homeless gypsies in that ugly, empty house. The only furniture we have is a huge kitchen table, a couple of kitchen chairs and the double bed. There is a square of floral carpet and a gas fire in the empty sitting room.

Every day I travel by bus to Heidelberg to help my mother look after Clancy. It is hard to walk now; blue, tissue-thin stretch marks crisscross my distended belly and I have cramps in bed at night. Les has found a job at Williamstown, driving off in the early mornings with the caked ice running down the windscreen. Sometimes, when the car won't start, he walks to the tram stop in total darkness, hearing the boots of our next-door neighbour echoing like a ghost on the opposite side of the street. They never meet.

On the night the pains begin, I crouch in front of the gas fire trying to take my mind off them with *The Fortunes of Richard Mahony*. Next morning Les takes me into the Queen Victoria Hospital, but it is two days before I give birth to an eleven-and-a-half-pound boy with long black hair and a big head. The baby is almost a breech birth, but he turns at the last moment when I am raw from elbow to wrist from bearing down uselessly for hours. Les walks down the ward smiling, with a branch of wild cherry he's picked over somebody's back fence.

As the nurse holds up the swaddled baby through the observation window, the awed father next to him says 'Jesus, mate, is that your kid? He's got a head like a robber's dog.'

'Mark my words,' says the hospital cleaner, 'that kid's been here before.'

We call him Joe, after Joe Hill, and maybe a little after Joe Stalin. At least we aren't like the woman in Marrickville who is famous for yelling out to her young son, 'Stalin, go and fetch a pound of potatoes.'

As I struggle backwards and forwards on the bus between North-cote and Heidelberg with the baby in his pram, I watch Clancy deteriorate from day to day. Joe lies out under the yellow roses and cries because I don't have enough milk for him any more. A crying baby is the last thing that miserable household needs, and I feel as if everybody resents the fact that he is alive.

'You can't expect to feed a big baby like this when you're doing all that travelling,' the clinic Sister tells me.

I walk to the telephone box on the corner and ring my mother. 'I'm losing my milk,' I tell her. 'It's too hard travelling to Heidelberg every day. Why can't I bring Clancy here? I'll look after him.'

'You?' she says. 'You couldn't look after him on your own in *that* place.'

'He's my child.'

'No,' she says. 'You deserted him long ago. Besides, I promised Lloyd I would never let him out of my sight.'

'You what?' I say.

'I promised Lloyd I wouldn't let you have him.'

'Lloyd's not even bloody well *here*,' I scream.

'I promised him.'

'You Judas!' I weep. 'You bloody Judas!' and bang the phone down. I am trembling.

Next day I am back on duty at Cape Street and there are more black looks from Les, home to an empty house, tired and dirty from the boiler shop, with no dinner ready.

Once we went to a party in Collingwood to raise money for the defence of Frank Hardy in the libel case brought against him for his novel *Power Without Glory*. Frank was riding high. *Power Without Glory* was a bestseller, and he was an Australian celebrity. He came into that crowded, drunken gathering of his fans, a slim, dark, Irish larrikin with a bit of a swagger befitting the hero of the hour. Frank's charm was always infectious. But suddenly I found myself arguing with him about his novel.

'It's a great story,' I said, 'but it makes a hero out of a criminal and it's clumsily written.'

Frank stared at me incredulously. 'And who the hell are you?' he said.

'She's Dorothy Hewett,' Les told him.

'Dorothy Hewett who wrote "Clancy and Dooley"?'

'That's right,' I mumbled.

'OK,' Frank grinned. 'You can criticize me if you like, but nobody else can tonight, only you.'

Retrieving the sleeping baby from underneath a pile of coats and a passionate couple in a spare bedroom, I fled out to the car feeling oddly disturbed.

'What are you writing now?' Frank had asked me.

'Nothing,' I'd said. 'I haven't got the time. I'm working for the Party.'

'Writing's your work,' he'd said. 'Let others who can't write do the rest,' and for the first time I'd felt ashamed. Had I sold my soul to save the world?

♠

On Clancy's third birthday he sits at the head of the polished dining-room table blowing out the candles, a paper cap on his head. Afterwards he sings 'Little Boy Blue' in his high sweet voice, and we all pretend to celebrate.

My father drives us out into the country to wildlife reserves where the white-faced child stares sadly at emus and kangaroos. My father, moving him in and out of the car with heartbreaking gentleness, seems to be the only one who can handle him without causing any more pain. 'Dai,' he says. 'I only want Dai to lift me.'

Sometimes I place him carefully at the foot of the baby's pram and push them both down the hill to the Heidelberg River, through wet dangling branches, past muddy streams, over dry leaves, the sky swollen and grey with unshed rain or suddenly illumined with spring sunlight.

The magpie swoops down from its nest in an overhanging tree and Clancy gives one sharp frightened cry. I hear the crack of its beak as it grazes his head, leaving a trickle of blood on his skin. The magpie keeps attacking, driving us out of the copse of trees, till I am running before the fury of its beating wings. It is like a bad omen.

My mother nurses Clancy devotedly, her eyes ringed with lack of sleep, until he goes back into the Children's Hospital for more drugs and blood transfusions. When I visit him in the ward he lies delirious and burning up with fever, his bed surrounded by hospital screens. There is a sign above it saying 'No fluids', but his lips are dry and cracked and he keeps whimpering for water. I remember my grandfather dying of pneumonia in the private hospital in Perth. Clancy looks just like him.

That night I ring the specialist. 'Clancy is very ill,' I tell him. 'I think he's dying of pneumonia.'

'I'll be in to see him first thing in the morning,' the specialist says, 'and don't worry. Children often show these alarming symptoms. Of course he's very ill, we all know that, but I think he's holding his own.'

'Why isn't he allowed any water?' I ask him. 'There's a sign above his bed, and he's terribly thirsty.'

'I'll ring the hospital straight away,' he says. 'Don't worry any more tonight.'

Next day he is as emaciated as a skeleton. How can any child lose that much weight so quickly? His breath rasps as he throws himself from one end of the bed to the other. Great blue bruises disfigure his face and body. There is a jug of water beside the bed. I moisten his lips. I wait. Silent tears drip down my face. He quietens down and takes my hand. 'Don't cry any more, Mummy,' he whispers. 'Don't be sad.'

I watch him lapse into the last coma. He is scarcely breathing. 'Die,' I whisper. 'Die now.'

Only when I am sure it is too late, I call the Charge Sister from her desk at the end of the ward. I have protected him. No more drugs, no more torture.

'My little boy's dying,' I say.

She takes one look and rushes to the phone. In a few seconds a young doctor runs into the ward and gives him a last hopeless injection. Too late. The specialist arrives. I stand out on the landing feeling a strange, dull triumph. I have defeated them. They are all too late.

A few minutes afterwards the specialist comes out to me. 'I'm sorry,' he says. 'It's all over. You were right. He was very ill. He died of pneumonia, but then it was always only a matter of time, wasn't it?' He looks at me with his dark, sad eyes. 'We did the best we could,' he said, 'and I do think it was worth it, don't you? He did enjoy those last months, didn't he – his little outings and his toys – and it wasn't all useless, you know. What we learned from him may help other children.'

I turn silently and walk alone down the concrete stairs, feeling clumsy and overweight in my cheap Woolworth cotton. My parents are waiting in the hospital parking lot. My mother takes one look at my face and helps me into the car.

'That's the end of it,' my father says bitterly. 'I'll never love another child again,' and I don't believe he ever did.

That night I take two Valium, weep, and can't feed the baby.

'You're only crying for yourself,' Les says. 'He's past crying for.'

But I keep on repeating over and over, 'It's the waste I can't bear.'

As we drive back to Sydney, with our bed roped on top of the Buick, kids in country towns stare and point at us. 'Look, Mum, gypsies!'

♠

'When I was a little boy, Mummy, I could run, couldn't I?' Clancy Davies in my parents' garden in Heidelberg, Victoria, September 1950. Photo: René Hewett

Toddy Flood speaking to 3900 workers at the Shanghai State Cotton Mill on the visit to China in 1952, with Chinese interpreter, and Sydney school teacher Madeleine Kempster, on her right.

In Peking, Les Flood (centre) visits the exhibition of the Bacteriological War Crimes committed by the Americans in Korea, 1952.

The June 1st kindergarten in Peking. From left to right: Madeleine Kempster, Mary Lewis, myself and friendly Chinese children.

Children at the Stalino Coal Combine Kindergarten in the Donbas present flowers to the secretary of the Kurri Kurri Miner's Women's Auxiliary, Les Flood and myself, during the visit of the Australian delegation to the USSR in April–May, 1952. Photo: Novrichevsky

Les Flood, a 'blue orchid', in the cockpit of his plane during the Second World War.

'Aren't we lucky, we've got three boys.' Mike and Joe Flood playing ball with Pommy looking on, Heidelberg, Victoria, 1956.

I never knew what my father did with the ugly house in Northcote. I never knew where Clancy was buried. I wrote Lloyd a letter telling him I wished I'd let Clancy die in peace without subjecting him to those months of hopeless treatment. I felt as if he'd been turned into a guinea pig. He replied indignantly, saying he couldn't understand how any Communist could have written such a hopeless, bitter letter.

When I looked back on those desolate months, we seemed to be continually driving in our Silver Anniversary Buick through the back streets of Melbourne with the windscreen wipers iced over, or lost and running out of petrol in pitch-black suburbs in the middle of the night. The black-and-white magpie would swoop down from an overhanging bough with a snap and a sharp beak and a trickle of bright blood on Clancy's brow, and I was running, pushing the pram over dry leaves with the wings beating in pursuit.

The cold back streets, the pursuing magpie, the big, white, snowy cat swarming with maggots I found one morning, stiff in the long wet grass by side of the house, led to it by the drone of blowflies . . . these ominous memories became like metaphors for the one memory I could never recall, until it became like a test I continually set myself. I would walk through the hospital doors, up the concrete stairs to the door of the ward, push it open, see the rows of children facing me, see his bed with the screens around it, and then . . . blackout . . . nothing.

It was then that the dream began – always the same dream, repeated month after month, year after year. I am walking through the dark, tussocky scrub along the cliff face at the South Coast, with a rush of white clouds and the wind blowing. As I come down the crest of the hill I can see a shallow rock pool, circular with a sandy bottom, above Jimmy Newell's Harbour. From this angle the pool looks innocent and clear. Only when I come closer I can see something lying on the bottom – a shadow? Puzzled, I lean over the surface and see the drowned child, the white face turned upwards, the floating sandy hair, the open eyes reflecting the sky. I am weeping uncontrollably, groping for the dead child in the limpid pool.

14

♦

D URING the day I never left myself time to think. If I thought, I would travel that same heartbreaking journey, up the concrete stairs, through the glass doors into the ward, the rows of neat white beds, and that one bed always waiting with the screens around it.

So I work hard to defeat the referendum. We all do – writing leaflets, some of them illegal; cutting stencils and printing them, smudged and inky, on the flatbed in the backyard shed. Late at night we paint signs in Jack Jackson's special non-removable luminous paint, and with Joe in his bassinet, swerve down back alleys escaping from Twenty-one Division (the political squad of the police force) on their souped-up motorbikes. Through Redfern, Waterloo and Alexandria, we leaflet the letter boxes and sell *Tribune* door to door, working for a united front with the South Sydney branch of the Labor Party. Our referendum 'No' campaign, much of it emanating from the house in Marriott Street, is the most successful in the whole of Sydney – maybe in the whole of Australia.

We never go to bed before 2 a.m., then up again at six o'clock in the morning, existing week after week on a few hours' sleep. No wonder tempers fray, and Les accuses me of turning off the alarm clock so that he sleeps in too late to get to work on time. If I did it, I did it in my sleep, but that was possible too.

Waking early one Sunday morning I lie for a moment bathed in that luminous golden light that transfigures Sydney in the early summer. Through the open window I can see the shabby line of little terraces lit up like children's birthday candles, and hear a woman's voice preaching fervently to the empty street. A Salvation Army lass, in her navy-blue uniform and poke bonnet, stands on the street corner, exhorting nobody at all to come to Jesus, and for a moment I have a sudden vision of myself. This must be the way the rest of the world sees us Communists. I giggle, I still haven't entirely lost my sense of the comic, but most of the time I am impossible – an ardent proselytizer, tired out with the desperate energy of belief.

How Len and Jean Flood manage to live in our house and stay apart from all this frenzied activity is one of the mysteries of our universe. Les tries to buttonhole Len late at night, demanding to know what has happened to his social conscience. He recruited Len to the Party in the old days when they shared a room together in the Adelaide city square. But now Len says he doesn't want to be involved any more. Les laughs incredulously. 'You've got no choice,' he says. 'You were involved when you were born to George and Clarice Blood in Tempe thirty years ago.'

But Len and Jean don't see it that way, and so their presence grows more and more untenable. The little wooden table in the kitchen becomes a kind of demarcation zone. On one side Jean lays her snowy ironed tablecloths, carefully folded in half to leave our side of the table bone bare. We don't possess any tablecloths, let alone ironed and starched ones. At night when I stagger home, pushing Joe in his pram, the two workable burners on the ancient gas stove are always in use. Their meals are well cooked and nicely served; ours are late, scrappy and slammed together. She walks for miles wearing out shoe leather, shopping for all the best bargains. I walk for miles working for the referendum – picking up whatever groceries I can on the way home. I am always boiling over the baby's milk or boiling the peas dry, while I argue political strategy over the kitchen table. Jean and I dodge each other as much as we can, but the silences grow and last for days. I resent them for taking up space in our house when they take no part in the struggle that dominates all our lives.

I have already worked out that if the referendum is lost, Les and I, with our house full of illegal literature and our notoriety as Communist Party activists in the district, will be amongst the first to go. If we are both jailed suddenly, I have asked Betty Maguire if she will take Joe and look after him until one of us is free. It sounds melodramatic, but in those fateful days it certainly wasn't outside the bounds of possibility.

One afternoon the district organizer takes me aside surreptitiously in the little back room. 'You've been chosen for a big responsibility, Toddy,' he tells me, 'but you must guarantee not to speak about it to anybody, not even Les. You're to be one of the Party's secret couriers in the underground organization.'

Until now I've never heard of an underground organization but I realize it is a sensible precaution. If the Party is declared illegal there has to be some kind of clandestine alternative already set up and viable. My heart beats faster. For a moment I feel like the heroine in a war movie about the anti-Nazi underground, but I soon learn that my role is nothing particularly exciting. Each week, as part of an underground money chain, I meet the district organizer in Moore Park and hand him the South Sydney Party funds, hidden under the pillow in Joe's pram. We become good friends. He is a university-educated

English intellectual from a rich Jewish family, who has left home to become, amongst other things, a sideshow barker travelling from town to town in the Midlands. Black-haired, bony-framed, with bowed shoulders and hornrimmed spectacles, he has the gift of the gab and can charm the branches with his rapid-fire delivery. But as the weeks go by he seems to grow paler and more intense, until one evening, just before the Section meeting, he corners me in the kitchen.

'Toddy, how much money have you got?'

'Not much.'

'Could you lend me something? I'm in a bit of a jam.'

I take my worn little purse and tip out everything it holds.

'Two quid,' he says bitterly, 'is that all you've got? I mean real money, Toddy – real money.'

As he lurches away down the front steps, his eyes glaze over with a kind of hangdog despair. I never see him again, but that night at the South Sydney Section meeting there are long faces and muttered conclaves, as Len Donald from the Sydney District Committee thunders out his denunciation.

The money I'd been secretly handing over every week in Moore Park had gone first of all on the horses and then, in a desperate attempt to recoup the losses, at the infamous Thommo's gambling school in Surry Hills. Two hundred pounds – it seemed like a fortune to us in Redfern in those days, and it was the workers' money, donated with real sacrifice by families who could ill afford it. The wrath of the Party exploded on my lost friend. He was summarily expelled, went back to a job at the glassworks and eventually repaid every penny of the lost funds, but the Party would never take him back.

The Communist Party did not easily forgive the slider from the paths of virtue. We had already been told to be careful of Snowy Baker. It was dangerous to have ex-crims in the Party. The bulls always kept their finger on anybody who'd been inside and Snowy had told us how, when he was coming home late at night from a meeting, he was often stopped and questioned by the local coppers.

I was angry that the Party could question Snowy's integrity. He was one of my favourite people in a Branch that sometimes drove me crazy with their sanctimonious speeches and holier-than-thou attitudes. In a world of lumpenproletarians, dropouts, small-time conmen and petty crims, the Redfern branch of the Communist Party sometimes behaved like a religious sect, a tiny island of rectitude in a corrupt sea. They frowned on Snowy and his nuggety mate Vic Boyle, hiding their bottles of cheap plonk in the hydrangea bush by the back step, bringing them out to drink with us after the wowsers had all gone home. Vic had a list of donors to the Party funds which remained his own mysterious property, but amongst them was Kate Leigh, the notorious Madam of the Surry Hills underworld. Rumour had it that Tilly Devine, her rival in Darlinghurst, voted for Menzies and had once been presented in feathers and lace at a Royal Garden Party at Buckingham Palace.

There were others who were considered a bit dodgy by Party standards. Handsome, black-haired Jimmy Washington had a record, and was only allowed to be a Party sympathizer. There was a big curly-haired ironworker with a high-coloured cherubic face who *was* a member of the Party. We were warned about him, but I wouldn't believe it until I saw him pointing out Communists to the coppers on the Domain, and stared at him with such accusation and disillusion-ment that he turned and ran away into Macquarie Street. To be a copper's nark in Redfern was the ultimate degradation. Otherwise, if you were going to survive and get on with the neighbours, it was better not to look too carefully into their pedigrees. They had their own rules of conduct, their own rough justice, and that was enough to get by on.

Teddy Watts was a veteran Communist who had lived in Redfern all his life. A little, round, pot-bellied boilermaker, he had a wealth of Redfern stories to tell. His favourite was the blazing-hot Christmas Day when the family were all together out in the back yard drinking beer, the turkey spitting away in the Early Kooka, and the table laid for Christmas dinner. But when they trooped inside the turkey had vanished – roast potatoes, baking dish and all. Redfern was like that, light-fingered and philosophical, yet there was a kind of fierce com-munal pride about living there.

And where are they now? Teddy Watts and Rachel, Snowy Baker and Vic Boyle, Bill the ironmoulder, Stan and May Webb the ex-Salvationists, Carol Jackson the Waterloo dressmaker and her hus-band Jack, who always needed carb soda for his ulcer before the meetings, Madge O'Grady with her home-made hats, Fred O'Grady the ex-pug with his cauliflower ear, Pat Gale and Red Siddy, Jimmy and beautiful Irene Washington, Charlie Newman with his spiky black hair on end, sitting up all night in front of our spitting coal fire, long after we'd gone to bed, arguing love and politics with his lovely new wife Joyce, my friend Ev with her broad, sweet, powdered face who lived in Alexandria behind the emblem of a Mexican asleep under a palm tree that Les Flood said was anti-working class.

All of them were there in the Pensioners' Hall on the night we gathered to celebrate prematurely the winning of the referendum.

Lance Sharkey, the general secretary of the Party, called in with his wife Cath, to say it looked as if we might have lost, and Jacky McPhillips, the Ironworkers' secretary, gave a speech about 'fighting the good fight but you have to face reality', until Vic Boyle stood up and castigated them both as 'weakies'. He said that as far as Redfern was concerned we'd won, and Pat Gale shouted, 'Up the fuckin' Commos,' and Vic was right, as we discovered the next day after we had made a bonfire of the illegal literature in the back yard. The NO vote had scraped home with a narrow margin, and democracy was safe in Australia for a little while. We wouldn't go to jail, and Joe wouldn't have to be brought up by the Maguires in Brighton-Le-Sands after all.

♦

So with a deep breath I am off again, pushing Joe through the streets of Redfern, collecting signatures against the atom bomb.

'Some of them look quite intelligent, don't they?' says a passing social worker, turning to her companion.

But Joe looks thin and peaky with big eyes in his big head. He is recovering from a bad bout of infant diarrhoea, a killer disease amongst Redfern babies, and can only suck Bengers Food from his bottle. Such a bright baby, he'll sit for hours turning over the printed pages of a book for all the world as if he is reading it. For three nights Les and I have sat up watching him vomit everything we give him – even boiled water. On the third night, when he is weak and dehydrated and burning up with fever, we hear his shallow breath and think we've lost him, but the crisis passes and by morning he is alive and asleep in the little canvas cot I worry about in case it gives him curvature of the spine.

He is an accommodating child. Taken to spend all day in his pram in the Ironworkers' Building, he plays with a packet of pink streamers, while his mother gives out leaflets and makes speeches on peace and democracy to the wharfies at the pick-up. Baby-sat by a succession of good-natured strangers, he regards them all with the same benign seriousness. He begins to talk very early, always greeting the branch members from his high-chair with a charming 'g'day'.

When Noel Dougan transfers to Sydney University to study for a diploma in Public Health and Tropical Medicine, he and Lesley rent a flat in Randwick for three months, and Joe christens her 'Dessie', twining himself around her heart. The name stays with her for the rest of her life, replacing her given name.

'It's your duty to look after Joe,' I tell my long-suffering sister.

'Don't forget I'm doing all this for you too, so that you can live in a better, peaceful world.'

How insufferable I am. When May Webb cries off a *Tribune* drive on Christmas Day to give her small son a proper celebration, I mock her for her bourgeois hang-ups.

Stunned by her obvious dislike, I castigate Jean Flood for her lack of political conscience. 'I am fighting for your son too,' I yell at her, 'so that he will never have to enlist in another war again.'

A last quarrel with Jean and I really lose my temper, taking her by the shoulders and running her down the hall. 'Get out!' I scream. 'Pack up tonight. I don't want you in my house.'

When Les comes home from work I expect ructions, but instead he good-humouredly helps Len load their furniture into the van, standing out in the street grinning after them.

'I thought you'd be furious,' I say.

'It's time they went,' he replies.

It is a relief to be on our own again, but now the last restraints have gone we often fight bitterly. Les doesn't relish living with this paragon of Communist virtue who puts the Party before everything else. The rifts in our relationship widen day by day. Once it was always possible, wordlessly, to repair the damage in bed at night. No matter what differences the day held, making love has always been our saving grace, but now even that is failing us.

We lie silently side by side in the darkness, or fall into bed at different times, both exhausted. At weekends Les takes Joe to visit his mother or the Maguires while I lead out the South Sydney comrades on yet another *Tribune* drive. Nothing can stop me. Some terrible emptiness of the heart drives me out week after week to tramp the lonely, often hostile streets, with my newspapers and petitions.

'We know who is the most important cadre in the Flood family,' says Len Donald, and my breast swells with my own self-sacrifice. Inverted vanity and pride inform everything I do. I have won. I have laid the judgemental ghost of Sam Aarons and the West Australian Communist Party. Not only have I rehabilitated myself, I have become the leading cadre in South Sydney. But the South Sydney Section calls on us to make even greater sacrifices. There is a Socialist Competition to see which comrade donates the most money to the cause. Les pledges more than half his wages and I am furious. We can't even live on his earnings now.

'You know Les,' the Section secretary says condescendingly. 'It's easy to get money out of him. He always has to be the first off the post.'

The Party is driving a wedge between us.

Stan Webb comes to the back door and stands appalled in front of our hatred. 'Don't make a habit of it,' he says quietly, 'or you'll find you don't know how to stop.'

But already the kitchen lino is littered with the remains of the 'utility set' the South Sydney Section has presented to us for the use of our house in the referendum campaign . . .

There is a two-week Marxist School at the Henry Lawson Hall. If Les will look after Joe at night I can go, but he won't agree, and as I stick my head round the wash-house door to swear at him, he throws the teapot full of boiling tea all over me. I am wearing my only 'good' dress. The tea stings and burns my face and my eyes. In a fury I pick the cups and plates up off the draining-board and hurl them at him one by one until his shoulder is bleeding and the floor is deep in broken china.

'Now you can clean it all up,' he says.

I arrange for Ev to take Joe for a fortnight and go to my Marxist School anyway, but when I get home on the first night Les has locked me out and I have to sleep, huddled and cold, on the back seat of the Buick.

One hot summer's night Les comes home drunk with a boiler-maker from Mort's Dock. We sit drinking beer in the kitchen until Les staggers into the bedroom and passes out, and I am left with Frank the boilermaker, tall, dark and good-looking in his late thirties.

'Let's go to a dance at the Workers' Club,' he says.

It's years since I've been dancing and suddenly I want to go. I want to be young and pretty and careless again, whirling round the dance floor. I go into the bedroom.

'Do you mind if I go to a dance at the Workers' Club with Frank?'

Les grunts and turns over. 'You're not going anywhere,' he says.

The first time Frank makes a grab at me I fend him off, but before long he is kissing me violently, my back pressed against the doorway of the wash house.

'No,' I say, 'no,' but soon he is leading me out into the back yard and I am going with him like a sleepwalker. When he lays me down on the old table in the shed and makes violent love to me, I don't stop him.

'You're so beautiful,' he murmurs. 'I've never been with such a beauty.'

It seems like years since anyone told me I was beautiful, years since a man looked at me with such desire.

'Come with me now,' he says urgently. 'Bring the baby and come. I can make you happy.'

But suddenly I am appalled. What am I doing?

'I can't come with you,' I tell him, 'I'm in love with Les.'

'You can't stay with him, he's a madman. Everybody knows it. He'll ruin your life.'

'But I've got to stay with him.'

'Why?'

'Because I've given up everything to be with him, because there will never be anyone else really.'

'Why did you lead me on, then?' he says bitterly.

'I'll have to tell him all about this,' I say. 'I always tell him everything.'

'He'll kill you,' he says, horrified. 'And me too probably. We've got to work together at the docks. His ego'll never stand this.'

'I'll still have to tell him.'

'Christ,' he says, 'are you a woman or a monster?' and goes stumbling out into the darkness of Marriott Street.

I stand beside the bed and tell Les everything. Is he too drunk to hear me? I fall on my knees, kissing his hand. 'Please let me come to bed with you,' I whisper.

He grabs me by the hair, drags me into the next room and throws me into a corner.

'Go to hell, you bitch,' he says between his teeth.

Hours later, while I am still sobbing hysterically, he comes in, takes me by the hand and leads me back into bed with him, holding me until I'm quiet again.

'Forgive me,' I whisper, and I think he has, but weeks later he stumbles in very late, very drunk, and Frank the boilermaker is with him. I can hardly believe my eyes.

'Well,' he says, with a malicious grin, 'I brought him home for you to fuck again. Aren't you pleased?'

He keeps mocking and goading until Frank makes a grab at me.

'Come on, then,' he says. 'Don't mind him. We'll have a fuck on the sofa in the front room.'

I slap him hard across the face. 'Go to hell,' I whisper and run out of the house, leaving them arguing drunkenly in the kitchen. It's well past midnight, and not a good time to be wandering the streets of Redfern alone, but I walk on blindly down Crown Street until I reach Surry Hills, and back again, hardly realizing where I am or what I'm doing.

As I move up one side of Marriott Street I can see Frank walking on the other. We pass silently, like shadows, and the only time I see him again is years later in the Domain, standing next to us amongst the crowd, listening to the speakers, a girl on his arm. Embarrassed, he pauses, says something banal and is glad to escape, a puzzled watchful smile on his mouth.

It is the only time I am ever unfaithful to Les in our nine years together, even during those long periods when I live unloved in the house of madness we will both share in Rockdale.

◆

A letter arrives from Lloyd. He wants a divorce, naming me as 'the guilty party'. He would have written before but decided to postpone it until after Clancy's death. I write back telling him I can't afford to pay for his divorce, that I'm perfectly happy 'living in sin'. When he answers that he's quite prepared to pay, I still feel hostile about it. I'm not sure why – probably because he wants to brand me as an adulteress, and I find this distasteful, opposed to all my concepts of sexual freedom.

Grahame Alcorn is working as a painter and docker in Balmain, living with a woman called Red Flo in Little Albion Street in Surry Hills. He tells me that Lloyd has asked him to be a witness for his divorce, but he has refused. So has Leah Healy, working as a kindergarten teacher in Sydney. Most of the old West Australian State Committee seem to have migrated overnight. Leah says it is to escape the heavy hand of Sam Aarons. One evening we are visited by Laurie Allen and her husband Bruce. After a few friendly preliminaries it's Bruce who says they have come to collect evidence for Lloyd in his divorce case. Bruce has to see our clothes hanging side by side in the wardrobe.

'Isn't he sufficient evidence?' I say bitterly, pointing at Joe smiling from his high chair. Bruce looks embarrassed.

I feel as if I've been tricked into a situation I loathe, but Les coolly signs the divorce papers, naming himself as co-re, and my first marriage is finally, legally, over.

Another visitor is Bill Woodlands. He appears without warning one hot Saturday as we are sitting out on the front step waiting for the Southerly Buster to blow up out of the stifling streets.

He seems older and tireder but more or less unchanged, although there is something lost and sad at the back of his eyes. But Les glares at him and makes me nervous until I wish he would leave. To get rid of him I suggest I walk him to the tram stop while I buy the weekend meat.

'Are you happy?' he asks me abruptly.

'Oh yes,' I say, 'quite happy . . . and you?'

'Not very.' I've heard he's married to a girl who works in the Ironworkers' office.

'I've joined the Party.' He grins at me. 'That's how I tracked you down. And I've almost finished my medical degree at Sydney Uni, but I'm not a very good Party member.'

I watch him swing on to the tram.

'If you need a friend,' he says, but I shake my head and walk back up the street to face Les's fury.

'Well,' he says. 'You couldn't get off with him quick enough, could you? Did you make a meet for afterwards?'

But I don't answer. I am too tired to quarrel about men or political commitment or anything else any more. All I want is peace.

Les picks up Joe and I hear the Anniversary Buick start up and chug down the street, leaving the usual cloud of kero fumes behind it.

Soon we will be leaving Redfern, this old world of the ice man, the baker's horse and cart, the man selling clothes props, the street vendors with their fruit and vegetable trucks on the corners, the *slap slap* of women's slippers on the footpaths of an evening. Once having left it, we will seldom see any of our old comrades again. Big cities are like that. Leaving a suburb, even if it's only a few miles away, is like moving to another country.

My mother has written to tell me that my grandmother has left me £4,000 in her will. I can buy a house with the money as long as it is registered in my name. My parents arrive in Sydney to visit Dessie and take me house-hunting.

In my wildest dreams I had never imagined my father sitting stiffly in the greasy, railway-fawn kitchen at Marriott Street, looking around him with ill-disguised contempt. I feel belligerent and ashamed and wish we'd done something to improve the house, but Les has always said that if we paint or repair it the landlord will only put up the rent.

I want to buy Marriott Street but my parents won't agree. I won't shift out of the inner suburbs so eventually we compromise on an ugly brick bungalow in Rosebery for £3,000, and look around for something to spend the rest of the money on. It never occurs to either of us to keep any of it for a rainy day. I feel the usual guilt about inheriting money from the bourgeoisie, so the best thing to do is get rid of the tainted stuff as quickly as possible. Les has a different attitude altogether. He believes that as one of the oppressed proletariat he has an absolute right to appropriate these ill-gotten gains and recycle them back into the working class.

In April 1952 there is a delegation going from the Union of Australian Women to a Conference in Defence of Children in Vienna, run by the Women's International Democratic Federation. Perhaps I might like to pay my own fare and join the Sydney delegation.

'Let's both go,' I suggest to Les. 'Mum will look after Joe for me.'

At first he is less than enthusiastic, but at last he agrees, and after only a few weeks in the house at Rosebery, we travel to Melbourne to leave Joe with my mother. Les books in on the *Toscano*, one of the Lloyd Triestino line, with the rest of the delegates, but I stay with Joe in my parents' house in Heidelberg until the last possible moment.

On the last night when I creep in to kiss him goodbye he is fast asleep in his safe cot with an old knitted animal toy lying beside him. Gently I extricate the toy without waking him. We have been asked to bring greetings from the children of the world to the Viennese conference – messages, cards, paintings, photographs, books or favourite toys. My little son is too small to donate anything, so I am making the donation for him.

My father is disgusted. 'She's a fanatic,' he says. 'Fancy taking the poor little kid's toy out of his cot when he's fast asleep.'

But as usual I am well away on a cloud of high-minded sacrifice in the cause of peace and international friendship. I go aboard the *Toscano* with a strange mixture of excitement and foreboding. It's my first trip to Europe, the trip I've been waiting for ever since I was a teenager, before the war broke out and marooned my generation in Australia.

Les has talked his sister Claire into paying her own fare and joining the delegation, and I have heard on the grapevine that Lloyd, his new wife and his mother are all going to the Vienna Conference. It's beginning to sound like a comic opera.

On board ship Les and I have been relegated to separate cabins, and he refuses to creep up on the top deck after midnight to make love under a tarp, in an empty lifeboat. He is treating me with cold indifference, more like an importuning harlot than a wife. It's almost as if he hated me, but for what reason? Sometimes he seems quite irrational, then the shadow passes and I wonder if I've imagined it. Is he still brooding over Frank the boilermaker from Mort's Dock?

I unpack my pale blue transparent nylon nightgown and my new pink plastic slippers (they seem completely wasted) and climb into the top bunk. I am sharing a cabin with Claire Flood and May Gregg, the secretary of the Miners' Women's Auxiliary from Kurri-Kurri in the northern coalfields. Neither of them trusts the ship's drying room, so as we begin to roll, their wet washing, draped from wall to wall, flaps in my face all night.

I am almost twenty-nine years old, the youngest member of the delegation on board, and my great adventure has begun.

CHAPTER

15 ♣

THE *Toscano* must be the slowest ship ever to run between Sydney and Venice. While I dose myself on Dramamine, keeping my eyes carefully averted from swaying centre lights and heaving seas through the portholes, she wallows along the Bight out into the silken waters of the Indian Ocean, circled by flying fish and whales spouting far off where the sea melts into the horizon.

Our delegation is composed of Communists and Christians and fellow-travellers; schoolteachers, miners' wives, members of the Union of Australian Women, a clerk, a Sydney barmaid and one lone Queensland Quaker. This little company of homesick restless women write long letters home to their husbands, do 'keep fit' exercises on the top deck in the early mornings, flirt with the Italian officers, promenade the deck, embark on brief shipboard romances, brew endless cups of tea on a little spirit stove in one of the cabins, or go quite spectacularly mad.

The delegation is a hotbed of sexual frustration and, tossing on my single bunk, watching Les flirting with the two beautiful Tahitians from Papeete, or playing 'Ragtime Cowboy Joe' by ear on the ship's piano . . .

> He's a high-falutin' rootin' tootin' shootin'
> Son of a gun from Arizona, ragtime cowboy Joe . . .

I am no better off than the rest of them.

As usual, when we reach Ceylon Les is one up on us all. While we are visiting a ward full of horrifyingly emaciated children lying like rows of dried-out mummies in their cots, he is off on his own, hiring a rickshaw and demanding to pull the astonished driver through the streets of Colombo. We act like an official delegation, but he spends the day in the rickshaw driver's hut, drinking tea with a real Ceylonese family, or wandering through the markets seeing a girl lying dead in the gutter covered in refuse while the unseeing crowds pass by . . . When we troop back on board, he is nowhere to be found.

'*Dov' è suo marito?*' asks the purser, wringing his hands in despair, and the cry is taken up all over the ship: '*Dov' è suo marito?*'. The

Toscano pulls out into the channel. '*Eccolo!*' they call, and across the water – standing up, grinning in triumph, the light bouncing off his gilt hair – comes Les, in a hired motorboat.

At Bombay we are met by a group of local Communists and driven off through the steamy night filled with the stink of India, the open fires, the shadowy forms of the myriad squatters along the street verges. The luxurious Soviet car is driven by a handsome film producer with ruby rings on his fingers and a tie-pin carved from a tiger's tooth.

'Who are they?' I ask him, pointing to the homeless, their dark faces lit up for a moment in the glare of the headlights.

'The squatters,' he sighs, lighting his cigarette from a silver-plated case. 'They are always with us. After a while you become hardened. You no longer notice them – or else you go mad.'

'*You* no longer notice them,' says the tiny, sardonic-voiced woman on my other side, pulling her sari irritably around her.

'We cannot all be saints like you, my dear,' he says, smiling benignly across her head. 'She is one of our great philanthropists, working without pay amongst the Untouchables.'

The film producer's half-French, half-Indian wife, a pale exhausted beauty, greets us lying on a carpeted divan in their flat on the heights of Bombay. She is recovering, she tells us, from cancer and has made a vow that if her life is spared she will dedicate it to the cause of world peace.

The flat is furnished with ornate Indian rugs, tiger skins spread-eagled on the walls, occasional tables balanced on elephants' feet with the autographs of the famous preserved under glass: Bernard Shaw, Picasso, Joliot-Curie, Nehru, Gandhi, Ilya Ehrenburg. Servants flit in and out carrying curries, seafood, fruit and alcohol. In the garden next door a wedding is taking place, the sitar music wailing through the magnolias.

Next day, with the little Indian doctor, we visit the Untouchables in their crazy, tiered, one-room apartments, with a tiny spirit stove for cooking on the balconies outside. The streets are full of beggars with mutilated arms and legs, thrusting the stumps into our faces, legless cripples pulling themselves along on handcarts, blind milky-eyed children – all the torment and misery of the human race seems to be gathered here, yet I have never seen such universal beauty: the fine dark profiles, the proud lift of the head, the melancholy dreaming faces.

Les and I make friends with two young Sikh Communists. They have very little English, but ragged and handsome, with wild liquid eyes and white smiles, they stand on the dock, clenched fists raised in a revolutionary salute as our ship pulls out of the harbour.

It is in Bombay that I first begin to comprehend the internation-
alism of the Communist movement. It is impossible ever to feel lonely
or isolated again. Wherever we go throughout the world they will
always be there to meet us, this shadowy army of activists who share
our beliefs and our vision of world socialism – Venice, Vienna,
Moscow, Leningrad, the Donbas, Peking, Shanghai, Canton, Hong
Kong, Darwin ... There are always the hands outstretched, the
welcoming banners.

But in Aden there is no welcome – only a shoving aside from
fierce-faced nationalists in white turbans, in a hellhole called the
Crater, amputees with the stumps of missing legs and arms, bleating
half-starved goats, bloat-bellied, begging children.

In Massawa graceful Abyssinian women in long, brightly coloured robes stand in front of earth houses with pitchers on their
heads. A girl plucks at her harp strings and they begin to dance,
circling slowly in the purple twilight.

In the Red Sea, at the ship's fancy-dress party, Les borrows
a grass skirt from one of the Tahitian women, dancing naked to the
waist, red with sunburn. Sunsets blaze, Arab dhows anchor like
ragged, winged insects in the harbours, khaki soldiers in military
formation jog along the banks of the Suez Canal. Out on deck I see
a mirage – a line of camels with their robed riders strung out across
the sky. Crossing the line, a fat-bearded passenger dressed up as
Neptune plunges my bare feet into a bucket of boiling spaghetti, tips
it over my head and upends me into the swimming pool.

That night the Tahitians dance an erotic hula on a canvas stage
swung between decks while the second-class male passengers try to
grab at their swaying hips and buttocks.

When we dock at Venice I am too ill to leave the ship. I have
picked up some bug, possibly from Bombay or Aden, or from the
supplies taken on board. Vomiting, shitting and sweating, with a high
temperature, I am left alone while the rest of the delegation go
ashore.

Some time during those hours I hear the chug of ship's engines
and stagger out into the corridor. Is the ship leaving port, has
everybody forgotten all about me? I grab the arm of a passing
stewardess. 'Where are we going?' But she can't speak a word of
English. Nobody left on board seems able to speak English. I wander
up and down the stairways. It's like a nightmare. At last one of the
stewards brings me to the ship's doctor. 'Nothing to be alarmed about,
we have shifted berth, that's all.'

Gravely he takes my temperature, shakes his head and gives me
a penicillin injection.

'You have a real *maladie*,' he says. 'Too ill for travelling.'

Les arrives, furious with me for spoiling everything. In a feverish daze I follow him over little bridges, past endless sluggish canals; feet clatter on stone steps, stout Venetian legs pass in the twilight. Here is the ship's doctor standing smoking with a group of officers, bowing and smiling courteously.

'You should be in bed, madame,' he says.

A Communist guide is taking us to a *pensione*, and at last amongst cool white sheets I fall asleep, waking hours later to hear the bells of St Mark's ringing from the square, Italian tenors singing outside my window, and think, for a moment, that I have died and heaven does exist after all.

Next morning we travel alone by train to Vienna through the Austrian Alps, the mountain streams swollen with melting snow. Polished wooden houses, the doors and windows painted bright blue, yellow, orange and red, cling to the mountainsides. Little girls dressed in dirndls and pinnies stand on station platforms, hand in hand with their brothers in their sweat-stained inherited leather shorts. Spring is coming again to Europe. The war has been over for seven years.

In the carriage opposite us sits a bitter one-armed veteran of Hitler's invasion of Moscow. Beside him a middle-aged Viennese businessman with a carnation in his buttonhole smiles at Les benignly.

'You are a honeymoon couple perhaps,' says the Viennese. 'These lakes we are passing now have always been a great favourite of your Prince of Wales.'

He leans forward, dropping his voice to a surreptitious murmur.

'I would advise you,' he says, 'we are soon reaching the border, where there is always trouble. The Russian soldiers will enter with their guns and their big dogs and if there is anything wrong with the passport they will take you off, any little thing at all, and *poof*' (he draws his hand across his throat) 'you are never heard of again. I advise you to be very careful of the Russian soldiers, who are all animals. Look what they did to this poor fellow at the Front.'

He gestures towards the empty sleeve of the veteran, speaking to him in German. The veteran nods his head morosely.

'He fought all through the war,' says the Viennese, 'and this is what he got from the Russian soldiers outside Moscow – his right arm too – he is useless now for anything.'

He continues with his diatribe against the Russians until we leave for the dining car. At the border, when the young, snub-nosed Soviet soldiers come down the corridors with their guns and their Alsatian dogs, a ripple of nervous alarm goes through the train. The Russians gaze stolidly at our passports for a while and then move on silently. We stay in the dining car until we reach Vienna. The station is alive with bands playing, bouquets of flowers and banners in a dozen different languages ... WELCOME TO THE CONFERENCE IN DEFENCE OF CHILDREN.

As we leave the train and are swept away by a group of excited Viennese I look back to see the faces of the businessman and the one-armed ex-soldier pressed against the window glass, their eyes wide and horrified, sure that we are Communist secret agents who at any moment will denounce them to the assembled Red authorities.

We are billeted in the Hotel Continentale in the Soviet zone. As I enter the shadowy foyer, Lloyd comes forward to greet me. It is the first time we have met since the bitter parting in Perth three years before. A girl with a black fringe (his new wife) is seated nearby with his mother, but neither of them speaks, and during the rest of our time in Vienna we do our best to avoid each other.

At that time the city was still divided by the Allies into four zones – English, American, French and Russian. Poverty and war damage were everywhere. The whole top floor of the Continentale was blown out and at head height, on the wall above the main stairs, there were bullet holes from the snipers who fought for this city, street by street.

But Vienna is still a place of legend and glamour. Marble statues still line the streets of pockmarked palaces, fountains play in the parks, crowds gather in the beer gardens and pavement cafés. The shops are full of fashionable, expensive clothing, confectionery and iced Viennese cakes toppling with cream. The rich lead their clipped poodles, dachshunds and Alsatians past the beggars on the pavement.

'You will remember Vienna,' I sang long ago, pedalling away at the player piano in the blue sitting room at 'Cathay'.

You will recall evenings in May,
Sweethearts who came and vanished away.

There are serious food shortages in post-war Vienna and once, when I unthinkingly order a boiled egg instead of the usual continental breakfast, it arrives, after long delay, borne before the waiter on a silver tray like an *objet d'art*.

We are taken on bus tours to see the house where the deaf Beethoven lived, always thrown out of his lodgings for playing the piano too loudly, singing at the top of his voice, or pitching the dinner at his landladies.

We sit in an outdoor café above the city in the Vienna woods – a bundle of black sticks waiting for their spring leaves – and drink the warm thin beer, gazing down on the Danube twisting in a grey ribbon through the valley.

Every day we visit the Conference, put on our earphones and listen to the speeches, translated into a dozen different languages.

Trembling with nervousness, I make an impassioned plea in support of the Chinese delegation, who are calling on the Conference to indict the Americans for germ warfare in Korea. Afterwards the Chinese give me a traditional landscape painted on silk to reward me for my support.

I meet Jewish survivors of the concentration camps who have returned to live in Vienna, the leaders of the Women's International Democratic Federation, the French women, Madame Eugène Cotton and Marie-Claude Vallient-Couturier, with the brand of Auschwitz tattooed on her forearm.

The secretary of the World Federation of Trade Unions is a Lancastrian who tells me my accent sounds just like 'our Gracie'. When I indignantly question the atrocity stories about the Russian troops pillaging and raping through the streets of Vienna at the end of the war, he scoffs at me.

'Who do you think they were,' he says, 'angels? They were soldiers, hungry and sex-starved, who'd fought the Nazis halfway across Europe.'

But I am horrified. What about Soviet man and the ideals of socialism?

He claps me on the back and laughs. 'Come on, girl,' he says, 'grow up. This is the real world. They were Nazis, you know, and many of them still are.'

At the end of the conference the whole Australian delegation, invited to the Soviet Union, sets out on a long, uncomfortable journey in carriages with wooden seats, through Hungary to the border of the Union of Soviet Socialist Republics. But I don't care what the train is like. I am almost delirious with excitement, wild with anticipation. I am on my way to the workers' paradise, the socialist homeland, the earthly Utopia.

Les and I are sharing a carriage with two Sydney women – Madeleine Kempster, a schoolteacher from the New England high country, and Mary Lewis, a Sydney barmaid. Next door to us are the Chinese delegation, who nearly all speak excellent English, so it isn't long before we are invited in for a talk, and to share the big box of chocolates they have been given as a farewell present at the station. We are all hungry but as I bite into the first chocolate I realize something is wrong – it tastes exactly like cardboard filled with sawdust. Determined to be polite, I make a valiant effort and swallow it whole. The Chinese are watching us very carefully, until Les reacts with predictable bluntness.

'Christ!' he says. 'What's this?' spitting out his chocolate. 'Cardboard and bloody sawdust! Whoever gave you these is no friend of yours.'

The Chinese look relieved and the ice is broken. Somebody has apparently presented them with one of those demonstration chocolate boxes kept in shops for 'display purposes only'.

'We thought it must be some new kind of Western chocolate,' they tell us.

After that Les can do no wrong, not even when he tells them that he didn't join up voluntarily to fight in the great Anti-Fascist People's War.

Before the journey is over the four of us have been invited to visit China, travelling on the Trans-Siberian railway from Moscow to Peking with all expenses paid. A tiny ancient man with a long white beard, dressed in a skullcap and traditional robes, rises to his feet to make a formal speech in Mandarin.

'This is Comrade X from the Presidium of the Chinese People's Republic,' they tell us, 'and he is inviting you to our country.'

We are inclined to discount it all as a polite fiction, but soon after our arrival in Moscow the invitations, in gold leaf and white satin, are delivered to our rooms at the Hotel Metropole.

But before they arrive there are several inexplicable incidents that leave us all puzzled. Why are the gypsy children in this border town begging, in the Union of Soviet Socialist Republics?

'Because they are gypsies and quite incorrigible, but we have resettled them and are rehabilitating them, Comrades.'

Why do the Ukrainian peasant women, peering from the doors of their wooden hovels, glare at us with such hostile unsmiling eyes? Why do they spit after the Soviet women officials in their fur coats and fur hats and high polished boots? Why do they point and laugh, nudging and whispering behind their hands, at the black American delegate, when Paul Robeson has told her this is the one country in the world where she will be treated as an equal? Why do these people live in such abject poverty, where the only footpaths are wooden planks placed over a sea of black mud?

'This, Comrades, is the legacy of the Anti-Fascist War.'

And when the train draws into Moscow station with the banners and the flowers to greet us and the loudspeakers blaring forth 'Soviet Land', who are this trainload of prisoners, their paper-white faces pressed against the barred window, while the young Soviet soldiers lounge, smoking between the carriages, their rifles slung across their shoulders?

'A trainload of Nazi collaborators, on their way to a rehabilitation camp.'

Yet when we cross the border in the USSR and I see the armed Russian soldiers on the railway platform I remember thinking: for the first time in my life I feel really safe at last. How unforgivably naive I was. Yet how can I, in 1990, attempt to remember the dangerous innocence of that first journey; how can I hope, after thirty-eight years, to hold on to that peculiar ardent cast of mind that censored all experience and saw only what it wished to see?

There was always an undercurrent of disquiet, hidden, pushed out of sight, but undeniably there, bumping into consciousness, often at the most inconvenient moments. Or am I speaking now from hindsight, overlaying this first journey with the second, thirteen years later, when the weight of history and evidence had dissolved that radiant film of falsehood for ever? Whatever the answers, on that first night in Moscow I stand at the window of our hotel bedroom, my eyes misty with images of gilded onion domes, the red star luminous on the Kremlin spire and the dark queues patiently edging towards Lenin's tomb.

The room is like an antique shop, heavy with dark, polished furniture and metal bears holding ashtrays in their paws. Our interpreter is Tamara – tall, long-legged, with swinging brown hair, in her early thirties – who dreams of a dacha in the country and complains of a husband who goes hunting for ducks and girls. With Tamara we see *Prince Igor* and *Swan Lake* at the Bolshoi and visit Leningrad, travelling through the night in those polished wooden compartments with pink-shaded lamps by the windows and a samovar bubbling at the end of the corridor. We walk by the Neva, stand awestruck before the Rembrandts in the Hermitage, and fly to the Donbas, crawling on our bellies down a coal mine with the roof only a few claustrophobic inches above our heads. In an iron foundry we try to speak with a young woman welder who sits dumb and terrified under our questioning. Outside our hotel, beneath the lime trees, a line of beggars with missing arms and legs and a mad-eyed belligerent girl rattle tin cups for kopecks, while Tamara flays them with her tongue.

The whole country stinks of shit, and once, when we are served a rissole in the exact shape of a large brown turd, Les's weak stomach rebels and he rushes for the toilet bowl. But when we pull the chain in the hotel lavatory the pedestal overflows with boiling water and burns our bums.

At the trade-union banquet in our honour Les stands up and criticizes the iron foundry for its lack of basic amenities, its shop floor littered with rubbish, its antique welding rods, the absence of any protective gloves for the welders.

'Back in Australia,' he says, 'no decent worker would be seen dead in a place like that. There'd be a mass walkout and a strike in the first couple of minutes.'

The Party trade-union officials are grieved and angry.

'Doesn't the Comrade realize we suffered, and still suffer, these conditions to save the working class of the world from Fascism and to maintain world peace?'

And of course it is partly true. They have suffered unbelievable devastation, unbelievable casualties. You can see it in the girls partnering each other at the dances, in the faces still strained with suffering and fatigue and chronic starvation, the corrosive memories that surface continually in their conversation. They have struggled back to a miracle of rebuilt cities, with scarcely any war damage showing at all.

But the great plains of the Donbas are dotted with sinister structures – high walls, pillboxes, sentries with rifles.

'What are they?' Les asks.

'Factory buildings,' says Tamara.

'Come off it,' he grins at her sardonically, 'out here in the middle of nowhere with sentries and rifles? I was in a military jail in the war; I know a prison camp when I see one.'

Tamara is furious. 'We had many traitors in the Anti-Fascist War. They have to be punished.'

'How come,' says Les, 'the workers' paradise had so many traitors? What went wrong?'

Back in Moscow we walk down factory avenues lined with monstrous blow-ups of the Heroes of Labour; we visit Lenin's tomb, circling that waxen idol with half his body eaten away, and gaze on the great cracked bell fallen in the Kremlin courtyard. On May Day we see Stalin standing on the platform wreathed in smiles, as the processions pass under the Kremlin towers. That night we watch his profile, with its Georgian moustache, traced in fireworks on the sky, and when we are shown the roomful of presents given to him on his last birthday by the world Communist movement, we are rather ashamed that Australia is not represented.

The delegation is breaking up: some are off to England, some to Europe, some back to Australia. Our leader, Rhoda Bell, has already left for Melbourne, the Queensland Quaker selflessly in attendance. The swollen leg Rhoda had first noticed in Colombo has been diagnosed as inoperable cancer, but nobody has the courage to tell her. Months later, when Les and I visit her in a dark bedroom in Kew in the depths of winter, she is still desperately maintaining that she hopes to get better soon. A big woman, she has shrunk to a bag of bones.

But now Madeleine, Mary, Les and I climb aboard the Trans-Siberian, four to a carriage, on the seven-day trip to Peking and the greatest adventure of all. It is a magical and contradictory journey. The fir forests have shaken off their mantle of snow, the ice is breaking up along the margins of the rivers, but outside the heated carriages the bitter cold numbs our lips and noses, and the sleet frosts our eyelashes.

When we stop at a Siberian station there are the inevitable ragged beggar children running alongside the train. A man sits in a doorway, naked to the waist in the terrible cold, a look of indescribable anguish on his face, a woman's arm flung across him for comfort. In the state store, smelling of unwashed bodies, footrags and sunflower seeds, a customer with furtive eyes jostles against me, muttering, trying to push something into my hand – a note, a cry for help, what is it? To my shame I shrink away and don't wait to see, outraged that a Soviet citizen should behave in this surreptitious manner. There is something about this village – the sordid, brutish, unshaven, haunted faces, the ragged clothing, the smell of misery and fear, the contempt on the faces of the Soviet officials. Are these the Nazi collaborators Tamara has warned us about? It is years before I realize that what we actually saw that day was a village of political exiles, the victims of a revolution that ate itself, turning paranoid, murderous and sour.

One evening, at a whistle stop on the flat Siberian plain, I leave the train and walk towards the station latrines, pushing open the swing doors to join a line of Siberian peasant girls standing shoulder to shoulder with their skirts hitched up, their stout legs astride two wooden blocks above a stinking ditch. Like great, friendly draught mares they stand in the half-darkness, the stench of their warm piss and shit filling the wooden shed, until, too inhibited to join in, I flee, pursued by their ribald laughter.

On the Mongolian border Les wakes me at dawn to see the magic mountain, conical, capped in snow, reflected in the blue ice of the lake, exactly like a Hans Andersen fairy tale, and I remember the princess who lived on top of the ice mountain. Then the dawn stains the snowy peak and the ice turns into a lake of blood and fire.

As we have drawn nearer to the border the faces in the villages have begun to change almost imperceptibly, until the horsemen reining in, dressed in furs, have coarse black hair and Asiatic eyes above their flat cheekbones. Wolves pace the train, panting, their great chests thrust out with each loping stride.

The Vietnamese, the Japanese and the Koreans leave on a branch line to travel back to their respective countries. The little Japanese mill worker with the broad flat face has tears in her eyes as she kisses me goodbye; the handsome Tokyo editor of a Communist newspaper writes out his address for us; the North Koreans are weeping in the washroom, going home to a country divided by war.

That afternoon we pull into the station, streaming with sunlight, and, arms laden with chrysanthemums, are borne off to our rooms in the Hotel Peking.

G AUZY white curtains filter the light, sunbeams dance off the carafe of boiled water. On the felt-topped card table, under the open windows, the glass dish is piled high with sweets. There are flowered kimonos and straw slippers in the bathroom and strawberries and cream for breakfast every morning in the dining room. It is a world away from all the darkness and ambiguity, the uncouth Baroque uneasiness of Moscow.

In the years before the Cultural Revolution the Chinese people were unfailingly courteous and modest, with a shrewd toughness and a surprisingly wry sense of humour.

'When the Revolution was over,' say the leaders of the Chinese Women's Democratic Federation, 'we thought: now we can relax and enjoy the fruits of our labours, but Comrade Mao Tse-tung has reminded us that our long struggle has only just begun.'

The navy-blue cadre's uniform is monotonous and militarized, but the small-boned Chinese women always manage to look graceful and delicately feminine.

'Our Soviet comrades,' they say with a sly smile, 'have warned us that we may lose our femininity,' and they laugh together, sardonic and amused, remembering the mannish Russian women in their ill-cut skirts and padded jackets.

It is the best time to experience a revolution, the time of exuberance and celebration, before the contradictions have surfaced and the bitter struggles for power have begun. In 1952 the proclamation of the People's Republic of China was only three years old, still young enough to seem almost as innocent as we were.

Under silken multicoloured flags and banners, workers march to the factories and children march to school, singing revolutionary songs at the tops of their voices. In the evenings we can see the people from rooftop to rooftop doing their 'keep-fit' exercises, instructed by radios. The walls of the city are covered with posters showing enthusiastic children with fly swats and butterfly nets pursuing flies and sparrows.

Moving through the teeming streets amongst carts and trishaws and unisex pedestrians in the standard navy-blue cotton tunic, cap and trousers, we suddenly find ourselves walking hand in hand with a stranger in a spontaneous, touching gesture of friendliness.

In the schools and kindergartens the charming Chinese children climb all over us, calling us 'Uncle and Aunty Bignoses', pushing our noses comically flat on our faces to match their own. There are moments of doubt when these children, separated from their cadre parents for months at a time, seem to vie hysterically for adult attention; or when toddlers, dressed in the uniform of the People's Liberation Army, enact a bloodthirsty Red Army charge, complete with toy bayonets and fierce yells. Perhaps, if we had read the signs correctly, we might have seen the shadow of their Red Guard future. But against this there are always the peace doves set loose above the roofs of the city, reflected in the stylized patterns on the cloisonné lamps and plates and ashtrays in the bazaars.

Our interpreters are young university students, deeply curious about our lives, determined to regard us as heroes and potential martyrs, fighting against a common capitalist enemy. One of the girls bursts into floods of tears when she leaves us at the border, before we cross over no-man's-land into Hong Kong, convinced that she is sending us to certain death. By that time we have travelled over large areas of China with these young interpreters, and they have become our friends and confidants.

Two disturbing events darken those first golden days in Peking. Dr John Burton, a former head of the External Affairs Department under Chifley, is in Peking with a peace delegation. Leaning across the breakfast table one morning, he says, 'I believe you knew Bill Woodlands. He was killed in a car smash on the northern beaches – crashed over a cliff with a rich young society woman, celebrating his medical degree.'

Remembering the sadness in Bill's eyes and the voice saying, 'If you ever need a friend', I wonder if it was an accident, and think of the long hard struggle of that Sydney washerwoman's son to become somebody. What a waste it has all been.

Ernie Thornton, former Secretary of the Ironworkers' Union, is now a professor at Peking University, lecturing on the Australian trade unions. One night he holds an impromptu party for the Australians in his suite at the Hotel Peking. Laurie Clancy, the secretary of the New South Wales Sheetmetal Workers' Union, has just finished singing 'The Foggy Foggy Dew'. He has a pleasant light baritone voice and the whole assembled company has applauded him – all except Les, who jeers at his choice of song. Drinking champagne, Laurie and I drift out on to the balcony in the half-darkness. Standing there with the lights of Peking beneath us, we talk about the Chinese

Communists, the high standards they set themselves and the vigorous meetings where criticism and self-criticism are always first on the agenda.

When we step back into the light of the room, the tension is electric. I can see Les glaring at me from the corner and my heart sinks.

'You don't mind Comrade Clancy taking your wife out on the balcony, do you, Les?' says Ernie Thornton, in a clumsy attempt to be jocular.

'She's fucked bigger men than Laurie Clancy,' says Les, with his vicious laugh. The room freezes, and Laurie Clancy hurriedly leaves the party.

But in spite of all this, China is good for us. Under the gaiety and openness of Chinese life, the constant activity and adventure, the brooding has left Les's face; sometimes even the infectious grin returns for a brief moment, reminding me of what he was like three years before when we had first run away together. Hope revives. Perhaps we will discover each other again in these ancient avenues of the Forbidden City, where the jade-green Chinese lions stand guard outside the temples and the roof tiles, azure blue and gold, glitter in the sunlight, cemented together by the egg whites brought to the city by starving peasants centuries before. The myriad clocks tick and chime in the rooms of the Dowager Empress, the mechanical nightin-gale opens its gilt throat to sing, and we are the bewitched Europeans wandering through these enchanted palaces and gardens, where the ancient and the new converge for one extraordinary moment in human history.

In early June we drive slowly through the streets of Hankow in open jeeps, shaking hands with the huge crowds who line the way until our fingers bruise and blister.

Cheering sailors see us off at the wharf and we sail upriver in the 'peace ship' that will transport us to a new Flood Diversion Project. Sitting in the stern at tables piled with flowers, sweets, cigarettes, oranges, apples and bananas, we watch a yellow moon rise up, outlined against the ancient square-rigged fishing boats. That night we fall asleep to the chug of the engines making upstream against the turbulent rushing of the Yangtze.

In the morning we wake to little boys skimming like small glistening Christs across the surface of the water, balanced on the backs of totally submerged buffaloes. Fishermen pass us, sitting on their decks under big red sunshades, sending out the tethered cor-morants with brass rings tight round their long necks to dive for fish. Along the shore, glistening with sweat, men roped to their boats tow them upstream against the savage current. A peasant in a dark jacket, white trousers and a big straw hat is sowing seed by hand, casting it into the furrows.

Here is a village with the washing hung out to dry, another circled with haystacks protected by straw roofs, another on wooden stilts built right down to the water's edge. A man and his wife walk together through the flat green fields. She carries a jade sunshade, he has a bundle of scarlet cloth on his back. The whole river bank is teeming with human life and energy, flowing like the river itself, ageless, yellow with mud and silt, rushing down from the snow-covered mountain of Tibet. Far away, a painted frieze on the horizon, are the blue peaked hills of China. As evening falls on that first day the water is like a moonstone, the surface chased with the blur of passing trees, the air full of the sweet smell of new-mown grass.

A peasant unyokes his oxen from a single-furrow plough, the children in their flowered jackets run out to watch us pass, serious under their black fringes. Smoke drifts up from the roofs of the villages. A brown foal frolics in a green field. A peasant drags a stubborn white donkey along a narrow path. Swallows swoop and dip in the wake of the ship, and I sit on the prow writing a clumsy ballad to the Yangtze, full of all the right revolutionary sentiments:

The Yangtze is a river that's broad and wide and strong,
And earth and child and river boat make up a Yangtze song.

Composing this doggerel, I feel exactly the same sense of exultation that I would feel if I were writing a great poem.

'Stand up,' said Chairman Mao, 'stand up and claim our lands. We'll take the Yangtze river and tame it with our hands.'

How do we ever know if what we are writing is any good or not? And the task becomes even more difficult when the critical faculty is atrophied by political blindness.

That night we hold a ship's concert – the two gentle Burmese women; the tiny, handsome Noda Mamoru from the Chaiyoda Poets' Group in Tokyo; the huge comical Pakistani in his ballooning white cotton trousers who insists on calling himself 'Pakistani Boy'; Ada Bonham, the English peace activist; the American China hand, with his big paunch and long white beard; and we four Australians, joined by a doctor of agriculture from the New South Wales Department of Agriculture.

He is a red-faced, sandy-headed, cheerful Sydneysider, who has already embarrassed us by howling with laughter at the Peking opera and staggering to his feet to propose a drunken toast – 'To Mao Tse-

tung, the Peking Duck' – at the big official banquet in Hankow. Now
the rest of the passengers are singing their national folk songs, but as
usual none of the Australians know any. The explosion of Australian
folk music into the ranks of the left wing is still a few years away.
Leaning forward, the doctor suggests that he and I sing a duet
together.

> On the road to Mandalay
> where the flying fishes play
> and the dawn comes up like thunder

he roars out, while the rest of us hide our blushes, praying he'll never
get to the giveaway lines about 'the little Burmese maiden'. I give him
a sharp nudge and break into 'Australia's a big country and freedom's
humpin' bluey' as loudly as I can. Bewildered, the doctor stops in mid
voice. 'I don't know that one,' he says, aggrieved, while the Burmese
women sit gracefully silent.

Next morning we reach the Flood Diversion Project spread out
along the banks of the Yangtze like a city of teeming ants. The straw-
hatted workers and soldiers in their white shirts and shorts run jog-
trotting up and down the dykes and the yellow mud walls carrying
baskets of earth on their shoulders, balanced on bamboo poles,
repeatedly singing 'Mao Tse-tung, Stalin' like a massed choir.

Docking at the wharf, we travel in jeeps through two and a
quarter miles of cheering Chinese, with banners flying and loudspeakers blaring forth revolutionary music and ear-splitting exhorta-
tions to work harder and better than before. Over hammers and
riveting guns, cymbals and drums, the commander in chief of the
Flood Diversion Works greets us on behalf of three hundred thousand Liberation soldiers, peasants and workers.

'We are moving rivers,' he thunders. 'Under the leadership of the
Communist Party and with the help of Soviet experts this great army
of river fighters are working diligently, day and night, in deep
channels and in spite of wind and rain, digging ditches and construct-
ing great earthen highways with spades and hoes.'

For days we drive across the Flood Diversion Project, talking to
the workers, watching the production of wall newspapers, attending
operas, films, drama and dance performances. Les is in his element
riveting two rivets into the north dyke sluicegate. At night we sleep
under canvas and mosquito nets, eating our breakfast with the Liberation Army. Then for five hours we travel in old American jeeps with
the springs gone, to the nearest airport to fly back to Shanghai.

What an odd foursome we must have looked. Madeleine Kempster, gamely hanging on to her black straw coolie hat, bony knees hooked up under her chin; Mary Lewis, freckled and sandy-haired in her limp rag sunhat, with her constant sad little cry of 'Pardon me for living'; Les, thickset and belligerent, hair gleaming above his nylon shirt and stamina trousers; and me, crop-headed, full of revolutionary fervour – all of us bouncing across the impossible roads of China.

Canton is a tropical city of palms, vines and pawpaws. Australian gums line the country roads and we roll the aromatic leaves between our fingers, feeling the first sting of homesickness. In the hotel we sleep on straw matting laid over the mattresses for coolness. All night we listen to the whirr of electric fans and the clip-clopping of wooden clogs in the streets outside.

The Cantonese are tall, handsome, slender people, in black silk tunics and trousers, the women with a long black plait bouncing down their backs. We sit by the Pearl River eating shrimps and cakes and drinking orange juice for afternoon tea, while the river women, who live out their lives, work, cook, eat, sleep, marry, give birth and die on the river, ferry their passengers from bank to bank.

Our interpreter is the Professor of English at Canton University, a tall bespectacled academic with a domed head who spent his youth in Lancashire preparing for his pre-revolutionary career as manager of a Canton cotton mill. As we sit under the palms in the university gardens drinking cold black tea with a frangipani floating on the surface, he tells us he is learning Russian as his third language. His favourite authors are Tolstoy, Dostoevsky, Dickens and Jane Austen. Remembering his background, I wonder what happened to our gentle Professor in the Cultural Revolution?

Idyllically I wander in the orchard of a peasant commune eating kiwi fruit from the sturdy trees, watching our young guide's face darken when she is asked what happened to the village landlords.

'We rose up and we dealt with them,' she says briefly, and I sense the pain and brutality that lie not far beneath the smiling surface of this country, the signs still left in commemoration in the old British quarter in Shanghai – 'Chinese and dogs not allowed'; the Party secretary in the peasant commune outside Peking making the brass spittoon ring as he spits savagely at the memory of the landlords; the old woman on tiny deformed feet, hobbling and waving beside the jeep as we drive into Shanghai.

The Chinese have been generous with pocket money, but Les donates all of his back to the cause of the Liberation Army fighting in Korea, earning smiles and congratulations from our hosts. With tears and kisses we cross the border between People's China and Hong

Kong, carrying our huge peasant straw hats with the red Chinese characters (months later we discover that they read 'Down with American Imperialists'). Since we left Vienna our passports don't mention where we have been. We have never received any mail from Australia; it's as if we have stepped into a void. In those days travel in the Soviet Union and China was forbidden for all Australian nationals. What are we doing here on the Hong Kong border, months of our lives unaccounted for? We are interrogated suspiciously by the Anglo-Indian guards in their khaki Bombay bloomers and British army tunics, and when the train draws into the Hong Kong station the reporters from the English-language newspapers cluster round us for a story, but we pretend we don't understand.

We are not sure of our status as former guests of an enemy country. Australian troops are still fighting the Chinese in Korea. What if our passports are impounded and we are left stateless in Hong Kong?

The streets are thronged with haggard Chinese women, babies strapped to their backs, trying to sell themselves cheaply to the passing European men. The beggars are everywhere and outside our hotel entrance a little girl offers a pathetic bunch of flowers to an American naval officer in his rickshaw, but he only laughs and butts out his lighted cigarette in her palm.

The Qantas plane seems to be full of escaping priests and nuns fleeing from People's China and rich Hong Kong businessmen flying to Sydney. Les says he has surprised a priest in the lavatory hiding emeralds in his soutane.

I look down, seeing a great mat of green jungle, lightless and impenetrable, spread out beneath us. The Qantas steward, who looks like Chips Rafferty, calls me mate and I almost kiss him.

When we touch down in Darwin at midnight for a three-hour stopover, the night air is so chilly I walk back across the tarmac to collect my coat from the baggage rack. Coming down the aisle, I interrupt the security men going meticulously through our cabin luggage.

This is my own, my native land, I think grimly. It is the first intimation of what will be waiting for us at the Mascot terminal in Sydney. Silently I take my coat and with Les, Madeleine and Mary spend the three hours sitting in the pleasant tropical living room of a big Communist wharfie. Little do I realize then the catastrophic effect this meeting will have on my future life.

At Mascot, where the vultures are waiting, we are treated like hard-drug couriers or the carriers of dangerous microbes. All our notes, posters, books, photographs and pamphlets – the cloisonné ashtrays, the china coral tree covered in white doves, the lamp base with the circling folk dancers, the straw hats with 'Down with American Imperialism', the wooden babushka, the wooden Pinocchio from Vienna – everything is impounded, to be returned intact months later. All we walk out in are our black cloth Chinese slippers and a raincoat from the People's Store in Peking.

The impact of inner-city Sydney is like a nightmare – the grind of traffic, the garish billboards, the neon signs hanging giddily on the skyline. For months we have lived in an advertisement-free world where the traffic was mostly people, trishaws, donkey carts and bullock drays. Now the weight on our nerves is almost insupportable.

Sitting up in the train at night, fighting for a share of the one foot-warmer in the freezing carriage, we travel to Melbourne for our reunion with the little son who probably won't remember us. I try to prepare myself for this, but when I crane through the carriage window for my first glimpse of Joe, and see him standing on Spencer Street station, I can hardly believe my eyes. He stands there, a replica of Clancy, dressed in my dead child's clothes, looking frightened and apprehensive, clinging to my mother's hand. It's as if the horror has risen up again to confront me from the grave. How dare they, I think, how dare they dress him up in the clothes of the dead? Where is the sunny-faced, talkative, self-confident little creature we left behind five months ago? But five months is a lifetime in a child's short memory. How could I have left him, even for my greatest adventure? Was I a bad mother? Had I failed again to be a 'proper woman'?

'Christ!' Les says. 'What've the bastards done to him?'

Guilt overwhelms me. I want to put everything right in an instant. All my good resolutions for a gentle beginning forgotten, I kneel down on the platform, holding out my arms, crying, 'Joey, Joey' but he shrinks away from me, hiding his face in my mother's skirt.

'Look!' she cries. 'It's Mummy and Daddy come home to you. You remember Mummy and Daddy?'

But Joe only juts out his lower lip, exactly like Les, and shakes his head.

'No Mummy, no Daddy,' he says firmly.

♥

Les refuses to stay at Heidelberg until Joe gets used to us again, so we return to Sydney with a disturbed child who can't piss for two days and keeps running away down the street screaming for 'Nanna'. Eventually Les lies down on the couch with him and holds him, weeping and pissing his pants, until the crisis is over.

It is a traumatic time . . . I have flu and a high fever, and now Les is demanding that we do our Party duty and travel to Newcastle and the northern coal fields on a speaking tour about our experiences in the Soviet Union and China. I can't face it. I want time to adjust, to get to know our son again, to recover from the flu and the jet lag, the exhaustion and the disorientation, but Les, as usual, won't listen. If I don't leave right away, he'll leave without me.

I am begging and crying. 'Just wait,' I say. 'Just give me another week, and I'll be okay,' but he only smiles, pushes some notes into my hand, and bends to kiss me. I go berserk, throw the notes back in his face, and hit him hard across the mouth, so, coolly and methodically, he beats the hell out of me. It seems to go on for ever, and I don't try to defend myself. I don't even know how to. What is the use when I am bouncing off the walls like a rag doll? When it is over, he throws me contemptuously into a corner.

'I haven't broken anything,' he says. 'Just taught you a lesson you won't forget.'

Joe is sobbing, crouched behind the furniture. I crawl over, rocking him in my arms.

'It's all right,' I say through rubbery lips. 'Mummy's all right.'

When he stops crying I get up and stagger into the bathroom – a face I hardly recognize stares back at me through swelling eyes. Les stands in the doorway.

'You'll look worse tomorrow,' he says, then he walks out of the house, slamming the front door.

Next morning I remember I am not penniless. I have five months of child endowment accrued in the Commonwealth Bank. I wait for a week for my face to go down, then, with only my eye still blackened, I catch the train to Newcastle with Joe.

Knowing Les is in Newcastle, I have made arrangements through the Union of Australian Women to go straight to Kurri and stay with May Gregg who shared a cabin with me on the *Toscana*. I haven't heard a word from Les since the beating, but when the train pulls into Newcastle there he is on the platform, grinning as if nothing at all has happened between us.

'I am going to May Gregg's,' I tell him. 'I don't want to see you just now, probably never again.'

He puts us on the branch line to Kurri, handing the luggage in through the open window.

'I'll see you, then,' he says, and I don't watch him walk away.

The miners are the soul of tact. Only May Gregg's black headed son mentions my eye.

'Ran into a door, did y'?' he says. 'Never mind that, plenty of miners' wives've run into doors. Nobody thinks nothin' of it in Kurri.'

May drives me from village to village in her battered little car, while I speak at pit-top and union meetings and Women's Auxiliaries. She knows there is something wrong but she never mentions it. A short, plump, squat woman, full of common sense and wisdom, she's lived in Kurri all her life. Her husband and sons are all coal miners, coming in, black with pit dust, for their evening meal at four o'clock every afternoon.

When Les rings her at the end of a fortnight to ask if he can stay for the weekend, she puts her hand over the receiver.

'Do you want him to come?'

'I don't know,' I say truthfully.

'Why don't you give him another chance?' she says. 'See how it turns out. You can have the double bedroom for the weekend.'

I wait in an open paddock with a black eye, a bruised face, and Joe beside me, for Les to disembark at the Kurri-Kurri railway station. And here he comes, walking down the slope, grinning, with that slightly jaunty swagger, the wind lifting his hair, the collar of his Chinese raincoat turned up against the cold. A slash of light parts the scurrying rain clouds and, hair and raincoat gleaming against the pale grass, he is, at that moment, illuminated in my memory for ever.

'Farver, Farver!' Pulling his hand away, Joe runs to meet him and we move together down the slope, with Joe riding on Les's shoulders, into May Gregg's weatherboard miner's cottage in the hollow.

That night in May Gregg's big bed, with the icy sheets and the starched, lace-edged pillow shams, I weep in Les's arms.

'I know I shouldn't have hit you,' I tell him. 'But look what you did to my eye.'

'You were asking for it,' he says.

'Kiss it better.'

'No,' but he does, and we are reconciled.

It's like a second honeymoon and I am incredulous, dazed with happiness, frightened every morning when I wake up that it will all have dissolved and this ardent, charming lover will have vanished overnight, transformed once again into the cold, brooding figure I've lived with for the last two years.

Together we travel through the coal fields, speaking at miners' lodges, dancing in union halls, and drinking in the Newcastle Workers' Club. At night we squeeze into a narrow single bed in a sympathizer's house, making rapturous love, with Joe asleep in an improvised cot beside us.

When we go home to Sydney the honeymoon continues. Les gets a job at Cockatoo Docks and on Sundays we speak on the Party platform in the Domain, until Len Donald takes us aside and suggests that it isn't really necessary to tell lies about the USSR and China.

'The achievements are great enough, Comrades. You don't have to gild the lily.'

But we are totally unconscious of doing any such thing, and rather scornful of Len Donald and his careful assessment of conditions in the Socialist Sixth of the world. After all, haven't we been there?

'Peace doves, Mummy, peace doves!' cries Joe, looking up at me in full flight on the platform, as the road-pecker pigeons whirr out from under the shade of the Moreton Bay figs, and cross the Domain in a flash like sunlight.

I am working hard to bring another dream to fruition. Appointed as the official reporter for the delegation, I have sent back thousands of words describing our experiences in Vienna, the Soviet Union and China, but none of them has ever been published, simply because there is nowhere to publish them. The *Tribune* has interviewed us about the Conference but there is no room in its pages, and no real interest in the affairs of women.

The dozens of women's radical magazines I've seen in Europe have fired me with a new idea. Why not start a left-wing Australian women's journal, published quarterly under the banner of the Union of Australian Women? My enthusiasm is infectious. The Party will put up some money, the Party press will publish it, and the UAW will raise the rest of the cost and take responsibility for distributing it. I arrange for photographers, supervise block-making, lay out the pages, invent the headlines, travel by bus from Circular Quay to Ryde to write the story of 'A day in the life of a Bussy', interview women union organizers, factory workers, teachers and housewives, write about equal pay, peace and international friendship, natural childbirth, the theatre and the Australian film industry. There are knitting and dress patterns, recipes, health hints and book reviews.

By March 1953 the first issue of *Our Women* has been coaxed and coerced into existence, but by that time my short period of happiness is over, the long nightmare has begun, and I will never again see the Les Flood I fell in love with in Perth in 1949.

When the wharfie we met in Darwin takes up Les's invitation to stay and arrives in Sydney for three weeks, we shift Joe's cot into our room and give the wharfie the second bedroom.

Not long after he's gone I realize I'm pregnant again, but even before that Les's face has begun to darken, particularly when he leaves for work and the wharfie is still eating his breakfast, and talking to me in the kitchen.

When he tells me the baby isn't his I can't believe it. I stare at him blankly.

'Whose is it, then?'

'Don't play the innocent with me,' he says. 'You know whose it is all right.'

Months later I discover he believes it is the wharfie's baby I am carrying.

'What are you talking about?' I scream. 'Have you gone mad? I hardly knew the man. I didn't even particularly like him.'

'Do you know how I found out?' he says triumphantly, pushing his flushed face into mine.

'No, I don't.'

'One morning I heard Joe, lying in his cot, say, "How about a fuck?" – that's how.'

I am silent, dumbfounded.

'He's like a little parrot. He repeats everything he hears, and where would a little kid hear that – except from that bastard while I was away at work. That's where he fucked you, there on that bed in front of Joe, didn't he, you filthy bitch!'

It isn't really a question, only a statement, and I think after that nothing much can surprise me ever again, but I'm wrong. Les loses his job and refuses to look for another. He gets the single man's dole but there is nothing for Joe or me. In late 1952 there is a kind of mini-Depression in Sydney. Jobs are harder to get, but they do exist. I put Joe in the Redfern Day Nursery, queue up at the Beautron Button Factory and am hired immediately, but I only last a fortnight. I can't stand the fumes from the plastic dip on the buttons, and when I find Joe, crouched and crying, in the bathroom in the Day Nursery with his soiled shorts around his ankles and nobody in charge, I give up and go home.

The poet and novelist, David Martin, who fought in Spain, arrives from Melbourne. Communist writers are finding it hard to get published, so they have started their own co-operative publishing company – The Australasian Book Society. Will I be their Sydney representative for £2 a week? I speak on the wharves and the ships, at union and Party meetings, I walk for miles and sell a few subscriptions, but the Sydney Union Movement – or the Party itself, for that matter – is not particularly interested in 'culture', or anything that derives from Melbourne.

It lasts for a few months, then Joe gets the measles and the Book Society tells me they can't afford my miserable £2 any longer, so I resign, and am humiliated when I discover that they have immediately employed someone else for £7 a week.

Les is covered in a weeping rash. He allows me to treat it with camomile lotion, but although we still share the same bedroom he sleeps with his back turned, as far away from me as possible. Our money is running out. There is never enough to eat in the house. To stem the hunger pangs I chew up handfuls of the wheat Rex Maguire stores in bags in the back of our garage.

Les suggests we put the house up for sale. There seems to be no other alternative. He has a dream of buying a big block of heavily timbered land he has discovered at Lake Macquarie. He will build a log cabin out of the timber, and we will find peace and contentment at last. I am not so sure. What will it be like, isolated in a spotted gum forest at the mercy of Les, with his crazy schemes and irrational hatreds?

Trying to be a smart operator, he plays one potential buyer off against another, only to discover, when it is too late, that they are the same people, moonlighting under two different names. We lose £1,000 on the deal and the land at Lake Macquarie fades away into another mirage.

I sit in a lounge chair, heavily pregnant, watching Les bullshit to the buyers. Taking their cue from him, they treat me like dirt, but there is a certain satisfaction in knowing that the house is in my name, and when it is sold I can leave, taking Joe, the new baby and the money with me.

The phone has been cut off. At least when I pick up the receiver I don't hear a click any more, and a voice saying, 'Did you get that?'

One morning I open the door to a bill collector.

'I've come about the overdue gas and electricity, Missus. We'll have to cut it off,' he says.

But when I tell him I haven't got any money he runs down the path muttering, 'Oh Christ! I can't stand this,' and we are reprieved.

Looking after him, with my belly sticking out and Joe by the hand, I marvel at my life and what it has become. Was it really me who sat up in a gilt and crimson velvet box at the Bolshoi watching *Prince Igor*, with the bones of my pale yellow 'strapless' bruising my flesh? Had I really stood on the Great Wall of China, made a speech to three thousand nine hundred workers in the Shanghai State Cotton Mill, sat at afternoon tea with Soong Ching Ling, the beautiful widow of Sun Yat-sen, in her black satin cheongsam, watched the swallows looping through the hotel window in Hankow?

Did Les, with his gold hair lifting in the wind, ever come striding down the slope to meet me at Kurri-Kurri, smiling in the cream-coloured raincoat he'd bought in the People's Store in Peking?

17

♠

T HE 'waiting patients' were incarcerated in a ramshackle outbuilding attached to Crown Street Women's Hospital in Surry Hills. Most of them were unmarried mothers, abandoned wives or, like myself, women who had exhausted all the possibilities of survival below the poverty line.

One of the tasks of a 'waiting patient' was to bottle-feed the illegitimate babies waiting for adoption in the special nursery upstairs. It wasn't unusual to see a heavily pregnant girl weeping bitterly over the newborn, knowing that in a few weeks her own baby would join these squawling bundles.

Other jobs for the 'waiting patients' were scrubbing the passage-ways, polishing the lino and the brasses, and peeling the vegetables for the hospital kitchen. Early in the morning the cry would echo through the narrow little fibro cubicles where the patients lived – 'All girls to vegetables' – and obediently we would troop down into a dank, ill-smelling cellar to sit for hours peeling potatoes, scraping carrots, stringing beans, shelling peas.

Sometimes we were ordered to cook rich butter cakes in the private kitchen of the ex-army matron who tyrannized over us. As all the 'waiting patients' were on extra-low-calorie, salt-free diets, and always hungry, this was a refined form of psychological torture.

I joined the 'waiting patients' in early May, sent there by the hospital almoner, who had managed to find out a few disturbing facts about my 'situation'. I had been referred to her from the prenatal clinic because I couldn't pay the outpatient's fee, and couldn't keep to the special diet. All I could afford were potatoes and bread and cups of tea, supplemented by handfuls of raw wheat from the garage.

The almoner was horrified. 'I don't understand how a girl of your obvious background could have got yourself into such a fix,' she said, and immediately suggested that I put the new baby 'out for adoption'.

'There's a long waiting list of adopting parents, and a great shortage of white babies with good backgrounds. Your child could have a marvellous home and all the advantages you'll never be able to give it.'

I was shocked. It had never occurred to me that I might lose my children, but she did convince me that I needed a rest, a decent diet and time to come to some serious decisions before the new baby was born.

So Betty and Rex Maguire had taken Joe to stay with them and I found myself amongst the 'waiting patients', treated like a delinquent charity case. I stayed there a fortnight. Les never came to see me, and at night I lay on a narrow single bed listening to the sounds of muffled weeping through the thin partitions, trying not to weep myself and wondering how I had made such a mess of my life. During visiting hours I walked round and round the concrete yard in the darkness or hid in my stuffy little cubicle.

When I wasn't peeling vegetables or polishing the brasses I was working on the next issue of *Our Women*, already due off the press. I had arranged for all the copy to be delivered to me at the hospital and pasted it up in the 'waiting patient's' dining room. The matron was astonished at this intellectual activity and from then on didn't know quite how to treat me. Was I some kind of duckling turned into a swan, a celebrity masquerading in the guise of an unmarried mother?

One morning, when the cry 'All girls to vegetables' echoed down the bleak corridors, I tried to get up and couldn't make it. I was in agony. The bad case of vaginal thrush I'd been suffering from had been daubed with copious amounts of gentian violet by the visiting staff doctor. Too late I discovered I was allergic to gentian violet. It stripped all the skin off my vagina until I felt as if I'd been flayed alive. I could hardly walk, and every time I wanted to piss I had to run myself a bath of lukewarm water. The baby was due in two weeks, and the thought of giving birth through a raw birth canal was becoming a nightmare.

It was the matron who saved the day. Taking me aside and swearing me to secrecy, she treated me with penicillin ointment, which she told me was 'strictly forbidden', but a miracle cure she'd discovered in the army. In a few days I was better again, and when my mother arrived to see me with a huge bunch of yellow and gold charm dahlias the matron said I didn't really need the 'waiting patients' any more, I'd be better off outside with my own people. The new tenant for my cubicle arrived before I left – a gentle Aboriginal woman with a soft, creased, dark face, a perfect victim for Matron's bullying.

Matron snatched the dahlias out of the vase, hissing in my ear: 'Give me those. Someone like that – *she* couldn't appreciate them.'

'Would you give me my flowers, please, Matron,' I said, presenting the bouquet with a flourish to the Aboriginal woman, who smiled with a sweetness I've never forgotten.

By lunch time I had left the 'waiting patients' for ever and sat eating ham sandwiches in my mother's pleasant room in a Kings Cross hotel. She was so horrified to find me in a 'charity ward', she didn't waste much time in recriminations. Sensing that something was wrong, and not having heard from me for some time, she had flown to Sydney on a rescue mission. It was one of the few times in my life when I was relieved to see her. As usual, my mother came good in a crisis.

We set out together on a tram for Rosebery. I was going to collect my clothes, join Joe at the Maguires' house and stay there until I could find a place of my own. My mother wanted me to fly back to Melbourne with her, but I was determined to make it alone and she didn't try to argue. On the Rosebery tram the first contractions hit me and the waters broke. Doubled over, trying to hide what had happened, I stumbled away from the tram stop shaking with laughter.

Rosebery was deserted. Stopping every few minutes to hang onto the furniture, I packed my case. The pains were coming uncomfortably close. I'd have to take a taxi straight back to Crown Street. This baby was not going to take two days to be born. Maybe the natural childbirth exercises, done religiously every morning in 'waiting patients', were going to pay off.

Michael arrived six hours later, blue in the face, with the cord wound tightly around his neck, a lusty eight and a half pounds, crowned with a mop of black curls. As they pushed me on the trolley from the labour ward with the baby in the crook of my arm, I looked up and saw Les walking beside me. Vulnerable with the excitement of childbirth, I was willing to forgive everything.

'Look,' I murmured. 'Isn't he a beautiful baby?'

'He doesn't look anything like Joe,' Les said, and walked away down the hospital corridor.

My first visitor was Colin Brindall, doing his internship in the maternity wards at Crown Street Hospital. He gazed at me speculatively. 'It's a wonder I wasn't on duty when you were admitted,' he said, and I had a sudden bizarre vision of myself, legs in the air, peering over the top of my giant belly at the ghost of a long-lost lover. As it was, I lay in the public ward, surreptitiously tipping the obligatory dose of purging cascara into a nearby potted palm, my convalescence enlivened by our heated discussions on the Malthus theory of overpopulation.

I stayed with Betty and Rex in Brighton-Le-Sands until Michael was two months old. Les was living in his mother's house in Rockdale. The moment I'd gone into hospital he'd found himself a job. Meticulously every weekend he'd call to take us for a drive, but never came inside, and when I tried to talk to him about our future he'd flatly refuse to answer. I couldn't stay with Betty and Rex forever. My mother had gone back to Melbourne and the money from the sale of the house at Rosebery was safely in my bank account, but I couldn't think about a job while the new baby was still so small. I had to keep enough money aside to live on for the next six months, and I had already discovered there wasn't enough left over to buy anything substantial. I'd dreamt of a small place on one of the southern waterways, but that was impossible. I couldn't afford it. The estate agents had shown me a ruined mansion looking out over Cockatoo Docks, and a tiny smelly terrace in East Balmain.

One morning, when Rex asked me if I had any plans about leaving, I realized I'd just about worn out my welcome. An unattached woman with two small children was a burden nobody wanted to bear. I had no choice. I would have to join my parents in Melbourne until I could put my life together again. I sent Les a telegram: 'Flying to Melbourne tomorrow'.

That night he came into the bedroom as I was putting the finishing touches to the packing. We faced each other across a room high with luggage, Joe asleep in the single bed, Michael in the cot in the corner.

'I've found us a house,' he said. 'In Rockdale above the railway line. It's a big place, needs a lot of fixing up, but I can do that, and it's a bargain, only one thousand two hundred.'

Nothing was said about love or commitment. The man with the gift of the gab was emotionally inarticulate, but it was his method of holding out the olive branch. I looked back at our sleeping children and made up my mind. After all, I had nowhere else I wanted to go.

So that was how we were reconciled, and came to Rockdale, picking up the threads of our lives together, building some kind of shaky structure in the ramshackle redwood house in Railway Parade, eaten out by white ants and borers.

There were no apologies, and no attempt to talk over the past or its problems. They were buried for the moment, only Les made an inordinate fuss of Michael, spoiling him and encouraging him in every act of mischief and defiance, as if he was trying to make up for the past repudiation of his own son.

Michael had a difficult babyhood. The rash I'd noticed in his first few weeks soon spread all over his body until he was tormented with a weeping infant eczema. At the age of two he contracted pneumonia and from then on had recurring attacks of bronchial asthma. During these attacks, when he panicked and struggled for breath, Les was the only who could calm him – not with sympathy (sympathy only made him worse) but there was a kind of tough demanding stoicism that Les taught him, and most of the time it seemed to work.

He was a brave, wild little creature with an inborn instinct for freedom. Put him in a highchair and he'd throw himself out of it, put him in his wooden cot and he'd demolish the dowelling and escape, put him in the water and he'd crawl towards the open sea. When he learned to walk, with great determination, at ten months, I'd find him heading down the road, or sitting in the middle of the railway line trying to change the points with his rubber hammer. Experimenting with a box of matches, he set fire to a heap of papers under the bookcase in the spare room.

'Tie him up to a tree,' said Clarice, 'and get on with your work. It's the only way.'

I stared at her in horror. I wasn't going to tether my child up like an animal.

Little by little the old house was becoming livable, but it was a hard time, cooking on a double-burner primus, balancing on a hardwood plank across the rooms, washing in a cracked brick copper while the new electric stove and the Bendix washer were still unusable, sheetmetal junk in the kitchen.

One morning, as I am cooking bacon and eggs for breakfast, Les says, 'Don't bother to cook anything for me any more, I don't want to be poisoned.'

I stand paralysed by the primus, fighting for control, then slowly I turn round.

'What the hell are you talking about?'

'You heard me. I don't want to be poisoned.'

My self-control cracks and I grab a carving knife off the table. I am halfway across the room, weeping and screaming, with the knife raised over my head to strike.

'I gave up everything to be with you,' I sob. 'I thought you were wonderful but you've destroyed the lot.'

We grapple until the knife falls clattering to the floor and I turn away.

'And you've done it without a tear,' I say. 'It's all gone. Where did it go, where did it all go to?'

Nobody answers. I turn round. He is standing in the middle of the room, the tears raining silently down his face. I've got to him at last. I can't believe it. I've never seen him cry before. It makes him seem vulnerable, like a child. I go to him and put my arms around him.

'Don't cry.' I say. 'It's not so bad really.'

'Life's so hard,' he whispers. 'It's so hard.'

We stand there for a long time, silent, with the sunlight moving across the floor and the oleander bush tapping away against the back wall, until it is time for Joe to go to kindergarten and Michael to have his morning bottle.

That night we are awakened by three drunks sitting up in the box trees along the railway embankment. Laughing, we lean out of the bedroom window. The winter sky is blazing with stars, an electric train whirls past on its way to Central.

'Lec lec lec,' murmurs Michael in his sleep.

'Good night Irene, good night Irene,' sing the drunks in the box trees. 'I'll see you in my dreams.' It is 1954. Stalin is dead, the Rosenbergs have been executed as spies, and Vladimir Petrov, Third Secretary in the Soviet Embassy in Canberra, has requested political asylum in Australia.

Two weeks later, as we are sitting by the Cosy stove in the completed living room, Les drops another bombshell.

'I think it'd be a good idea if you and the kids went to stay with your parents for a while.'

I can't believe my ears. He could never stand my family, and never wanted any of us to have anything to do with them.

'Go away?' I say stupidly. 'But why, and how would we get there?'

'I'd drive you.'

'I don't want to go.'

But he goes on talking as if he hasn't heard me.

'It'll give me a chance to finish the house without any interruptions, and it'll be better for you and the kids. It's a strain on all of us living like this.'

I stare at him in the firelight, trying to work out what is going on behind that deadly calm, those evasive eyes. He is trying to protect us. He wants us to go away because he is afraid of what he might do if we stay. For the first time I face the truth. He is going mad. He is getting out of control, he knows it and is afraid, and I, who have done a university course in Abnormal Psychology, have refused to face the truth that has been staring me in the face for months, years, maybe always.

Had he always been mad? And I remembered the warning on the Adelaide railway station, the irrational jealousy that had begun in a hamburger bar in Perth one night when a passing sailor called out to me, 'How are you, blondie?' and continued with the fantasy of the Darwin wharfie. I remembered Leah Healy's story of the night Les, crazy with laughter, threw a beer bottle straight at the windscreen of Kevin Healy's oncoming car, nearly causing a serious accident. And he was growing worse, moving from fantasies of infidelity and random violence to fantasies of murder. Maybe the only thing to do was pack up and go, but what would become of him, left alone in the half-renovated house with no one to anchor him to reality any more?

Strangely enough, it was almost a relief to find out the truth. What had seemed deliberately cruel and destructive was explained as a sickness beyond his control, something he couldn't be blamed for. What could be done about madness? I remembered the patients paraded before us in Claremont Mental Hospital when we were doing the course in Abnormal Psychology; the girl I'd gone to school with who'd moved away beyond reach into her own world of schizophrenic fantasy; the paranoid schizophrenic who'd begged us to procure his release. He'd seemed so sane until his face swelled and his voice rose as he confessed his central delusion – he was the victim of a Catholic plot. Afterwards they told us he was dangerous, never to be released. He'd taken an axe to a stranger and almost decapitated him.

Within the week Les has driven us to Heidelberg, and my mother, smiling but bewildered, is meeting us on the stone steps edged with blue hydrangeas. The following night Les leaves for the long drive back to Sydney with a thermos of chicken noodle soup I've made up for the journey.

Two days later he is on the phone. The chicken noodle soup has poisoned him, he's been vomiting for days. One of us is mad and it is time we made an appointment to see a doctor.

I find out the name of a well-known Party psychiatrist and go to see him.

'It sounds like a well-developed paranoid schizophrenia,' he tells me.

'Can anything be done to help him?'

'The prognosis isn't good,' he says. 'But if we can get him to commit himself voluntarily we can at least begin treatment.'

'What would you do?' I say trying to be calm, envisioning shock treatment and other horrors I'd read about.

'I've been experimenting with sleep therapy,' he tells me. 'They're using it in the Soviet Union now.'

When Les arrives from Sydney we sit silently in the doctor's waiting room until his name is called. I pick up a magazine, turning the pages, trying to concentrate while a girl twitches and jerks in the chair opposite, and a middle-aged woman sits with tears running silently down her face.

'No, no, no, no, no!' Les is yelling down the corridor. He comes out, walking quickly, head down, agitated, muttering. I follow him across the park, running to keep up, the Flame of Remembrance on the War Memorial is burning steadily in the winter chill.

'What happened?' I ask.

He stops and turns to me, looking cornered. 'He said one of us is mad but he can't tell which one.'

I struggle to keep my voice totally noncommittal. 'What did he suggest?'

'Nothing, he said there's nothing to be done.'

That night, while I am upstairs putting the children to bed, Les disappears, walking out of my parents' house without a word, and nobody sees him go.

I ring the psychiatrist. 'What really happened?'

'I told him he was suffering from paranoid schizophrenia and if he came into hospital immediately I might be able to do something for him – but he just ran out of the surgery. They usually know something's wrong,' he says.

I visit the clinic again, haunted by guilt and the necessity to understand. Perhaps it is all my fault. Perhaps if Les had found somebody else, somebody who hadn't challenged him intellectually, who didn't come from the middle classes he despised, who hadn't had the education he wanted so badly . . .?

'That kind of thinking is counterproductive,' says the psychiatrist. 'If he'd wanted a different kind of woman he'd have found one. It's nothing to do with you.'

'Should I go back to him?' I ask. 'Should I try again?'

'It's my duty to warn you he's dangerous. You might lose your life, and then again there might be a spontaneous remission. It happens sometimes.'

'For how long?'

'A month, a year, three years, for ever – nobody knows.'

Time passed. I discovered I was pregnant again. Les rang once more.

'I think it'd be a good idea if we didn't see each other for quite a while,' he said coldly. 'I've been much better since there's been nobody here to poison my food.'

'I'm having another baby,' I told him.

I found a job as a nurse's aide in the male paraplegic ward at the Austin Hospital in Heidelberg. Some days the alarm clock woke me at six and I walked to the hospital for a seven o'clock start. Other days I started late and worked night shift until ten o'clock. My mother looked after the children and taught Joe to read. Everybody was calm and supportive. Nobody said, 'I told you so'. In the hospital I helped

paraplegics into wheelchairs, washed bedridden patients, fed men
who couldn't even hold a spoon and learned to make beds with
hospital corners.

To a chorus of ribald comments I tried to adjust a urine bottle for
a man in an iron lung. As I leaned across to fix a pillow, somebody
made a grab at my breast. As I passed with a bedpan somebody else
pinched my bottom. A big, fair-headed coalminer, paralysed from the
waist down, was always losing his catheter.

'And we know why, don't we?' said the bitchy Ward Sister. 'If you
stopped playing with yourself it'd stay put all right.'

There was an audible hiss as she flounced out into the pan room.
'He's got six kids already,' she grumbled, 'and he can't wait to get
home next weekend and give that poor wife of his another one.'

There was a man with Parkinson's disease out on the balcony.
He'd been there for years, slowly turning into a vegetable, but there
was a flicker of life left in him yet as he beckoned the cleaning woman
over to whisper in her ear.

'How about a fuck?'

'You filthy thing,' she shouted.

'I would have smacked his face,' said the Ward Sister.

The boy who had broken his spine in a motorbike accident when
he was sixteen, turned twenty-one. Singing 'Happy Birthday to You',
the kitchen staff wheeled in a huge iced cake with twenty-one candles,
but he sat up and hurled it at the wall.

'He's so ungrateful,' they said. 'You can't do anything for him.'

Big scooped scars of old bedsores pitted his back. He shivered
with cold out on the balcony, until I made sure I brought him an extra
blanket every night before I signed off to go home. At weekends and
on my days off, I hunted out pop songs for his record-player.

Only one patient walked out of the hospital on crutches while
I was there, pretending to chase the nurse down the aisle to the cheers
of the bedridden. He was a red-headed building worker who'd fallen
from a multistoreyed building.

One day, as I was lifting a teenager with burnt feet like two lumps
of twisted concrete, I felt a dull pain. Something wet trickled between
my legs.

In the women's toilet I discovered I was bleeding. I spent
a fortnight in the Austin Hospital before they sent me home. My
mother said it was a blessing in disguise, but I managed to keep the
baby, and was glad. It was the only positive thing I had managed to
salvage out of the wreckage of our life together.

My father had a sheep farm at Sunbury outside Melbourne
where we often spent three or four days a week. Wearing a leather

coat and earmuffs against the cold, he was happy riding over those freezing denuded uplands on a huge dapple-grey ex-racehorse called Matchless Mathias. Once when I lost Michael I found him gazing up, sucking his thumb, almost under the hoofs of the great horse, which was sniffing at him curiously.

'Big Poosy,' he said gravely.

The children, in lumberjackets and woollen beanies, played at being Edmund Hillary and Sherpa Tensing, scaling Mount Everest.

Sometimes in the evenings I'd go with my father to search for the lost sheep, climbing through the valleys where icy streams gushed down from the hills. He had all sorts of trouble with his sheep. He had mated the ewes with big-shouldered rams and when the lambs were ready to be born they were caught by their shoulders in the birth canal. The ewes lay dying all over the hillsides with only the lambs' heads protruding. If the lambs managed to struggle out, the foxes were waiting behind the rocks, picking them off before they gave their first bleat. At weekends Dessie and Noel had their surgical instruments out, easing the lambs, trying to save whatever they could.

After this disaster the itch attacked the flock and they staggered through the paddocks with their wool hanging in rags, rubbing themselves raw against the granite boulders.

But when the spring came the survivors recovered, and all my mother's yellow roses bloomed at once along the picket fences in Heidelberg.

Patiently my father taught me to drive in his pale-grey Austin, paying for a driving instructor for the last finishing touches. The day I got my licence I passed Wally Thomas on a Melbourne pedestrian crossing, hand in hand with two little boys, but I didn't speak and he didn't notice me.

Just before Christmas a letter came from Les: 'Dear Toddy, I think for the sake of the children we should give it another try, don't you? Love, Les.'

I went back to the clinic and asked the psychiatrist what I should do. I suppose what I was really looking for was some kind of sanction to say 'yes'.

'If you go back,' he said, 'you must remain absolutely calm at all times, and remember how important it is to try and shield him from any conflict or strain.'

I passed the Flame of Remembrance still glowing in the park, and shivered remembering that first visit months ago, but now, basking in the calm confidence of pregnancy, I felt I could accomplish anything.

The taxi from Mascot dropped us at Railway Parade. The sunflowers were out, the cicadas were already whirring in the box trees along the railway line, and the glider in the front yard of the house next door still hadn't got off the ground. Les was mowing the lawn, stripped to the waist, in an old pair of khaki shorts. Unable to bear the loneliness, he had been staying with his mother for months and the grass had grown up, dry and tall under the coconut palm.

'We're home, Farvie, we're home,' Joe shouted, running up the driveway, 'and guess what, I can read.'

We went inside to the coolness of the kitchen, Michael riding on Les's shoulders, and made a cup of tea.

Two months later I opened the front door to a plain-clothes copper and a shorthand writer with a subpoena for me to appear before the Petrov Spy Commission. I laughed incredulously.

'It's no laughing matter,' the copper said. 'Can we come inside and read the subpoena? The light's bad out here on the verandah.'

'Read it from there,' I said, as Les came down the hall in a pair of shorts, grinning, determined to give them as much cheek as he could get away with.

'Haven't you got anything better to do than this?' he said.

'Watch your mouth,' said the copper, 'and keep a civil tongue in your head, or I'll run you in for contempt.'

In April 1954 Vladimir Petrov and his wife had both defected from the Soviet Embassy in Canberra for an Australian Security Intelligence Organization promise of £5,000 and a secure income for life in Australia.

The defection of the Petrovs inaugurated Australia's own little McCarthy spy hunt. It was a small chapter in a long history of spy mania in the West: Alger Hiss, the American atomic scientist found guilty of spying for the USSR; Klaus Fuchs, the British atomic scientist also found guilty of betraying atomic secrets; the infamous McCarthy witch-hunts in the United States, the defection of Burgess and Maclean to Moscow, and the execution of the Rosenbergs.

Since December 1945, when he passed his Act for the dissolution of the Australian Communist Party, Menzies had been trying unsuccessfully to destroy the Communists. Now, ironically, he was able to use the Communist bogey – Petrov, his defection and his secret documents – to split the Australian Labor Party, discredit Dr Evatt, the leader of the Opposition, and save the 1954 elections for himself and his Party.

Although it had maligned Dr Evatt and his staff and blackened the names of many intellectuals, the Commission by this time had been revealed as something of a paper tiger. The original promise of sensational revelations, about a secret spy ring operating in Australia under the control of the Soviet Embassy in Canberra, had never been delivered. Trade-union radicals jeered at the Commissioners in open court. But it still seemed worthwhile to hold the proceedings up to a little extra ridicule.

In the light of the narrow-minded attitudes towards pregnant women, who should neither be seen nor heard in public places, my appearance might hammer another small nail into its coffin. When the Commission presented me with further ammunition I made the decision that it was my political duty to appear.

I arrived home that afternoon to find a Commonwealth car waiting outside the house, with a drunken messenger who said he had come from the office of the Public Prosecutor to tell me I had been excused from appearing in court.

'Why?' I asked, unconvinced.

The messenger suggested that 'since I was in a delicate condition' my lawyer must have asked for me to be excused.

'I have just been to see my lawyer,' I said, 'and he has done no such thing.'

The drunk on the doorstep looked confused and staggered off down the driveway. I didn't really believe he had come from the Commission at all. I imagined he was some kind of political provocateur. The political climate of the time was so thick with suspicion that we all felt threatened. For weeks cars had been parked outside our house, their occupants obviously taking notes and watching every move we made. It was probably only provocation, but it worked. The drunken messenger turned out to be absolutely genuine, but he had given me some more comic ammunition to help discredit the Commission.

I went to see Dixon, the small, grey, anonymous-looking man who, with Lance Sharkey, ran the Australian Communist Party.

'Were you at the last Central Committee meeting?' Dixon asked me.

I stared at him in astonishment. What on earth would I have been doing at a meeting of the upper echelons of the Party hierarchy?

'No,' I said.

'So you don't know anything that occurred at that meeting?'

'No.'

'So you wouldn't be able to answer any questions about the proceedings?'

I shook my head.

'Then I can see no reason why you shouldn't attend the Commission. It might be politically useful.'

To this day I have no idea what Dixon was referring to or what had occurred at that Central Committee meeting of the Australian Communist Party.

Appearing before the Petrov Commission was like *Alice in Wonderland*. At any moment I expected the Red Queen to scream, 'Off with their heads', but instead the three old, desiccated men nodding away on the bench carried out their appointed tasks like senile marionettes, conferring and muttering to each other in a travesty of justice.

When Petrov and Mrs Petrov enter the court, there is a slight stir of interest. An attractive blonde woman in an ill-fitting Soviet costume, she looks nervous but controlled. Little, fat Petrov is sweating profusely. In the front row I see Ron Richards, the dark-joweled, heavy-shouldered plainclothes detective who used to run the Special Branch in Western Australia. For his skill in harassing Communists and radicals he has now been elevated to Deputy Director of the Australian Security Service.

Claire Flood, Mary Lewis and I have all been called as witnesses. Apparently the plan is to link certain members of the Australian delegation to the Conference in Defence of Children with Petrov's infamous list of Soviet sympathizers and potential spies. I wonder why Claire, Mary and I have been chosen. Les, annoyed that he hasn't been subpoenaed, says it is because the Commission has picked us out as potential 'weakies', easily intimidated by the court.

The prosecutor produces a photograph of myself and Michael, supposedly taken from Petrov's files, but the dates are all wrong. It is a copy of a photograph that has appeared in an issue of *Our Women*, taken long after Petrov's papers were handed over to the Security Service, proving once again that his original files have been tampered with to add more names and more validity.

When I tell the story of the drunken messenger there is a slight uproar in the court. The three Commissioners start banging on the bench, and the Prosecutor's face is swollen with indignation.

'What are you doing here?' says the Prosecutor. 'Because of your condition you were excused from appearing.'

'I didn't believe the word of a drunkard,' I tell the court as innocently as I could manage.

'It's no use, Mr Windeyer, trying to treat these people with common decency. They don't understand the meaning of the word,' says one of the Commissioners bitterly.

Did I really achieve anything at all by appearing before the Petrov Royal Commission? Who knows, but at least I had the satisfaction of helping to hold it up to more ridicule. Six months after it was inaugurated, the Commission issued an interim report saying it had found no evidence of criminal activities by any Australian, but it had served its purpose – the election of Menzies and his Liberals, who remained in power for the next eighteen years.

♠

Myself at thirty-six years, the time of my
publication of *Bobbin Up*, 1959.

Borrowing Barbara Ball's cardigan and hooped silver earrings, I had my hair done and was photographed as one of the finalists in the *Australian Women's Weekly* Short Story Competition, 1957.
Photo: Consolidated Press

'We'll never come back.' Dessie and I at the turn-off to Wickepin, Western Australia, in the summer of 1987. Photo: Merv Lilley

'Nobody plays Rock of Ages on the untuned piano now', (from 'Legend of the Green Country'). Lambton Downs in 1987. Photo: Merv Lilley

On St Patrick's night 1955 I give birth to my third son in Crown Street Maternity Hospital. Taken by surprise, because he is a month early, I have made no booking at any Sydney hospital, nor have I been to any maternity clinic. I am irresponsible, but somehow the struggle to stay calm and controlled in that uneasy household in Railway Parade has taken up every ounce of energy I possess.

When the first contractions come Les refuses to walk to the nearest phone box and book me in at Crown Street.

'Just turn up,' he says. 'They've got to take you.' But I know that without a booking the hospital administration can refuse to admit me.

Hanging on to walls and electric light poles, I stagger a quarter of a mile down the road and phone Crown Street, pretending I am a patient at the Queen Vic, on holiday from Melbourne.

In the labour ward three staff doctors bluster and bully around my bed accusing me of lying, telling me I deserve to be thrown out in the street to have my baby in the gutter. As the pains come closer and closer the room seems to darken and quiver, the faces around the high, hard hospital bed distort to a circle of judges out of the Inquisition.

'We can easily check the records from the Queen Vic, you know,' they are crowing. 'We can prove you are a liar.'

'Just leave me alone,' I say grimly. 'Just leave me in peace to get on with it. I'm having this baby,' and such is the force of my conviction, they slink silently away.

In the public ward the same almoner passes my bed, shaking her head over me. She has given me up as a lost cause, but after two days I am translated into paradise, sent to convalesce in the Crown Street Annexe, a former Rose Bay mansion on the margin of the Harbour opposite Taronga Park Zoo. One problem mother who can't decide on a name for her new baby entertains herself by making lists of all our suggestions until one morning, with a scream of triumph, she tips her bedpan over once again and announces dramatically: 'I know – I'll call her Taronga!'

Because he is born on St Patrick's Day, it seems appropriate to call our new baby Patrick, but Les objects. 'Joe, Mike and Pat,' he says. 'First thing you'll have the priest calling.'

And he's right. A few days after I bring the new baby home the local priest is knocking on the door of Railway Parade, enquiring if there are any Catholics in the house. 'No, only Communists,' I tell him blithely, and he flees down the path as if pursued by demons. Eventually we call our third son Tom, after Tom Mooney, the American labour leader.

I push the pram over the Railway Bridge into Five Ways with Joe trotting at my side and Michael sitting at the feet of the new baby. 'Aren't we lucky?' Joe announces to the passing parade. 'We've got three boys,' but there is only a dubious response.

Michael has tantrums standing on his head in the shopping centre, shying the newly bought potatoes out of the pram to bounce away down the hill, or without warning leaping into the mainstream of traffic across the Bridge.

'Why don't y' take care of y' kid, Missus,' shouts a passing motorist.

'It's all right, love, I know what it's like,' interjects another more compassionate voice.

It seems years since masculine heads turned when I walked laughing past the Quay on a spring afternoon, my cotton skirt blowing in the wind off the Harbour. The butcher calls me 'Missus' these days and, as my seamed and roughened hands accept the change, the grocer comments, 'There's a pair of hard-working hands for y'.' The passing ladies peer under the hood of the pram at the benign pink-cheeked creature with the lint-white hair. 'What a lovely little girl,' they coo.

Consumed by a guilty jealousy he hardly understands, Michael bashes Pom (as he calls Tom) over the temple with a metal duck, or upsets him, cot and all, off the front verandah into a prickly bush. I sit in the darkened bedroom, trying to manufacture enough milk for a hungry baby, while Michael stands in the doorway sucking a rebellious thumb. 'Take it back,' he mutters darkly, 'take it back.'

IN February 1956 Nikita Khrushchev denounces Stalin at the Twentieth Congress of the Communist Party of the Soviet Union. We find
the printed speech pushed under the back door one summer evening
when we come back from driving down the South Coast. We argue
over it for weeks. Is it really genuine, or a skilful forgery by some anti-
Soviet writer?

If it is genuine, the ramifications are unbelievable, the crimes
monstrous, our beliefs and our lives made ludicrous, naive, even
criminal, because we have lived this lie for years, and preached it
everywhere – the lie of the perfection of Soviet society under its great
leader, Joseph Stalin.

The Australian Communist Party does its utmost to keep the
Twentieth Congress report from its members, expelling Jimmy Sta-
ples, the schoolteacher, who has dared to publish and distribute it.

Dissent and argument in the Branches, demands that the Central
Committee verify or deny the report, and at last we are told the truth.
The report is absolutely genuine. The crimes of Stalin are document-
ed. The 'Cult of the Individual' is the culprit, and Stalin's body has
been removed from the Mausoleum in Red Square. He will no longer
lie with Lenin as one of the embalmed saints of the Revolution.

What now? Shaken but determined not to 'throw the baby out
with the bath water', we will continue the struggle for socialism, but
something has happened to us. Some ultimate innocence has been
destroyed for ever, some uneasy voice lies at the back of the mind
asking interminable questions: What if . . .? How do we know . . .?
From now on we will never be quite so gullible again, but surely this is
a good thing – to question, to learn, to discover, is one of the basic
methods of dialectics. Only sometimes we long for the old settled
security, the old untainted certainty before the Twentieth Congress
and the deposition of the man-God Joseph Stalin, floating in fireworks over Moscow with his moustache ends dripping stars. Who now
are the heroes and who the villains, after the Twentieth Congress?

Perhaps this is one of the reasons why one day we pack up our
belongings, leaving Sydney, 'the big smoke' and the class struggle, all

that has defined our lives for the past seven years, to go back to the bush – to 'the radical innocence of communities living close to the earth', back to another Australian dream of 'the rugged individualist'. A dream we never even thought we had.

'Piccaninny daylight,' says Les, as we drive away from Rockdale in the dawn, making for Western Australia in our new second-hand Buick, loaded to the running boards; Joe and Michael clamouring amongst the luggage on the back seat and Pom sitting up, pink-cheeked and cherubic, on my knee.

'Now our new life is just beginning,' says Les, and I look across at him, beaming with excitement, wondering how long it will last this time, trying not to be a killjoy but knowing we carry all our problems and contradictions with us across three thousand miles of desert, along the Great Australian Bight, through the rabbit-proof fence on to the plains of the Great Southern.

We have sold our house in Rockdale to Clarice and are on our way to share-farm Lambton Downs with my father. I am going home to the first house in the hollow of the heart. Surely I can at least pretend to a confidence I no longer feel.

Dessie has a residency at Royal Perth Hospital and a baby boy, a few months older than Pom. So my whole family have migrated back across the Nullarbor to South Perth. Whatever happens, there will be protection. We won't starve, we won't be destitute or homeless; why then do I feel this peculiar sense of foreboding, as if we are moving into a future that darkens as we drive?

It has been a hard year and when my mother writes to say that Lambton Downs is empty and its future undecided, the Sartoris having left to live on their own farm near Malyalling siding, Les begs me to ask if we can lease the farm.

'I'll do better in the bush,' he says. 'I can't stand the noise or the strain of the boilershop any longer.'

My father writes back to Les, agreeing to take him on as 'a working partner', on one condition – he must marry me immediately.

'Surely,' writes my Methodist father, 'even if you don't wish to regularize Dorothy's position, you will want to make your children's future secure.'

I am angry with my father for meddling in our private lives. A forced marriage fills me with disgust – yet I remember the shame of facing up to the Registry Office to register Pom, the pitying looks of the Registrar and his offer to arrange an immediate marriage, while Les turns away silently with that cruel little smile curving one corner of his mouth. I remember filling in Pom's name as our third son and the Registrar explaining kindly that each illegitimate has to be registered separately. Bastards have no familial relationship.

But Les just laughs, ignoring my father's letter. Clarice has paid us a deposit on Railway Parade. She is planning to turn it into a boarding house. The rest of the money will arrive in three monthly instalments, allowing us an income while we get on our feet in Western Australia.

So we leave Sydney, travelling through country towns, across creeks and rivers, through forests and cities, past farms and sidings, while Michael sings '. . . dog dadogdadog, mandamandaman, cow-decowdecow, 'orsedorsedorse' from the back seat of the Buick. Across the potholed roads of the desert, thick with bull dust, we dodge the wombats mesmerized by the glare of the headlights. The gate on the rabbit-proof fence is icy with frost, burning my palm as I close it.

Arriving at Eucla on the West Australian border late at night, I knock on the door of the one store for petrol. There is a light burning, a radio turned up high, the sound of a man shouting. He appears in the doorway, drunk and cursing, letting a pack of snarling terriers loose at my heels. I run for the car and we wait, shivering until morning, when the petrol pumps open up again.

At the next station a gaunt, ghastly woman, with a bundle of keys jangling at her waist, overcharges us for her brackish showers. A breakdown on the saltbush plain and I stand at the edge of the road to flag down the first passing motorist. 'Eastern Staters,' snarls his companion. 'Drive on.'

Outside Norseman a kangaroo springs from the low scrub to smash into our windscreen. We limp into town covered in dust to stay for one night in a big wooden pub on a wide street where the children jet the tap water into their mouths like little desert rats.

As we drive through the goldfields, the trunks of the gimlets twist like polished wooden corkscrews along the road to Coolgardie.

Les has decided that we must call in at Lambton Downs. He is impatient to see this farm he has heard so much about, but my heart is sinking. What will he think of it?

Reaching Wickepin in the dusk, I have to guide us to the farm along roads lost in the drift of memory. Wickepin is deserted; a run-down country town with one single dusty street. Where is the turn-off past the Showgrounds, the track to Malyalling along the railway line? If I keep the line on our right, we must reach the boundary gate eventually. The stars wheel and blaze overhead and I am drunk on the scent of the dew-drenched stubble under the moon. I can see the silver wheat silos glistening at Malyalling siding, see the lights of Tony Sartori's farm with the sheepdogs barking.

'Where's home?' wails Michael from the back seat.

'Let's call in,' I beg, and so we drive into the yard and Tony comes out, carrying a hurricane lantern, the dogs leaping around his knees.

'It's me, Tony, it's me!' I cry out.

'Doff, it's Doff!' he says, in his husky accented voice, the light from the hurricane lantern held high to play across my face.

Next morning, following Tony in his big American Ford, we cross the railway line – LOOK OUT FOR THE ENGINE – pass through the iron gate on the boundary, the rock hill on our left, the creek trickling with the first autumn rains, but the banks are peculiarly empty – where have the wattle, the tea-tree and the bottlebrush gone?

My heart leaps. I can see the house lying in the hollow amongst almond and fig trees, its corrugated-iron roof gleaming, but except for one hardy quince, dressed in white rags to keep off the parrots, the orchard is dead behind it. Here are the stables with their brush thatching, the shearing shed leaning sideways in a sudden shaft of light, but there are no animals, no dogs, no horses, no cows, no turkeys, no fowl-yard. Only the everlasting sheep, with their melancholy baa-ing, move like grey clouds through the paddocks.

The garden has gone, the sleepout wrecked in the path of the hurricanes that sweep through these regions once every twenty years. The children stand, small and desolate, on the verandah, staring out across the empty flats; town children lost under all this immensity of light and air. I glance at Les nervously, trying to see the farm through his eyes – three thousand run-down acres, bordered with sagging fences.

'Christ!' he says. 'What the fuck have you brought us to?'

But my father has great plans for Lambton Downs – we will deflect the salted creek into new channels and regenerate the land. We will plant new trees to replace the dead, dig new wells, replant the orchard, using the one remaining soak across the creek to bring fresh water into the house.

'What if the new channel doesn't work?' I ask him. 'What if it just turns salt again?'

'Then we'll dig another one,' he says.

But until these marvels can be carried out we have to depend on the two rainwater tanks at the back step, washing in a tin dish on the verandah, pissing and shitting in the creek bed, because Les refuses to empty the old pan lavatory.

I struggle with the ancient fuel stove in the kitchen, the cracked brick copper in the wash house, while the children run and crawl around the verandahs coated with thick black sump oil to keep off the white ants.

I have already insulted my mother by taking down the old paintings in their ornate gilt frames, the ones I used to love – 'The Watcher on the Hill', 'The Wild Horses', 'The Stag at Bay', 'The Deer in the Forest', 'The Newfoundland Dog Rescuing the Drowning Girl',

'The English Children Roasting Chestnuts in the Grate'. I simply can't tolerate them any more. It's sad to grow up, to go back through the mirror on the wall. My mother gives the paintings to the Sartoris, who are delighted with them.

When seeding starts and Les has to balance on the tray of Tony Sartori's truck, pouring the superphosphate from open bags while Tony drives flat out around the paddocks, he rages against these primitive farming methods. He wants the latest in expensive farm machinery, but we have no money to buy it and my father won't even listen. He has agreed to stake us for our groceries at the local Co-op, but only after my mother intervenes. He complains about Les constantly, but only behind his back. Les is a bludger, he won't get out of bed in the mornings, all he wants to do is spend my father's money on luxuries.

The Golden Valley of my childhood has gone for ever. I am reliving my mother's life on the farm, finding out the difference between illusion and reality. A child's vision has turned into a grown-up woman's nightmare. Standing by the kitchen window, staring out across the creek bed, I even experience the identical loneliness my mother must have felt, the sense of hopeless entrapment. We cannot stay here any longer, not with Les and my father's hostility picking away behind my back. I remember the Melbourne psychiatrist's advice: 'He must have absolute peace and contentment'.

When the morning sickness begins and I know I am pregnant again, there is only one thing left to do. I go out to say goodbye to my father, digging in the garden under the kitchen window. I can hear the scrape of his spade against the clods of damp earth.

Feeling guilty, I kiss his cheek. 'We're going now, Dad,' I tell him.

'You never even gave it a chance,' he grumbles.

'It wouldn't have worked.'

And so I leave him there, head bent, still digging, sour with his lost dreams. We will never run horses on the hundred acres now. He will never rechannel the salty creek through the paddocks or replant the farm with new trees.

We drive away in the late afternoon, leaving the house huddled under watery clouds, and I am not sorry. There is nothing left of the dreams of childhood. We can never relive them. Thomas Wolfe was right, you can't go home again.

In Perth I make an appointment to see the same doctor who arranged my last abortion years ago. These days he calls himself a psychiatrist. When I tell him the story of Les's mental illness he leans forward, his eyes glistening like a voyeur.

'I suppose he is very sexually demanding,' he says. 'They usually are.'

I smile grimly. 'No, he hardly ever touches me.'

His face falls. He suggests that it would be a good idea if I am sterilized at the same time as the fetus is aborted.

'After all, you don't want another child to this man,' he says, 'and it's very unlikely, at your age and with three children, that you'll ever marry again.'

A fitted rubber pessary, orthogynal and a douche have never been a spectacular contraceptive success, but I can't agree to be mutilated, to be turned into a sterile doll. I think of my mother, her frigidity, her madness, her early menopause. Nobody is going to do that to me at thirty-three.

Les doesn't object to the abortion, only makes one of his dark remarks – that it 'might be used against us later' – but when the time comes he doesn't turn up to drive me to The Mount Hospital. I have to ring for an ambulance and lie alone in the hospital room, drugged and shaved, wondering if it's too late to change my mind.

After the abortion we leave for Albany with my mother to stay in the little jarrah house on the beach, dragging home driftwood from the storms breaking along the shore to build giant fires in the whitewashed fireplace. At night through the rusty windows Breaksea flickers on the horizon, and I lie listening to the wind rising, the pulse and rock of the little house, moving out across the ocean like a wooden ark at sea.

There are new, wild plans afoot for us to buy a guest house at Middleton Beach, or a school bus at Yarloop. Les seems to think that I could run the guest house more or less single-handed, or drive the school bus on the days when he doesn't feel like it, but I am not very enthusiastic.

When we arrive back in Perth he announces that we are leaving immediately for a holiday in Geraldton.

'But you've just had a holiday,' says my mother.

As we drive away she pushes £20 through the window.

'You'd better take this,' she says, 'you might need it.'

'We'll be back in two weeks,' I tell her, but it is two years before I see her again.

I look at Les's profile, relaxed, smiling, as if he hasn't a care in the world. What is going to happen to us? Our money is running out. We have no future plans, and now here we are practically broke, driving off to Geraldton like a bunch of tourists.

'We can't afford this, you know,' I tell him.

'Okay,' he says. 'Let's go home then,' and turns the car around towards the Great Eastern Highway.

Two nights later, driving through the dark across the desert, he tells me he is probably wanted by the Sydney police for a 'hit-and-run' on the road to Newcastle. It all turns out to be fantasy. At least no policeman ever knocks on our door in Sydney to accuse him, but the whole journey is darkened by the thought that for all I know it might possibly be true.

After driving day and night we arrive at Railway Parade to be greeted by a disgruntled Clarice, whose last words to me had been: 'If it doesn't work out in the West I want you to know I can't have you and the kids back here living on top of me.'

But we have nowhere else to go, so she crowds us all into one single room, maybe hoping we will be so uncomfortable that we will make other arrangements.

'If you could buy the house back from me I'd be willing to find somewhere else,' she says.

'But we haven't got the money,' I tell her.

'Perhaps you could ask your mother.'

There seems to be no other solution. I hate asking, but I write for £2,000. Clarice has spent the extra money laying lino in all the rooms and hanging Venetian blinds at the windows. She has tidied up the garden, cutting back the red oleander to a mutilated stump. I loathe all her 'improvements' but there is nothing to be done about them. My mother sends me the money, Clarice buys herself a smaller place in Rockdale, and with a sigh of relief we settle down in our own house again.

How wonderful it is to move through these rooms knowing they are my own – the coconut palms soughing in the wind off Botany Bay, brushing against the bedroom windows; the Venetian blinds rattling as the trains rush past to Central.

But there is no money, and Les seems sublimely indifferent to getting a job. I will have to find one myself, and this time, as the breadwinner of the family, I can't afford a low-paid factory job or working for the Party for £2 a week or less.

Putting aside my ideals, I will have to sell myself to the highest bidder, but what have I got to sell? There is only one skill I have ever possessed – writing. That is how I became a 'prostitute of the pen' for Walton-Sears.

I read the advertisement in the *Sydney Morning Herald*:

Creative copywriters, ex-journalists, girls with a flair for writing, wanted to join the staff of huge mail-order firm with international links. Great opportunities for advancement, American scholarship training scheme, profit sharing and pension fund. Ring for appointment.

I blonde my hair with Napro blonding emulsion and invest in a new blue woolknit, with a tiny hat made from blue tulle roses and a wisp of veiling. Les says I look like 'a moll on holiday'. Next morning I catch the train to Central, walking through a subway of echoing footfalls and drawings of women's genitals. Waltons and Sears-Roebuck have taken over the old Murdoch building in Riley Street, where a huge twenty-stone Swedish masseuse runs the Turkish bath as a blind for Thommo's Gambling School. The side entrance opens into a lane where the derros sit against the wall all morning, waiting for the Sydney City Mission to open up its soup kitchen. Next door is the Sydney Refuge for Mothers and Children, up the hill the juvenile lockup and the Children's Court.

The floors click past like a camera shutter and I step out into the Advertising Department, an echoing vault with a pitted concrete floor, where I am interviewed by Mr Ken, the advertising manager.

Mr Ken is a handsome, elegant man in a cutaway coat and a swagger. One day, when he grows older, that icy debonair charm will flake off like gold leaf, leaving him sleazy.

'You've never worked in advertising before,' he says. 'There are only a few psychological truths to remember. Human beings are composed of four basic instincts: sex, greed, fear and envy!'

Through the glass I can see the commercial artists bent over their drawing boards, swimming in the tea-coloured light; can see myself reflected, bowing and nodding and scraping like a blue marionette, hopelessly compromised.

'What does your father do?' he says.

'My father is a grazier.'

He struggles to adjust to this . . . 'Sheep or cattle?'

'Oh! sheep,' I say arrogantly.

But he is determined to resurrect himself as the boss.

'Well, I think we will find each other very satisfactory. I want to build up a skilful writing team and I need intelligent people – so shall we say tomorrow morning, somewhere after nine – no time clock to punch here. You copywriters will have a very privileged position.'

'And what about the salary?' I ask him.

'Oh! let's say twelve a week, typist's wages to start.'

I am stunned with disappointment. How can I hope to keep the whole family on a wage like that? I struggle for the right degree of contempt in my voice.

'I've never worked for a salary like that before.'

But all the time I am hooting with silent laughter, remembering the Alexandria Spinning Mills, sorting buttons at Beutrons, nurse's aide on the basic wage for women.

'Then how about £14 to start?' he says, backtracking hastily. 'And we'll discuss a raise later. Remember you're beginning in a new profession – unskilled.'

As I exit through the baize door he writes the one word 'sharp' on his blotter; a word, mistrustful but realistic, that will colour our relationship for the next two years.

On the stairs I pass a girl, long-legged, russet-haired, in a suede reefer jacket. She bounds into Mr Ken's office, sees that word on his blotter, and tells me about it a week later.

On my first day at work the copywriters and artists are given their first professional assignment – buckets and washcloths to clean down the filthy third-floor windows.

Les has mixed reactions to my new job.

'Toddy never tells me anything,' he grumbles, 'just goes her own sweet bitchy way.' Or, 'Housework drives her mad. She can't stand it, but you've got to face facts. We don't live in a perfect society. We haven't got equality, and it's the woman's job to stay home and look after the kids. That's part of the bargain.'

In the mornings he puts on his lambswoool slippers and sits under the light in his vinyl chair reading Balzac from the Rockdale library, his finger carefully tracing the sentences.

'I'm retired,' he tells anyone who will listen, 'bludging! Toddy's gone off to work to keep me and the kids.'

He leaves most of the housework to Joe, paying him pocket money to do the weekend shopping, hang out the washing, and vacuum the house. At six years old this is an unfair burden, but Joe is a phenomenon. Skipping classes, he is sent around the schoolroom to demonstrate his astounding reading skills. But there is a nervous, unchildlike line etched permanently between his eyebrows, as if he carries a weight too heavy for a child's shoulders.

Michael and Pom are both at home all day, because Michael refuses to go to kindergarten. Kicking and swearing, he escapes over the wall, teachers and children streaming after him, up and down the streets of Rockdale. 'Dear little yellow duck, fartin' down the parf,' he chants round and round the 'kindy' playground.

'I've never been beaten by a child before,' sighs the Principal. 'He's a dear little thing but I do think he might be better off at home.'

At night I often dream the same nightmare about Michael: I am running after him down the railway line when he disappears into a long tunnel. I can hear his laughter echoing back, and see his curls bobbing up ahead. Then the train enters the tunnel; it is coming closer. I can smell the acrid smoke and see the sparks flying. The noise bounds and thunders off the concrete walls.

'Mikey, Mikey!' I scream, and wake up shaking in the double bed.

While Les reads Balzac and Zola, or works out in the shed inventing a new rotary clothes hoist that folds up like an umbrella, Michael and Pom wreck the house – mixing eggs, golden syrup and flour amongst the clothes in their divan drawers, or painting neat sticky stripes of indelible red nail polish down the pink blankets on our bed.

'Mum, Mum, Pom's deaded the cat!' Michael cries, and I run in to find Pom dunking the half-drowned tortoiseshell in the old baby's bath. I wrap it up in a blanket in front of the heater, feed it warm milk with brandy out of an eye dropper, and save its life, but it is always neurotic and shits regularly in the shower recess. We have two cats, the tortoiseshell and a big clever tabby Pom has christened 'Tom Scatch Cat'. Les rescues a starving lop-eared, half-foxie, half-cattle dog from the Tempe Tip and it goes everywhere with us, riding in the Buick to National Park, the Hawkesbury, Woy Woy and Lake Macquarie.

Our life seems much like that of any other Sydney working-class family, but underneath the facade there are those dark moments when the shadow of madness comes closer and then recedes again. We seldom make love any more, and when we do I find myself shrinking away from him. There is some primitive part of me that cannot lie easily with a madman. Maybe it's an instinctive fear of reproducing abnormal genes. When Les uses me as a guinea pig for his latest and weirdest invention, I feel outraged. A tiny 'French letter' made out of a child's balloon, it just fits over the tip of the penis and is designed to give maximum sexual pleasure, but it has one basic fault. It invariably falls off at the moment of climax, only proving, Les says, 'my insatiable sexuality'.

He continues to manufacture hundreds of these condoms in the shed in the back yard, until one day I come home from work to find the children blowing them up and letting them float over the picket fences into the neighbours' yards.

Les replaces the condom manufacture with a different dream – a fantasy of a gentleman's existence in a ramshackle mansion amongst the Arncliffe rocks, where we will let out rooms to ideal tenants and never have to go to work again.

From the outside the whole place is a folly, as if he has fabricated it as the outward sign of his own craziness. If I wind down the car window and shout 'Fake', it will surely dissolve in the mists above Cook's River.

Up and down the stairs, through innumerable pigsties of little outhouses and washrooms, the existing tenant scuttles in front of us, twisting a dish rag in her ancient hands, mortally afraid that we'll buy the house and turn her out into the street.

I long to tell her: 'Don't worry, it's all right, we'll be gone soon and you'll never see us again. In a week or two he won't even remember that you exist.'

Gold-headed and smelling of shaving lotion, with only his train fare in his pocket, Les leaves for lunch at the Rex to discuss finance on a £4,000 deposit with the owner of the Arncliffe residential.

'The car looks a bit beat-up for this kind of thing,' he says.

The following week, omitting to confess his discharge from the RAAF for 'nervous instability', he is negotiating with the owner of a fleet of aircraft for a job as a commercial pilot. Adopting the pseudonym 'Frank Hardy', he cons a real estate agent into driving him twenty-five miles to view a secluded house on the beach at Stanwell Park for 'a writer's hideaway'.

Sometimes I even welcome these delusions because they leave me in peace, but straphanging amongst the suffocating crowds on the train to Central, I often feel guilty and mortally afraid. Each time I agree to a new fantasy, each time I play along, it is as if I give him another little shove down the incline of madness. One day perhaps he will never come back, and I will have farewelled him – striding, jaunty, bright-haired, even whistling – into Bedlam.

But my heart is so hardened that I try to forget about it and save myself. Besides don't I leave this madman's castle each day to enter into my own 'Grub Street', my hell of lost talent and wasted opportunity? But it doesn't comfort me. I am free and guilty as well because with each insane dream Les is holding in his hand some crazy gift for me: a rotary clothesline patented to make our fortune, a toppling house on the edge of a cliff face, a secret hideout by the sea, or a vision of himself as he once was: the hero, climbing into a cockpit, grinning, in his blue uniform with the white wings on the pocket.

Perched up on the top floor of the old warehouse in Riley Street, pounding out mountains of trash – lettuce-crisp sundresses, bunny-warm twinsets, Sinatra-red pure wool jumpers, tangerine lipsticks, throbbing with the savagery of tom-toms under a tropic moon, I sometimes wonder which of us inhabits the craziest world.

The Advertising Department is organised on hierarchical lines – artists on one side, copywriters on the other, with a phalanx of junior executives down the middle, phoning, posturing, flaunting their petty authority over us all.

They are all members of the Walton-Sears 'Knights of the Round Table' – a five-foot mannikin called Mr Bigger, Kerry Vere de Vere, who has come to us from *House and Garden*, and Harry Garlick, a BA dropout from Sydney University, a satirist who outrages the office girls by saying 'fuck'. Each month they compete for 'the blue vase', a miniature china object that habitually graces Mr Bigger's desk alone.

In the darkroom a pale-faced hump-shouldered photographer called Johnny Ray concocts diabolical schemes to bring them all down. Together we devise a fake illustrated proclamation presenting each one of them with the Order of the Pink Chamber Pot and drop lewd suggestions in the new 'suggestion box'. At night the young executives try to trace the origin of these outrages by checking all our typewriter keys, but their detective work is never successful.

> There is a woman in my life
> with tongue as sharp as any knife
> and hair made gold as Sydney beaches
> with bleaches

writes Johnny Ray, propping it on my desk as a morning greeting. His pensioner father is in hospital, so he brings their white cockatoo to sit out on the roof and scream all day.

'Where's that bunny in the darkroom?' cries Mr Ken, darting across the floor holding a full point on the end of his tweezers.

'Dance cocky, dance cocky, dance cocky,' squawks the white cockatoo from the balcony, while the models circle slowly, displaying their whirly-skirted polished cottons. ('Through these portals pass the most beautiful girls in Australia.') Only when they turn their backs the illusion is dispelled, the 'whirly skirts' cut down the centre seam with a razor blade, leaving their panties exposed.

'We are not after the carriage trade,' says Mr Ken, pirouetting under the giddy blaze of fluorescent lights, 'we want the good solid middle-class custom, the Holdens, not the Packards and the Rolls.'

He is restoring a run-down mansion on the north shore, once the residence of the dead poetess Dorothea McKellar, to 'its former glory'.

A blow-up of himself and two models in Walton-Sears 'separates', posing in front of the pillared portico, will adorn the front cover of the catalogue.

There are five copywriters – including my russet-haired friend Barbara, a twenty-three-year-old English migrant whose last job was writing blurbs for the book covers at Angus & Robertson. Contemptuous of Australian men with their short back and sides and stamina trousers, she has nevertheless fallen in love with red-headed Harry Garlick, who has kissed her at the Advertising Department Christmas Party.

Peter Bonner is a nineteen-year-old whizz kid with a yacht on Sydney harbour called *Peter Pan* and a girlfriend called Wendy. One day he will be promoted to writing washing-machine jingles for television and take out American citizenship. Monica, who dyes her hair weekly from red to black, is writing a novel called 'Tainted Eyeballs'. Changing her name to 'Monique', she will become a fashion writer for a glossy magazine. Marie, the head copywriter, is a middle-aged spinster from Melbourne with a peculiarly pungent body odour. Behind her back Peter calls her 'Old Yellow-Stain Blues'.

Secretly modelling the fitted red velvet coat with the grey fake fur collar, I admire my reflection in the full-length mirror in the stock-room. I think it makes me look a little like Marlene Dietrich. Dreaming of owning it, I steal a pair of boots for Michael instead – my first crime ever. Walton-Sears has succeeded in corrupting me, but when I bring them home my punishment is that they don't even fit.

My eyes are swollen and smarting, giving out under the flickering fluorescents. We are all working overtime, going home after dark down Riley Street, past the clamorous interior of Thommo's where the 'cocka-toos' spring up, negligently lighting cigarettes all along the pavement, and in the upstairs windows of the semi-detached brothels girls in kimonos sit outlined under pink lightshades, open for business.

'Toddy,' calls Peter Bonner in the blue dusk, 'did you dance the charleston and the black bottom when you were young?'

19
♣

B UT now the miracle happens – between one catalogue and the next, while the buyers are hustling up the next lot of merchandise, the rain is splashing through the roof and the typewriters are empty, I begin to write again after ten silent years.

Sitting at my desk, pretending to be busy, I find myself typing a story about Jeanie, one of the girls at the Alexandria Spinning Mills, a story that will become the catalyst for my novel *Bobbin Up*. I can hardly believe it – are the weary years of exile over, is the long endurance of silence ended? Clumsy, awkward from disuse, the words are tumbling out of me. I am possessed again, writing wherever or whenever I can find the time or the space. I resent every time-consuming moment wasted on the wretched catalogue: writing copy, choosing typefaces, laying out the pages in millimetres so that not one line of space is wasted. Les is being extraordinarily supportive, designing a table of mathematical calculations that makes my task magically easy, even finding me a second-hand Olivetti in a hock shop.

I finish a second story, 'The Wire Fences of Jarrabin', set in the Corrigin of my childhood. There we are walking to school together with Edna and Irene McLimmens, watching their red-headed mother feed the newborn baby, watching Duncan Waldon standing at the door of the Co-op in his white apron, with the midges biting in the dusk.

At the Rockdale branch of the Party I meet a small dark woman called Enid with one dropped eyelid who introduces me to the Sydney Realist Writers. The Realist literary movement was begun by a group of Communists and left-wingers in Melbourne. Melbourne always had the reputation of being the centre of any intellectual life that existed in Australia. Frank Hardy, Judah Waten, Alan Marshall, John Morrison, David Martin, Eric Lambert, Ralph De Bossiere, Stephen Murray-Smith and Ian Turner were amongst the founding fathers of the Realist Writers and the Australasian Book Society.

Moving to Sydney, Frank Hardy has inaugurated the first Realist Writers' meeting in his house above the lakes at Narrabeen. Frank is riding high. His novel *Power Without Glory*, and short stories like 'The Load of Wood', have made him famous.

He is in many ways a charming larrikin but in others a dedicated Communist with a burning – almost biblical – belief in the power of the word. Some Party members complain that he has used them up shamelessly, but in those years, when I needed someone to believe in me as a writer, he never faltered.

As a committed Socialist Realist I have given 'The Wire Fences of Jarrabin' a 'positive' ending – a strike against the Shell Oil Company led by McLimmens, the Aboriginal truck driver. When I read the story at the Realist Writers' meeting and come to McLimmens' penultimate speech – 'It's my country. I been here for thirty thousand years' – Frank slaps his knee in genuine delight.

'He would too, the bastard,' he shouts.

It is that capacity for spontaneous empathy that I love and value in Frank Hardy, but it isn't all praise. When I write a clumsy poem about meeting the ghost of Henry Lawson in Redfern Street, and a worse one about the execution of the Rosenbergs, Frank says: 'For Christ's sake, Toddy, write a poem about the death of your mother or something.'

This is probably the most crucial thing ever said to me as a writer. It will take a long while, but it starts me on the long road back to freedom from doctrinaire Marxism. For I am still a dogmatist, nothing has fundamentally changed, and I write bad sentimental stories with 'positive endings' like 'Joey' and 'Pink Blankets for Kathy and Blue', heavily loaded with sympathy for the suffering working class. They are praised, win prizes in Communist circles, and are translated into foreign languages in Eastern bloc countries, so that it takes me years to realize how dishonest and saccharine they are, how the bias and propaganda distort the style.

I am still preaching Marxism in a different form, struggling to find my own ways of doing so. It's true that the rock-hard certainty of belief has trembled a little – more than a little – under the impact of the Twentieth Congress. Maybe that is the main reason why I have found my way back again to the country of the imagination.

When the *Australian Women's Weekly* advertises a short-story competition I enter 'The Wire Fences of Jarrabin', but realizing it will never be acceptable in its present form, I eliminate the strike and the 'positive ending', retitling it 'My Mother Said I Never Should'. I feel politically compromised, but Frank says it is good tactics to get yourself published, and the story has a pro-Aboriginal message anyway. The rest of the Realist Writers are not so sure, and – probably for all the wrong reasons – this is the one time when they are right. 'The Wire Fences of Jarrabin' has integrity. It is an incomparably better story than the truncated version tailor-made for the *Women's Weekly*.

When 'My Mother Said I Never Should' is chosen as one of the six finalists, and published in the magazine, my mother's friends ring her to say they didn't know she had Aboriginal blood in her family, and Aunty Daisy is upset because the grandfather of the story is the town drunk.

It is my first experience of the Australian habit of equating fiction with reality.

'My Mother Said . . .' disappears into the ephemeral pages of the *Weekly*, but 'The Wire Fences' is anthologized in 'The Tracks We Travel', published by the Australasian Book Society. With 'The Wire Fences' I begin on a book of interrelated stories set in the wheatbelt of Western Australia. In the first story Dolly Cracker, the storekeeper's daughter, is kicking a spirit stove down the main street of Jarrabin while the local carpenter prances past on his big black stallion.

There is much that is lively, even new, in these stories, but again I spoil them with my heavy hand, twisting them out of shape. My middle-class characters are not allowed to develop under their own impetus. Without softness or humanity they are all ultimately present-ed as scavengers against society, giving the stories a sour, lopsided atmosphere. The copywriters at Walton-Sears read them all. Marie says I must have known a lot of nasty people in my life.

Frank Hardy is the only real writer I know. The Sydney Realist Writers are mainly composed of Lawson's 'wanter writes an' can't', a beleaguered little group in a philistine Communist Party in a philis-tine Australia, but they do provide the necessary support system for a new left-wing writer struggling to survive in a hostile environment.

We foregather at these meetings to argue about Socialist Realism, and the problems we will face writing literature in a Communist society. It wasn't unusual in those days, whenever Communists came together to discuss these and similar utopian questions.

'When all the contradictions have withered away,' somebody says, 'there'll be nothing left to write about any more.'

'People will still die,' says Frank. 'They'll still have tragic love affairs and broken marriages and sick children.'

It has never occurred to me before – the chilly perfection of a Communist paradise will never exist because it isn't even human.

That night, his narrow Irish face concentrated with energy, Frank stands to read W. B. Yeats's 'Easter 1916'.

'Too great a sacrifice can make a stone of the heart' – the room hushes, and it is months before I have the gall to try and write another poem. When I do I borrow Barbara's fawn sheath and hooped silver earrings, have my hair styled, and read a poem against atomic war on the Women's Session on Channel 2:

> Have you heard the children singing
> As they march through field and town,
> Hiroshima Hiroshima now we all fall down.

The Aldermaston marchers against the terrors of the bomb are massing in the London streets, but in Sydney a viewer rings ABC to say that she has heard this poor woman reading a poem on Channel 2 who seems to be very upset about something, but she has no idea what it is.

In October 1956 there are demonstrations in Hungary demanding an elected democratic government. By 4 November the Soviet tanks are rumbling through the streets of Budapest, and the Australian Communist Party is torn apart by the Hungarian Revolution. The majority of its intellectuals are questioning the official Party line that the Soviets' tanks are defending socialism against the counter-revolution.

When Les and I ask questions about 'the counter-revolution in Hungary' at a Party fraction in Rockdale, we are told there is nothing further to talk about as the Party is now concentrating on the 'campaign against monopoly'.

Worried at the expulsion of so many dissidents, I stand up at a meeting of hundreds of South Sydney Communists and ask the chairman, Eddie Roe, Secretary of the NSW Sheetmetal Workers' Union, to open up a discussion on the dangerous political situation in the Party. Instead I am virtually threatened with expulsion myself.

'These comrades,' screams Eddie in his orator's voice, sandpaper scraping against skin, 'these comrades have been with us for a long time, but now the day has come to say "goodbye"; our paths divide – they to move back into the ranks of the capitalist class they never really abandoned, we to go on together to fight in the great struggles that lie ahead, the struggles of the working class of Australia against monopoly, for jobs, socialism and world peace.'

As I move out of the hall the comrades make a great path for me to pass through, as if I have some form of political pox.

At a meeting of a national fraction of Communist writers and intellectuals, held in a private house near the harbour, I tell the story of the Hurstville meeting, quoting Eddie Roe word for word.

'What beautiful prose!' cries Communist poet John Manifold, his sleepy-lidded malicious eyes springing wide open.

It is early summer and the golden light glows across the harbour, illuminating the circle of faces. What an extraordinary group they are, this pantheon of men, these stars of the Australian Communist intelligentsia, many of whom will have such a profound effect on my life. We are gathered together on a quiet Australian weekend in the calm suburb of Castlecrag (houses designed by Walter Burley Griffin) to discuss these cataclysmic upheavals that are tearing the Communist Parties of Europe apart: John Manifold from Queensland, handsome, cherub-faced, Oxford-educated, dispossessed son of the New South Wales squattocracy; David Martin, novelist, poet, journalist, an intense, myopic, Hungarian Jew who by background and experience has more at stake in these discussions than any of us; Stephen Murray-Smith from Melbourne, editor of the left-wing literary magazine *Overland*, big, baby-faced, defector from the Toorak bourgeoisie, educated at Melbourne Grammar, leaning back in an armchair, puffing on his pipe, with that deceptive, benign calm that hides the fighter; Frank Hardy, one of that rare breed, a writer from the Australian working class; and Laurie Aarons, son of Sam, the new general secretary of the Australian Communist Party, a devious, wary, political animal who has dedicated his life to the cause of Communism.

The arguments are heated and bitter. Writers in the Soviet Union and the People's Democracies who were shot as enemies of the Revolution under Stalin are being 'rehabilitated' daily, and now Khrushchev, the engineer of the Twentieth Congress Report, is crushing democracy in Hungary.

'Mistakes have been made in the past, Comrades,' says Laurie Aarons, 'but the disturbances in Hungary are counter-revolutionary, and engineered by the CIA.' But there are too many graves, too many ghosts that won't lie down.

A meeting of the Realist Writers at Frank Hardy's is interrupted by a phone call from Ian Turner, member of the Victorian State Committee and secretary of the Australasian Book Society, in Melbourne. Eric Lambert, the left-wing novelist famous for his war novel *Twenty Thousand Thieves*, is imprisoned in Hungary for demonstrating with the 'counter-revolutionaries'. What are the Party writers, and Frank Hardy in particular, going to do about it?

'Nothing,' says Frank. 'It's all bullshit. Lambert always was a lying bastard.'

Soon afterwards I am called into Laurie Aarons's office at 40 Market Street to discuss my 'differences with the Party'.

'Have you any doubts about the counter-revolution in Hungary?'

'No, I just think it should have been handled differently. If it had been properly discussed instead of just pushing it under the carpet we wouldn't have lost so many good comrades.'

It never occurs to me that I might be expelled, but years later Frank Hardy tells me that at this time my name was on the list for immediate expulsion, and only his intervention saved me.

Ian Turner has been expelled and Stephen Murray-Smith has followed him out of the Party, taking *Overland* with him. (We hear the news on the ABC.) Helen Palmer, daughter of novelist Vance and critic Nettie Palmer, has started a new political magazine called *Outlook*. Any Communist writing for it will be instantly expelled. The nasty gossip amongst the male Communist hierarchy is that Helen is 'an old maid gone mad with the change of life', and therefore can't really be held responsible for her actions. But that doesn't stop her expulsion.

A surprising number of ex-Communists are joining the Scientologists. There must be something about their rigid methodology and thought-police processes that makes them feel at home. Out of curiosity I attend a Scientology meeting on the north shore, where one of Ron Hubbard's disciples presents us with a weird mixture of pop psychology and brainwashing.

'There is,' he says, glaring at me, 'a hostile presence in this room.'

It never enters my head to leave the Party, because I simply cannot imagine any life outside it. Not only have I spent the last twelve years of my life defending its causes, but it has structured my whole existence, given it a special meaning. Without the Communist Party I will be adrift again, at the mercy of a hostile world, with all my old fears and inadequacies waiting to destroy me. The Communist Party once saved my life. I dare not put it aside, for maybe that way the old madness lies: the resurrection of the weeping girl with a Lysol bottle in her hand. So I tell myself there is nothing wrong with the principles of Marxism–Leninism, only deviations, human errors, that can always be rectified. I think about the Chinese Communists and their rooftop meetings in Peking. Honest unafraid criticism and self-criticism are obviously the answer, but the Australian Party leadership seems remarkably unenthusiastic about this method.

One stormy night, when the oleander is bashing its dark-red petals against the glass doors, the Rockdale Branch of the Party send round a young comrade to sit in front of our cosy fire and argue us out on the error of our 'revisionist' ways, but we are not convinced. Some time in the next few months Les leaves the Party without even mentioning it to me. He takes a job on night shift in Balmain and every morning, too frightened to leave the children alone in the house, I run to the corner, waiting to see the Buick topping the rise, then race to catch the train already pulling into the Rockdale station. It's a nerve-racking business, and when he decides to leave, because he maintains that the New Australians are trying to kill him by dropping angle iron on his head from a great height, I'm not really sorry.

The rituals of our life continue – fish and chips on Brighton Beach on Friday nights, then across to Mascot aerodrome to park and watch the planes take off, south to the tree ferns, north to the pandanus palms at weekends, driving down the Hawkesbury pass to see the river flashing like a great reflector in the sunlight.

'Some people are too sensitive to survive under capitalism,' says Les, his profile driven and tight above the steering wheel.

One night, catching the train home from Central, I run into Grahame Alcorn.

'When are you going to write that novel, Toddy?'

'I'm not ready yet,' I tell him. 'I don't know enough.'

But all the time, as I move through the clamorous streets, I am gathering my material – the eccentric Bea Miles in a man's old overcoat and felt hat, reciting Shakespeare for two bob a time, pinching fruit off the barrow man on the corner of Riley Street: 'To be or not to be, that is the question.' The little man in the high-crowned Akubra hat printing 'Eternity' in copperplate on the inner-city pavements. Riding pillion behind Barbara on her scooter, my crepe-soled shoes smoking on the exhaust pipe, we pass the lighted interiors of dance halls where boys in ducktails and pegtop trousers, and girls in layers of roped petticoats, swing in the square dances.

On 4 October 1957 the first Sputnik circles the globe for ninety-five minutes and is seen clearly in the night sky over Sydney. On 2 November Sputnik 2 is sent into orbit carrying a dog, to study living conditions in space. That summer in Sydney the wonders of these first man-made satellites are on everybody's lips, so that when I actually come to write my first novel the following winter, it's not really surprising that I use Sputnik as an emblem of revolution and hope.

Sometimes in my lunch hour I walk up to Mark Foy's store and sit on the terrace, drinking cappuccinos amongst the strutting road-pecker pigeons, pretending I am in Paris. Remembering Tiger, I take the tram up to the Cross to sit in the Apollyan amongst Rosalie Norton's murals of leaping black panthers chasing naked women along the coffee-shop walls.

Sometimes we copywriters give ourselves a special treat and have lunch together in a café behind the Tivoli, where George Wallace, the Tiv comedian, with his sad rubbery clown's face, tells loud jokes at the opposite table. A couple of the artists often come with us: the daughter of the children's writer and illustrator Pixie O'Harris, or the granddaughter of Hugh McCrae, now living out his old age in a retirement home – 'I am the Lord, I am the Lord, I am the Lord of everything' – Hugh McCrae who used to stand at the top of William Street declaiming Greek verses to Christopher Brennan, rolling drunk up the hill to meet him in his flowing black cloak. How sad life is.

Remembering how Bill Hart-Smith used to praise Mary Gilmore for her selfless assistance to young writers, I make an appointment to see her in her flat above the King's Cross Library. Clutching the precious manuscript of 'The Wire Fences of Jarrabin', I am ushered into her presence. An imperious figure dressed entirely in black and blind in one eye is sitting on a throne-like chair with a hassock at her feet, looking exactly like the Dobell portrait of a slightly later.date.

I am motioned to the hassock but decline to take it. She turns her intimidating profile towards the window light. 'That is where I stood with Henry, looking down on the crowds below, and helped him write "Faces in the Street".'

Silence falls; there seems nothing to say to this. Timidly I hand her my manuscript. She reads through the first few pages, then puts it aside impatiently.

'Why do your characters refer to the Aborigines as "niggers"? No Australian has ever referred to an Aborigine as a "nigger".'

'They did where I come from,' I venture.

She turns her hooded eyes on me: 'Australians are not racists.'

Another silence, broken only by the muted sound of the traffic in the street below.

'Your story is not good,' she says. 'I advise you to throw it away.'

Dismissed, I pass another mendicant waiting nervously in the foyer, and shout myself a cappuccino in Repin's Coffee Shop, to recover.

Peter Bonner is writing pulp novels for the paperback trade; producing a novel a fortnight in his spare time, hoping to emulate Carter Brown and make his fortune. Perhaps this is one way out of slavery at Walton-Sears. I can work at home, dash off a pulp novel, and do my own writing in between. Then I see the advertisement in the *Sydney Morning Herald*: 'Australian Writers Wanted'. Nobody, as far as I can see, ever wants Australian writers in Australia. Excited, I make an appointment and take out a 'sickie'.

He is waiting in his tiny eyrie high above Hyde Park, a Canadian in a loud checked suit with a plot-wheel and all sorts of bright ideas about bestselling paperbacks: one to be set in hospital corridors amongst doctors and nurses; one in a Lemmy Caution underworld of tough private eyes, coppers and crims; one in an evil psychiatrist's clinic, all the characters to be modelled on Hollywood stars.

'No, we don't want novels with Australian settings. Nobody's gonna buy them. They stink of the gum leaves, stink of the gum leaves, Sister.'

He sends me away to concoct a chapter or two of Gothic romance in the deep South and, to my shame, I do it and am given an 'assignment', with the plot and characters already invented. But the story has an anti-Communist twist at the end, so I ignore that and invent another one. Delivering the manuscript, I never hear from 'Australian Writers Wanted' again, and when I call to enquire the phone always rings in an empty room.

I salve a guilty conscience by writing the verse commentary of 'Words for Freedom'. A documentary, directed by the left-wing film-maker Cecil Holmes, it traces the history of radical newspapers and journals in Australia.

> There are men like Maxie Thomas,
> There are men like Jim McNeil,
> Who've knocked around the country
> Until they're made of steel.
> It doesn't matter who they are,
> We don't remember names,
> But they're men who've got the sunlight
> Of Australia in their veins . . .

I declaim with more enthusiasm than art, determined to have it both ways, a pantheon of Communist heroes plus an awareness of the cult of the individual.

I have already profited from my brief encounter with the paperback trade. Inventing the offer of a lucrative full-time job writing pulp literature, I have put in my resignation from Walton's.

'There's no need to noise it around the office,' says Mr Ken, raising my wages to £17 a week. 'This is between you and me.'

When I tell Barbara, Monica, and Peter Bonner, and they all demand the same wage, I do not make myself particularly popular with the Advertising Department. I follow this up by inventing yet another, even more glamorous job to go to, but I have overplayed my hand. They congratulate me on my initiative and make up my severance pay. Unmasked, I have to eat humble pie and beg for my old job back again.

'We'll take you back,' purrs Mr Ken, 'and we won't penalize you for it, but remember we expect you to work harder now. Marie tells me you've been slacking a bit lately.'

One Friday night we are sent home from work. The big Yank bosses from the Sears-Roebuck Catalogue Department are arriving on Monday from America, and the Advertising Department has to have a complete and miraculous facelift. When we arrive on Monday morning we blink our eyes in disbelief. Has the lift let us out on the wrong floor? This showroom, painted, lushly carpeted, transformed, the desks arranged in neatly regimented rows, an instant roof garden blooming overnight through the windows – can this be our old leaking warehouse with the pitted cement floor that wrenched the stilt heels off our shoes? In the reverent hush we are ushered into our new seats to sit like automatons while an American executive who looks like Edward G. Robinson inspects us in our new environment. Marie has stubbed out her constant cigarette. The new American boss doesn't approve of women smoking, and Marie is a 'trusty'.

The workload gets heavier, the number of pages we are expected to complete per day is stepped up. In this manic atmosphere Barbara marries Harry Garlick, and both of them leave Walton-Sears – Harry to go back to Sydney University, Barbara to work for Sydney University Press. Isolated amongst strangers, I go for job interviews at all the big advertising agencies, trying to sell myself, taking examples of my work, telling them about my publications, and small literary successes.

'I'm afraid you're too highbrow for us,' they say. 'Why not try Farmer's? Your style is very upmarket, tailor-made for them.'

But I have already spent hours in the public library copying Farmer's ads until I think I've got them down perfectly, only to be turned down at the first interview. I try the *Sydney Sun*, John Thompson at the ABC. I even track down Peter Foulkes and ring him at one of the commercial radio stations.

'Now is the time, Peter,' I tell him, 'to find me one of those jobs that was going to make me so famous,' but he doesn't even want to see me.

When I am told about a vacancy on *Common Cause*, the Miners' Federation paper, I go to see the Communist editor, Edgar Ross, in the Ironworkers' building.

Edgar is enthusiastic about giving me the job, and I am delighted to get it. It means £2 a week drop in salary, but how wonderful to be able to write honestly for the first time in years.

In the winter of 1958 I resign from Walton's. Not long after I leave, seeing the writing on the wall, Sears withdraw all their capital and the catalogue folds. Marie has been unmasked as a secret drinker with a stash of hard liquor hidden in the women's toilets. She is dispatched, at the firm's expense, to an isolated sanatorium for alcoholics in the dark scrub at Waterfall.

There is a two-week waiting period before I start my new job, and Frank Hardy has suggested we have a 'socialist competition', both of us writing a novel for the Mary Gilmore Novel Competition.

Abandoning the eight completed chapters of 'The Wire Fences of Jarrabin', I decide to write about the girls in the Alexandria Spinning Mill. Taking my notebook I wander through Paddo, Redfern, Waterloo and Alexandria, hanging around outside the mill as the girls leave work, travelling in buses, trams and trains, watching, listening, taking notes, remembering. Then the telegram comes from Edgar Ross: the Miners' Federation has refused to employ me on *Common Cause* because I am a married woman. Angry and devastated, I throw myself on the mercy of the Party, applying for jobs on *Tribune*, in the Party offices and the trade unions, but nobody is prepared to help me.

All that happens is that the Rockdale Branch of the Party castigates me because I can't pay my usual pledge into the Branch funds.

I go home and begin to write, sitting at the end of the kitchen table, listening to 'Top of the Pops' on the radio, incorporating them into the texture of the story. It is a freezing Sydney winter, but we can't afford to buy coke for the Cosy fire, so when my fingers freeze on the typewriter, I warm them over the ring on the electric stove.

As I write, the novel becomes a kind of poem to Sydney, all those places we lived in when I first arrived from Perth, the stories Les has told me over the years, the rough, slangy speech of the mill girls, weaving a web of correspondence across the city, binding this book of episodic stories together.

In the midst of the novel I take time out to write to Dessie and my parents:

Dearest Dessie,
I am developing as a writer every day, and it interests me above everything else until I think people will find me terribly boring because it's all I want to talk about. It's as if I've been damming back for years all this spate of storytelling and now there seems so much to write and not enough time to do it all and I don't develop fast enough. But I feel as if I had to wait till now because I wasn't adult enough.

Dearest Folks,
I am still jobless but have a few irons in the fire – writing flat out and have done four chapters of my book. I've got a long way to go of course, and the things I want to say are not too popular. Maybe I'll be famous when I'm dead like poor old Henry Lawson – something to look forward to. Sometimes I wonder am I kidding myself. Maybe it's all vanity and self-delusion. But I believe that I am a writer, no matter what the critics say, and I have been getting a lot of criticism lately. For some I'm too political, for others not political enough, for some clumsy and amateurish, not up to standard, for others, polished but too obtuse, and oh! yes, too much sex and rather coarse.
All the characters are based on real women in the mill, but it is a pretty radical sort of book and will not be popular.

My predictions about *Bobbin Up*'s unpopularity turn out to be untrue. The first and only Australian edition sells out in six weeks but is never reprinted. It is reprinted, however, by Seven Seas in East Berlin, and in four foreign-language editions in the Communist countries. Finally it is republished by Virago Press in London in 1985. Some male Communists maintained that it was really written by Les Flood, who 'allowed me to put my name to it'.

Working a backbreaking schedule, I finish the novel in eight weeks and dispatch it to the Mary Gilmore Novel Competition. Broke and unemployed, I am offered a job by Peter Leyden and his wife Elsie, two ex-Communist English schoolteachers who have set themselves up in a small publishing company in North Sydney, publishing educational paperbacks.

Manic, wildly enthusiastic, in love with literature and ideas, Peter employs me to write 'social studies' comic books for children on subjects like 'The History of Federation' and 'The Story of Henry Parkes'. Peter is the ideas man, Elsie is the practical organizer who keeps the day-to-day life of the firm together. They are an unbeatable combination. Always running close to the wind, the little company is operating on a series of bank loans.

'Put your low-necked blouse on, El,' says Peter, 'and run around and vamp the bank manager.' It always seems to work.

Curly-headed, opinionated, lovable, half-Irish, originally trained in a Catholic seminary to become a priest. Peter becomes my friend and loyal supporter. All writers need a patron, and Peter is mine. Sometimes at night I go back to their house in Turramurra to sit with my feet up by the gas fire drinking tea while I read him extracts from 'The Wire Fences of Jarrabin'.

'You've got to finish it, Toddy' he says, his blue eyes bulging with fervour, 'and when you do I'll publish it. It's your great novel.'

The Communist Party warn me about Peter. They suspect he works for ASIO; Frank Hardy calls him 'a Jesuit bastard'.

When Peter tells me he can't afford to employ me any longer I burst into a flood of tears, so he keeps me on, out of the goodness of his heart – tying up parcels, typing up labels, answering the odd letter, and the phone. I'm sure I'm not worth the wage, but it is all that stands between us and destitution. Les has bought himself a second-hand banjo and sits strumming 'O lonesome me' far into the night. Perhaps he is transported back to that golden time before the war when, a fifteen-year-old in a hired tux, he played the double bass by ear in a jazz 'combo' at the Trocadero dances. Perhaps he is remembering the likely lad who dreamed up the Hawaiian Guitar Club, advertising it by playing his guitar nonstop one weekend in a shop-front window in the Rockdale shopping centre.

He seems to be going mad again. Accused of having sex with his morose eighty-five-year-old uncle, who is living in the shed in our back yard, I am also supposed to be having a secret love affair with Peter Leyden.

'All you've ever wanted', he tells me, 'is for a prince to come riding up on a big white charger, and fuck you and fuck you until you're dead.'

Although we sleep in the same bed, we haven't made love for more than six months now. One night after the Rockdale pub closes he brings home a sad, rheumy-eyed drunk and his frightened wife. The children are in bed and I am reading them a bedtime story as I always do. Their favourite is an old Russian fairy tale called 'The Old Man's Mitten'.

When I come into the kitchen, Les jeers at me. 'Here comes the dinosaur,' he says, 'big arse, little head and no brain.'

The woman is staring at me with bulbous eyes. 'She doesn't look a bad sort. I dunno what I expected but you told us she was such a terrible bitch.'

Silently I turn and go inside, sitting shaking on the edge of the bed, listening to them growing drunker and more quarrelsome round the kitchen table.

Next morning he sits there glaring, his face red and swollen. 'If I get crook again after I've drunk this tea, I'm going to deal with you,' he says.

This time I'm supposed not only to be lacing *his* tea, but drugging the children's food *and* slowly poisoning the dog. When they catch measles he says that ASIO is using germ warfare against them. Driving in the car he tells them to keep a sharp lookout for ASIO who, he says, have developed new techniques of driving in *front* of their victims.

I travel backwards and forwards from North Sydney, giddy with misery. Sometimes I even play a kind of chicken, hanging out over the rails in the underground as the packed train pulls into Wynyard station and the blank-faced crowd press to the edge of the platform fighting for a toehold. I wander up and down the concrete stairways dazed and exhausted, like a somnambulist. Everything seems to be swimming in a sickly, livid, yellow light. Sometimes I stop for coffee, sitting for hours in the station café, too frightened to go home.

Les has taken to whispering in the shower, or pacing up and down the hall all night, muttering, arguing with himself, as if he is possessed by two warring personalities.

'Will I kill her tonight? Will I kill her tomorrow?'

I climb into bed with Pommy, clinging to him, listening to the nightmare arguments, the steps pausing at the door, then continuing on. Surely he won't murder me as I lie in bed with our children. If he comes into the bedroom to attack me, can I possibly escape through the front door and run into the street for help? But the street is dark and empty and the neighbours never want to get involved in a 'domestic'.

Sometimes I sit out on the front verandah after midnight, shivering in my old fur fabric coat, or go walking through the Rockdale streets playing another kind of chicken with the passing cars. If suicide has ever been a solution it is always there, as a possible way out, but now I have three children to consider. If I die, what will happen to them? They will be at the mercy of a madman. Already, at eight years old, Joe is beginning to question the crazy logic of Les's theories and arguments; already he too is becoming 'the enemy' accused of being bourgeois and devious, 'just like his mother'.

One night three shocked boilermakers, standing outside the glass door leading into the sitting room, see Joe huddled up on the floor in a fetal crouch, with Les kicking him. As I make my futile efforts to intervene, Les spins me across the room to crash into a corner, hitting my leg on the iron pipe of the chair. I lie there, half-stunned and breathless, while the three men stare in horror at this domestic scene. Then suddenly Les notices them, and in a moment he is all charm and hospitality, welcoming them into the room, opening up a bottle of beer, while Joe and I creep away into the bedroom, where I hold him in my arms to comfort his sobbing. The three men don't stay long. They are nervous, watching Les with uneasy faces. He is not often caught red-handed like this.

'What a charming man your husband is,' the neighbours tell me.

'Will you come with me to see a psychiatrist?' I beg him.

'The class position is too strong,' he says seriously. 'Any psychiatrist will automatically side with you. What kind of justice can you expect in a set-up like that?'

'Let's part, then. We can't go on living like this.'

'You can leave whenever you like,' he says, 'but the kids are staying with me. A good worker doesn't desert his children, and if you try for custody I'll go to a doctor, and when he finds out I'm full up to the neck with seven years of drugs you won't stand a chance . . . so you see there's nothing to be done,' and he sits there smiling with that eerie smile, like a reasonable man.

He doesn't know it but I've already been to a lawyer and discovered that as our children are illegitimate he has no rights over them whatsoever. It seems unfair to the natural father, but perhaps it is the payoff for those cruel words he once said to me: 'Who'd marry a moll like you who deserted her husband and child?'

We go on a miserable family visit to Les's brother Paul, at Engadine. As we walk through the bush amongst the giant Illawarra lilies, I drop behind with Joe. 'What's the matter, darling?' but he pulls away and won't answer me.

'Is something worrying you?'

'Dad says you're drugging us,' he whispers.

I kneel down and put my arms around him. 'You don't believe that, do you?'

'I don't know.'

'You know I wouldn't do anything to hurt you, don't you?'

'Yes,' he says, dropping his eyes. 'Why does Dad say it then?'

'He's sick, and he doesn't know *what* he's saying. I know it's hard for you to understand, but it'll be all right. I love you and it'll be all right.'

All this time I am keeping a careful eye on Les, walking with Mike and Pom up ahead. Now he stops and turns, eyeing me suspiciously. I take Joe's hand and we walk on through the blackbutts and the fleshy red lilies.

The following night, as I come up the driveway, Michael runs out to tell me about the great bonfire Dad has made in the back yard. Heart in mouth, I go round the side of the house. The children are standing watching the flames, sucking their thumbs, while Les works with a sort of gleeful intensity, throwing all my manuscripts, files of letters, notebooks and cosmetics on to the fire. Amongst the manuscripts is a love poem I have written to him:

My body turns to you as the earth turns
Oh! from such bitter need you've taken me
to dub me lover friend enemy
that neither one can set the other free
but still there is a loveliness that burns
that burns between us two so tenderly.

And now everything is burning, even the first act of the play called 'This Old Man Comes Rolling Home', and another poem that will survive from this period, remembered and reprinted in *Windmill Country*, my first book of poems, in 1968:

Once I rode with Clancy
Through the wet hills of Wickepin,
Through Kunjin and Corrigin
With moonlight on the roofs,
And the iron shone faint and ghostly
On the lonely moonlit sidings
And the salt earth rang like crystal
Underneath our flying hoofs.

Enid had criticized this literary ballad on the tram taking us to yet another Realist Writers' meeting.

My golden hair has faded,
My tender flesh is dark,
My voice has learned a wet and windy sigh,
And I lean above the creek bed,
Catch my breath upon a ghost,
With a great rapacious nose and sombre eye.

'I'd keep off that tack if I were you,' she'd said.
    Now I stand beside the choko vine, the smoke stinging my eyes.
    'Why have you done this to me?' I cry out, bursting into tears.
    'I'm burning your lies against me,' he tells me simply.
    The only writing he has spared is the first eight chapters of *The Wire Fences of Jarrabin*.
    'Why didn't you burn them too?' I asked bitterly.
    'Because that's real working-class literature,' he says.
    The next night when I get home from work the house is deserted

and the car gone. I sit for a long time in the kitchen waiting for the Buick to come home, but nothing happens. I walk round to Clarice's place, but she treats me as if I'm being unnecessarily hysterical.

'They've probably only gone for a drive,' she says.

At two o'clock in the morning I wonder if I should call the police. Then the headlights reflect off the louvre windows and Les comes in laughing, carrying a sleeping Pom over his shoulder.

'Where have you been?' I cry out. 'I've been worried to death.'

But he just keeps on laughing.

Silently I take the children and put them to bed. 'You don't know where we've been, Mum,' Michael tells me solemnly. 'We've got a secret and you're not supposed to know.'

'Aren't I?'

Michael leans forward conspiratorially. He can never keep a secret. 'Dad's taking us to Lake Macquarie to live with a lady, while he works in the Newcastle Steel Works, and you'll never find us again.'

So this is it. I walk out of the room, my mind full of plans of escape. In spite of all this horror I have found myself a new job writing copy for film ads, due to start in two days' time, but if I leave and find a room somewhere in Sydney Les will track us down and take the children.

The next day I ring my father from Peter Leyden's office and ask him to send me the plane fare to Western Australia, addressing the bank draft to North Sydney Post Office.

He doesn't ask any questions. 'It'll be there tomorrow,' he says.

For weeks I have been organizing an Australia Night celebration with the Realist Writers and the Bush Music Club. Now, oddly enough, the celebration has fallen on my last night in Sydney. When I stand up to recite Henry Lawson's 'The Lights of Sydneyside', my voice cracks and I can hardly finish the poem.

> Run of rocky shelves at sunrise with their base an ocean's bed,
> Homes of Coogee, homes of Bondi, and the lighthouse on South
>   Head,
> For in loneliness and hardship – and with just a touch of pride
> Has my heart been taught to whisper, 'You belong to Sydneyside'.

As I stand on the sidelines, watching the folk dancers circling the room, a big, good-looking man with fair-cropped hair and golden eyes like a sleepy cat, is standing beside me.

'Enid tells me you've been having a bit of trouble,' he says.

I long to confide in him but I am too proud or too shy. How can I ask this almost complete stranger to take on any of my burdens?

There is something about him, some strength and compassion that inspires confidence, but I've met him only twice before, and then only briefly. The first time was in the Domain with Enid, when I asked them both to dinner, but they never turned up.

'You keep your baby blue eyes off him,' she told me afterwards.

The second time was at a Realist Writers' meeting when he read a poem that reminded me of *The Ballad of Reading Gaol*. Riding home that night in the back seat of a car with him, I had a sudden surprising urge to throw myself into his arms and disappear into the night somewhere, but now I say nothing and the moment passes.

Eighteen months later Merv Lilley writes me a letter addressed to 'Dorothy Hewett, Poet, Perth, Western Australia', but it is never delivered.

Coming back over the bridge, there is a lump in my throat. I am leaving Sydney, the magic city where I came with a lover to find happiness. The bridge spanning the harbour arches over our heads, singing in the wind, and I remember the first time I saw it when I was only five years old: two incomplete arches, and a space in the middle waiting to be filled.

Late that night I creep out of the house and throw a pathetic bag of children's clothing – three little shirts and a change of underwear – over the back fence, hoping nobody will steal them before morning.

Les has been visiting Charlie Newman in Ryde Mental Hospital. Charlie has acute manic depression, babbling incessantly and writing indecipherable meaningless words on scraps of paper. Les tells me that they sat out in the grounds all day arguing politics with Mao Tse-tung. Soon afterwards Charlie disappears and is never heard of again. Sometimes I imagine him lying dead somewhere by the Parramatta River with a drift of leaves covering his face.

Next morning the children leave for school and kindergarten as usual, Joe dinking Pom in front of his scooter, as I pretend to get ready for work. I stand in the bedroom doorway looking at Les, lying with the *Herald* spread out in front of his face.

'Goodbye,' I say, and cross over to kiss him, but he jerks his head away. I never see him again.

I pick up the children's clothes and catch a cab, first to the kindergarten, then to the school.

'Joe seems to be in a very bad way lately,' says the headmaster.

'So would you be if you lived in our house,' I say bitterly.

'Where are we going, Mum?' the kids are asking me.

'We're going on a holiday to see Nanna and Dai,' I tell them.

'Is Dad coming too?'

'No, Dad's sick. He has to stay at home.'

They seem to accept it all with the strange fatalism of children.

I have booked our tickets in a false name but the plane doesn't leave until late in the afternoon, so we wait in Vera Deacon's house at Milson's Point. A pretty, fragile, ex-Salvation Army lass from Newcastle, Vera is the devoted secretary of the Realist Writers, who has helped me type up the first draft of *Bobbin Up*.

Enid arrives from work, Peter Leyden pulls up in his car to drive us to the airport. I shepherd the children out through the gate, but suddenly Pom turns and runs down the road, sobbing hysterically.

We are walking across the tarmac. I am wearing the teal-blue serge Barbara gave me because it never really fitted her properly. I look back, seeing Peter, Enid and Vera waving behind the barrier, and have a sudden yearning to turn and run myself, back the way I have come – all the way, to relive it and make it work this time, but of course I will never go back. Or if I do I will be somebody different who remembers this only like a long-ago horror movie I once lived through. I will weep and dream about my return, but it will never happen. It will be only a fantasy.

I ponder on the repeated obsessive dreams of these last years – wading with Les through seas of bright blood along the Sydney coastline, escaping from some kind of Fascist putsch on shore, or dreaming my revenge and becoming a sexual predator, a beautiful blond young man making cynical love to dozens of adoring women.

Why am I leaving this city of dreams and nightmares, with the Harbour swinging at the end of its narrow streets? Where am I going, creeping back with my tail between my legs to watch the pitying glances, the knowing silences, the 'I told you so's' and the loneliness? What will happen to Les now that we have gone? Who will look after him, who will shield him from madness, how will he live?

The plane banks and sweeps across our back yard in Railway Parade, where he is waiting for us all to come home, but of course by this time he'll have gone to the kindergarten and school, questioning everyone, picking up the abandoned scooters he reconditioned from the Tempe Tip.

Now we are crossing the waterways of Cooks River and Botany Bay, all the places where we have wandered and driven, explored and swum, for the past nine years. The smoke from Bunnerong Power Station hangs in the wintry air and drifts across the bay. It's over and I'm going back to Western Australia – tired, defeated, sadder, older, wiser perhaps, but miraculously still alive with my children beside me. I have saved us, but we have no home – we are homeless. For the rest of my life I will dream about us walking down unknown roads together with the darkness falling, or sleeping cold, with our arms around each other in half-ruined, abandoned houses.

Night and the children sleep. Underneath lies the darkening Nullarbor with the waters of the Great Australian Bight breaking against its giddy limestone cliffs.

Perhaps now that I have nothing I can find that empty space of sunlight, 'the clean well-lighted place' in the middle of the world.

'The only unreconcilable loss,' writes Sylvia Townsend Warner, 'is the loss of one's private solitude . . . but one morning you will walk into an empty room and be cheerful.'

EPILOGUE

The little sour apples still grow in my heart's orchard,
Bitten with grief, coming up out of the dead country.
Here I will eat their salt and speak my truth.
'Legend of the Green Country'

EPILOGUE

LAST summer Dessie, Merv Lilley and I went back to the bend in two creeks, dropping down through the Darling Ranges into the Avon Valley and out across the plains of the Great Southern.

We arrived in Yealering late on Saturday afternoon but the town was deserted, only the shadows of Arthur Kelly's river gums stretching across the road from the station as if he had planted his own epitaph. Where had they all gone and what had happened to Saturday, when everyone came to town, when the main street was alive with cars and trucks and sulkies and we collected our *Puck* and *Tiger Tim* from our Co-op pigeonhole? Now the only place open was Paul Kingston's Cool Drinks and Ice-Cream Shop, where we bought our weekly acid drops, and the stranger behind the counter had never heard of anybody we ever knew.

I can shut my eyes against the glare and smell my way up this street . . . Paul Kingston's, Kingston & Salter's General Store, the Co-op, the bank, and the post office, Mr Honeyman the saddler's, the pub, the butcher's shop and on the rise opposite Lou Fuller's, Mr Coxon the blacksmith, in a grease-stained leather apron, black hair sprouting out of his nostrils. These shades, more real to me than the people I met last week or last year – perhaps I will bring them out once again, carrying their wooden chairs from the shop fronts to sit under Arthur Kelly's trees waiting for the Albany Doctor to ruffle the surface of the salt lake, waiting for the hush before the lights come up.

We drove past Rae Kelly's house facing the golf links where the 'Silvertails' frittered away their farms, past the tennis courts where my young uncles, immaculate in white flannels, played Country Week tennis. Why did the lake look so miniature, shrunken to a parody of itself, the dead trees along the opposite bank too close for comfort? Impossible now to imagine Kingston & Salter's pleasure launch hooting as it pulled away from the jetty for a cruise on Boxing Day. But the river gums were rattling gently in the evening breeze and here comes Arthur Kelly in a panama hat staggering under a giant watering can. We parked by the RSL Hall where I danced at the Fancy

270
♥

Dress Ball in white spangled tulle with a silver wand, a silver cardboard star in the middle of my forehead, gauze wings sprouting from
my shoulder blades.

'When are we going home?' wails Dessie, and I turn on her in
tragic disgust and fury: 'Go home, what do you want to go home for?'

What indeed? Driving out past the railway embankment where
we used to straggle in single file carrying our groceries across the
flooded creek, we were searching through fifty years for familiar
landmarks, but nothing was the same. Why should it be? Only for one
brief instant, catching us unawares, the paddocks were ambered in
light, the wheat whispered beside the road, there was a whirr of quails
rising up, the plovers wheeled and cried through the radiant air.

We were taking the back road, fourteen miles to Wickepin. It
hadn't changed much – a new swimming pool and a craft shop where
we could buy facsimiles of Albert Facey postcards decorated with
violets and forget-me-nots . . . 'Happy Birthday Albert, hoping this
finds you as well as I am at present' . . . Albert Facey the farm
labourer whose handwritten memoirs, *A Fortunate Life*, became a
posthumous bestseller. His old house was on show on the edge of the
town. We could even book a bus tour through 'Albert Facey Country'.

We stayed overnight in the Wickepin pub, pondering how our
grandfather could have fitted the great rump of his ginger gelding
under that low front lintel.

> Next Saturday night he rode his horse
> Up the turkey red carpet into the bar, smashing the bottles and
>   glasses.
> Tipping the counter, sending the barmaid screaming, her breasts
>   tilting with joy.

In the morning we stared out of the upstairs dining room into the
empty street, seeing the tour bus passing with the little blank Japanese
faces pressed against the windows, going no doubt to view the Albert
Facey Pioneer Homestead. Did they imagine him, perhaps, as some
venerable ancestor or household god?

We were going to visit our own pioneer homestead, following the
railway line to Malyalling. The siding had vanished but there was the
turn-off to the Sartoris' place, the dark brick bungalow with the wide
terrazzo verandahs, deserted and melancholy.

Tony's granddaughter came up from the stables and told us the
story: 'I s'pose you haven't heard,' she said. 'I do a bit of watering, but
nobody's lived on the place for eighteen months. All hell's broken
loose here.'

Tragedy had struck the Sartoris and they had fled to Perth: Hilda
with a weak heart, Pommy in a wheelchair, one leg amputated from
gangrene, Tony old and cranky with family squabbles. When he died
three months later his mystery Italian daughters sent condolences to
his 'Australian family' through the 'In Memoriam' columns of the
West Australian.

We drove on across the railway line to the boundary of Lambton
Downs. On the other side of the iron gates was a hose running
hopelessly into a sheep trough, with a hole in it. Nobody came this
way now. The roads were grown over, the gates wired up. Desolate,
treeless except for the hardy York gums and jams, the crossing over
the creek was barely distinguishable, but lying in the hollow were
a scatter of corrugated-iron sheds and a single brick chimney.

'Oh God!' we cried. 'Oh God! Is that the house?'

Two almonds, a few figs and one quince had survived. No she-
oaks, no wattles, no tea-tree, no paperbarks, no bottlebrush, no salmon
gums, no stables or sheds or post and rail sheep yards, only the
concrete dip left like a scar in the home paddock, littered with iron
and rusty machinery. Day's timber all gone – a denuded landscape.

> This land is not mine to give or trade,
>
> I have no lien on these sad acres,
>
> where the crow flies home,
>
> a solitary reaper.
>
> The milky creek runs death,
>
> the wattle and the tea-tree are all gone.

The loose roofing iron flapped up and down over the broken boards
on the verandah. Rabbits started up under our feet, a well-fed feral
cat glared and ran, swallows had nested in the sitting-room cornices.
Only the four main rooms, with glassless windows, and the old dunny,
had survived.

I used to sit in there for hours, hiding from the drying-up,
reading 'Pip Squeak and Wilfred' in the *Illustrated London News*,
scratching my first boyfriend's name, Max Green, on the weatherboard walls, but my mother made me take the scrubbing brush and
scrub it all off again. When I write him my first love letter, secretly
posting it without a stamp, she storms into the Yealering Post Office
to retrieve it.

'Dear Max,' it says, 'What kind of sums do you do now? Love
from Dorothy.'

Sitting by the cold black stove in the kitchen, looking out towards
the creek bed, listening for the inevitable crow, I heard the scrape of

my dead father's spade in the orchard. When Dutchy Butler's 'brudders' come out from the 'old country', they follow my father for days, plodding silently in the furrows of his plough.

'But why do they do it?' he asks, puzzled.

'Dey like to see de earth turn,' says Dutchy Butler.

Shadows creep into the corners of the rooms. We are waiting for 'the men' to come in on a Sunday evening, transformed into dandies in their striped flannel blazers. Tying on our white pinnies, embroidered with 'Dolly Vardens', we stick the stub of a pencil behind our ears and set up a makeshift counter with its weights and scales, its currants and sultanas, sugar and tea, new-laid eggs, pats of yellow butter, jars of chutney, pickles, pears, apricots and peaches, mounds of potatoes and onions, pyramids of apples and oranges. 'Playing shop', we repeat the rituals of our tribe, weighing and wrapping, adding and subtracting, smiling graciously while the grown-ups queue for the phantom merchandise.

'Let none go by while this house lives.' In the first bedroom the dust motes are dancing on the silver hand mirror embossed with Sir Joshua Reynolds's cherubs. In the tarnished glass there is a card house made of fibro, weatherboard and corrugated iron bowling over and over through the empty paddocks, torn apart and scattered across the sunstruck miles with nothing left to show that once a family worked and loved and quarrelled here, planted orchards, gardens and crops, raised animals and children, grew angry, sentimental, passionate, proud and sad.

An Irish farm girl from Belturbot ran off with a sailor; a Cornish servant girl emigrated to Beechworth; a Methodist preacher from Norfolk and a Scot with a Jewish wife sailed for Bendigo; a charming counter-jumper sold a few yards of silk to a South Melbourne dressmaker; an Anzac with crow-black hair dived overboard from a troopship into Princess Royal Harbour; a pretty postmistress kicked an exploding primus down the main street of Corrigin.

Dessie and I sank down on the broken verandah and wept silently together. There was no one left but us to remember them now, no one but us to mourn for our tender fragile country.

I lie warm on my belly on that same verandah, reading about Kylie Tennant in the *Australian Woman's Mirror*, smiling, Eton-cropped, from a tobacco kiosk at Central.

One day I too will smile from *my* tobacco kiosk, Eton-cropped, one of the 'new women', gathering material for my latest novel. A plane passes over, spinning against the clouds. 'Aeroplane, aeroplane!' we scream, staring into the void, shading our eyes against the sun, because if you don't you'll go blind. Is it Kingsford Smith, Amy Johnson or Bert Hinkler?

♥

Turning away we climbed into the car, saying, 'We'll never come back'. There is no need because in the Dream Girl's Garden, in Golden Valley, in the districts of Jarrabin and Mukinupin, the first house lies secure in the hollow of the heart. Only the ghosts keep walking in our sleep, ringing us up out of nowhere . . . 'Wally Mundy here, just wanted to tell you I'd shorn with the blades before the Queen and danced with René Coade in Wickepin.'

'Malcolm McAuley here, just thought I'd give yous a ring for old times' sake.'

'Do you remember how you once wrote MM loves DH in the girls' shed at South Perth Primary?'

''Course I do.' But he doesn't.

'Tuesday's child is full of grace,' chants my mother on her good days. 'Great gawk!' she screams on her bad days.

Probably both are true. A great gawk full of grace, a Tuesday's child, I stagger forth to make my history.

'You've said enough,' snaps the ghost of my grandmother, 'so hold your tongue.'

WILD CARD